P9-CKE-492

DARK HORSES
&UNDERDOGS

DARK HORSES

&UNDERDOGS

The Greatest Sports Upsets of All Time

LES KRANTZ

WARNER BOOKS

NEW YORK   BOSTON

• • •

CONTRIBUTING WRITERS:
David Aretha, Bill Chastain
Tim Knight, Sue Sveum

• • •

Warner Books, Inc.
1271 Avenue of the Americas
New York, NY 10020

Visit our Web site at www.twbookmark.com.

WARNER BOOKS

Printed in the United States of America

First Printing: October 2005
10 9 8 7 6 5 4 3 2 1

• • •

Library of Congress Cataloging-in-Publication Data
Krantz, Les.
Dark horses and underdogs : the greatest sports upsets of all time / Les Krantz.— 1st ed.
p. cm.
ISBN 0-446-57703-0
1. Sports upsets. 2. Sports stories. I. Title.
GV576.K76   2005
796—dc22   2005014855

• • •

Book Design: Judith Turziano

To Billy and Buster
and Broadway Joe
whom I think about every time
I want to do the impossible

Contents

Acknowledgments

I am very grateful to my contributing writers who so diligently helped me choose the events in this book and, of course, gave me some marvelous text to work with. They are, in alphabetical order: David Aretha, Bill Chastain, Tim Knight and Sue Sveum. Andy Horner also assisted in flushing out their text in spots, making it far better for telling the story. Sportswriter Marty Strasen, too, helped immeasurably.

Rick Wolff, my editor at Warner Books, proved to be one of my biggest assets and went far beyond his duties as my editor. His knowledge of sports and books is unequalled and his stamp on my book will always be appreciated. I am also grateful to Jamie Raab and Maureen Egen, who have looked at many of my projects through the years and eventually settled on this one as my first Warner book. Jason Pinter, also of Warner, could not have been more helpful and supportive. Flamur Tonuzi, ace designer of Warner, provided an exciting cover and was a joy to work with. So was Chris DuBois who tracked me half way around the world to negotiate our contract.

Jim Lampley, thank you, for your wonderful reading of the script, and your expert consultation on it; and to Lou Oppenheim for putting us together. Other sports figures helped us rank the upsets including: Ross Greenburg of HBO, Jay Rizick and Crowley Sullivan of ESPN, Mark Mravic of *Sports Illustrated*, Jim Litke of the Associated Press, Mark Geddis of Collegiate Images, Steve Cangelosi of Topps Baseball Cards, Alex Sachere, formerly of the NBA, and many others.

I am also grateful to many who helped with our documentary including Louise Argianas of ABC-TV, Peter Bregman of Fox Movie Tone, Meredith Fox of the NBA, Peter Helfer of Major League Baseball, Greg Weitekamp of the NCAA and Tamera Reub of the United States Olympic Committee.

Our television crew who worked on the DVD documentary couldn't have been better, including Marcus Yasui, Mike Johnson, Toni Johnson, Pamela Lljubo and Peter Levermann. The post production folks too, including Jeff Pulera of Digital Vision and Jack Piantino of Creative Edge Video.

Help and support came from many others including: Nicole DiGiacomo and Andy Hill of AP Wide World Photos; John Kirchner of Datasis; Jack Huckel of the National Soccer Hall of Fame; Detlev Boschung of the Fédération Internationale de Football Association (FIFA); Tony Randolph, Chaminade Alumni; Mark Weinstein, and many others.

Thank you all!   —LES KRANTZ

Introduction

How does a 45-to-one shot knock out the fiercest warrior to enter the boxing ring in 40 years? By what twist of fate can a bunch of college boys beat the greatest Olympic hockey team in history? What would allow a five-foot-eight-inch NBA "midget" to win a slam dunk tournament, humiliating even the seven-foot giants of the sport?

Things like this have puzzled me for most of my life. But they have also inspired me. Each time I hear of some underestimated athlete knocking off the competition, my skin breaks out in goose bumps.

Of course, from the fan's standpoint, these things are only vicarious thrills, but that's not necessarily such a bad thing. Knowing full well that we may personally never be able to accomplish world-class athletic achievements, seemingly unrelated things can provide solace. Take that nerdy-looking geek with glasses who dropped out of college to become the greatest business success of the 20th century with his computer software company. And there's that soft-spoken, milk-toast intellectual who founded a girly magazine in the 1950s and even today gets those great-looking center-fold types to stop by his mansion for a little fun.

Unlikely achievers are part of the landscape of life, not just somebody or something that surfaces on the playing field. Regardless of what you do for a living, there's always the possibility you can triumph over the giants in your profession. Simply put, sometimes David does slay Goliath. It's literally been going on since Biblical days and has never stopped. In truth, every sports season there's a new dark horse or underdog to capture our imagination.

Please don't confuse the events in "The Greatest Sports Upsets of All Time" with the subject of my previous book, *Not Till the Fat Lady Sings*, which was about the greatest sports *finishes*. This one pertains to upsets, which means unexpected victories, though there's more to it.

The 50 upsets in this book were chosen by myself and my contributing writers. The most important factors in our choice were not only the unevenness of the match, but other things too, such as "how unlikely the competitor." For example, we included Jim Abbott, a one-handed baseball pitcher and Ed Furgol, a physically challenged golfer. We also chose Kerri Strug and Tenley Albright, both Olympians who were seriously injured when they competed. Most fans would never expect disabled or injured athletes to beat the pants off the world's best competitors who were in their best form, but they did. In sum, the 50 sports events we chose weren't *just* the most uneven matches; the choices were tempered by an "underdog factor," which made the victor's triumph over the odds *incredible*.

Please also note that a few, and just a few, famously uneven match-ups weren't included in this volume. We went for those which we considered to be the "greatest sports upsets," since they were the best examples we could find of unanticipated and dramatic victories that defied almost all odds. Of course, any red-blooded sports fan might challenge the selection of these upsets. But in truth, that's the beauty of sports.

We also ranked the 50 major upsets. This was achieved by circulating ballots among sportswriters, sports broadcasters and various sports professionals. Their professional affiliations include the Associated Press, ESPN, HBO Sports, *Sports Illustrated* and other well-known organizations involved in sports. Each balloter assigned a one to five numerical score to each of the 50 events, and we then averaged the scores.

Adam Vinatieri's 48-yard field goal as time expired in Super Bowl XXXVI gave New England a championship and marked the first time the game had been decided on the final play.

There were several averaged scores that tied, but these ties were broken by a blue-ribbon panel, which reviewed them and adjusted the rankings based on their knowledge of the events.

So here it is, a ranking and relating of the greatest sports upsets of all time.

ॐ

Perhaps retired heavyweight champion George Foreman best summed up this uniting "underdog" quality when he regained the world title at age 45, despite the naysayers who said it was impossible. I remember his message to them well, though I could never find his exact words in print, so I shall paraphrase:

Don't make any difference what anyone thinks but me. I'm the guy that has to do the fighting.

Foreman's words translate to a powerful message about sports and life in general: No matter how commanding and powerful a foe, and regardless of what the so-called experts predict, what *you* think is far more important than what *they* think.

The late N.C. State basketball coach Jim Valvano said it a bit differently, but the message was the same. The night he and his Cinderella team upset number-one ranked Houston University to win the national NCAA title in 1983 he told the press: "The national title is defended on the floor, not in the polls."

And so, we now go to the floor, to the bedrock of dreams that have come true, to hopes that have actually happened because of what athletic competitors unshakingly believed in their hearts—that they could do it!

Here's what they believed...and what they accomplished because they believed it.

—LES KRANTZ

UNEXPECTED VICTORIES

Chapter One

Yes, I Believe in Miracles

Winter Olympics, Hockey Semifinal
United States vs. Soviet Union
Lake Placid, New York, February 22, 1980

Three days before the Opening Ceremonies of the 1980 Winter Olympics, the U.S. hockey club faced the fearsome Soviet national team in an exhibition in New York City. Team USA, tutored and driven for months by coach Herb Brooks, seemed ready for the challenge. The puck was dropped, they played their guts out...and the Soviets won 10–3. "Can you imagine," some said, "if this was more than an exhibition game?" The implication was clear: If the Soviets had a serious game against the U.S., they'd really smash the American boys but good, far worse than this.

Exhibition, competition, who cares—this was the Soviets, renowned for their conditioning and skill—a team many believed to be the equal of any in the National Hockey League. And Team USA was nothing but a bunch of college boys, with little more to bring on the ice than their enthusiasm.

After the humiliating defeat, Brooks's prediction that his club would challenge for a bronze medal seemed like a pipe dream. Indeed, as the U.S. players

U.S. goalie James Craig protected the
net against constant Soviet attacks.

arrived in Lake Placid, New York, they were seeded seventh in the 12-team Olympic field.

For Brooks, who had coached the University of Minnesota to three NCAA championships, this Olympics was a shot at redemption: As a player, he had been the last man cut from the 1960 U.S. Olympic team, which won a gold medal. Brooks pushed this team hard, emphasizing conditioning and discipline. He persistently challenged and sometimes deliberately angered his players. "You're playing worse every day," he once said, "and right now you're playing like the middle of the next month."

Knowing that American collegians couldn't match the skill level of the Europeans, Brooks utilized players who were speedy, aggressive, and mentally tough. Forward Mark Johnson, whose father, Bob, coached the U.S. team in 1976, packed the most offensive punch. Moreover, Neal Broten, Dave Christian, Ken Morrow, and Mike Ramsey were promising NHL prospects. Mike Eruzione was considered too small and slow for the NHL, but no one played with more heart. Brooks named him team captain.

Team USA opened the Games sluggishly against Sweden, falling behind 2–1 in the third period. The U.S. eked out a tie, however, thanks to a last-minute goal by Bill Baker. An assist should have been credited to the raucous pro-American fans in the cozy Olympic Arena. "The people refused to let you play flat," said forward John Harrington. "There was so much electricity in the air."

In game two, USA stuck it to Czechoslovakia 7–3, a game that boosted the club's confidence. "We were maybe better than even *we* thought we were," said Eruzione, who emphasized the club's strong coaching and teamwork. "We worked hard for each other," he said. "It was 20 guys; it really was."

Spurred on by chants of "U-S-A, U-S-A," the Americans knocked off Norway and Romania, then notched a 4–2 comeback victory over a tough German squad. By this time, Brooks's club had captured the country's imagination. The U.S. club replaced the Dallas Cowboys as "America's Team." "It was nuts," recalled Harrington.

USA coach Herb Brooks could only look on stoically during the closing minutes with his team protecting a one-point lead.

"And as the tournament went on, it got crazier."

Along with Sweden, Finland, and the USSR, the U.S.—with a 4-0-1 record—advanced to the medal round. In the first game, they drew the Soviets.

Only dreamers thought the U.S. could defeat the Big Red Machine. Forget the 10–3 thumping two weeks earlier; the Soviets had blown out a team of *NHL All-Stars* 6–0 in a challenge series. The Soviet Union had won not just four straight Olympic gold medals, but 21 consecutive Olympic games.

Millions of Americans planned their Friday night on February 22 around this game, broadcast on ABC on tape delay. At the arena, scalpers were demanding $340 a ticket. Brooks, meanwhile, motivated the troops. Recalled Harrington, "Herb was drilling it into us: 'They're an old team. They're ready to be beaten. Our youth and young legs will win out.'"

The Soviets took a 2–1 lead in the first period, but brilliant saves by goalie Jim Craig kept the U.S. in the game. A stunning goal by Mark Johnson off a rebound, with just one second remaining, sent the two teams to the locker room tied 2–2.

The Soviets pulled goalie Vladislav Tretiak after Johnson's goal, but the move hardly seemed to matter since the U.S. could muster only two shots in the second period. Craig stopped everything but an Alexander Maltsev breakaway shot, which gave the USSR a 3–2 lead through two.

In the final period, the younger, well-conditioned Americans took advantage of the Soviets' old legs—and mistakes. Johnson capitalized on a Soviet turnover by converting on a power play. Then Eruzione—whose name means "explosion" in Italian—snared a loose puck and fired in a 30-foot shot that replacement goalie

THE GOLDEN PATH TO THE NHL

For decades, Canadians have dominated the NHL, with only a smattering of American players on league rosters. Few of Team USA's players had been coveted NHL prospects in 1980—until they won the gold medal. Subsequently, 10 of the American players went on to NHL careers, including the following:

- Neal Broten, F, 17 NHL seasons, 289 goals
- Dave Christian, D/F, 15 NHL seasons, 340 goals (includes one year in WHA)
- Steve Christoff, F, 5 NHL seasons, 77 goals
- Jim Craig, G, 3 NHL seasons, 11 wins
- Rob McClanahan, F, 5 NHL seasons, 38 goals
- Ken Morrow, D, 10 NHL seasons, 17 goals
- Jack O'Callahan, D, 7 NHL seasons, 27 goals
- Mark Pavelich, F, 7 NHL seasons, 137 goals
- Mike Ramsey, D, 18 NHL seasons, 79 goals
- Dave Silk, F, 7 NHL seasons, 54 goals

Of note: USA captain Mike Eruzione retired from hockey after winning the gold medal. Ken Morrow won a Stanley Cup with the New York Islanders four months after winning the gold. Steve Christoff became an airline pilot after his NHL career. And defenseman Bill Baker went on to become an oral surgeon.

Vladimir Myshkin did not see leave the stick. The puck found space between the Russian goaltender's bulky pads and kissed the back of the net. *The U.S. was up 4 to 3!*

The building rocked with chants of "U-S-A!" "Man, did we hear it!" Eruzione said.

Ten minutes remained, and the Soviets, not used to close games—much less being behind—were as shocked as they were desperate. Panicked, they dumped purposeless pass after purposeless pass. Each time the Soviets fired a shot at goalie Craig, you could almost feel the fans' hearts drop into their mouths. Each time, Craig made a sensational stop, including a lunging skate save on a backhander.

The crowd was erupting into wild cheers and rafter-rattling chants of "U-S-A, U-S-A!" that would only grow in intensity as the period wound down. When the final buzzer sounded, pandemonium broke loose, both in the stands and on the ice. The American players threw their equipment into the air and embraced in wonder at their achievement. Draped in the Stars-and-Stripes, Craig, one of the heroes of the game, sought out his family in the stands. Though the match was not broadcast live on television, news of the tremendous upset spread like wildfire across the country. When the final score was announced at Radio City Music Hall in New York City, the crowd cheered and began an impromptu singing of the national anthem. All over the nation, Americans embraced in bars and living rooms as the astonishing final score flashed across their television screens.

"I'm sure the 20 guys won't believe it," said Johnson of his victorious teammates. "They'll probably wake up tomorrow morning and still won't believe it."

The quest for gold was not over, of course. There was still Finland in the final. But after the miraculous victory over the Soviet powerhouse, that match was all but a formality, as the U.S. won 4–2 to earn hockey gold for the first time since the equally stunning victory in Squaw Valley twenty years earlier.

In 1980, America embraced its young heroes as it had no hockey players before. For one glorious moment, the Cold War was won—the United States could boast of having the best hockey team in the world.

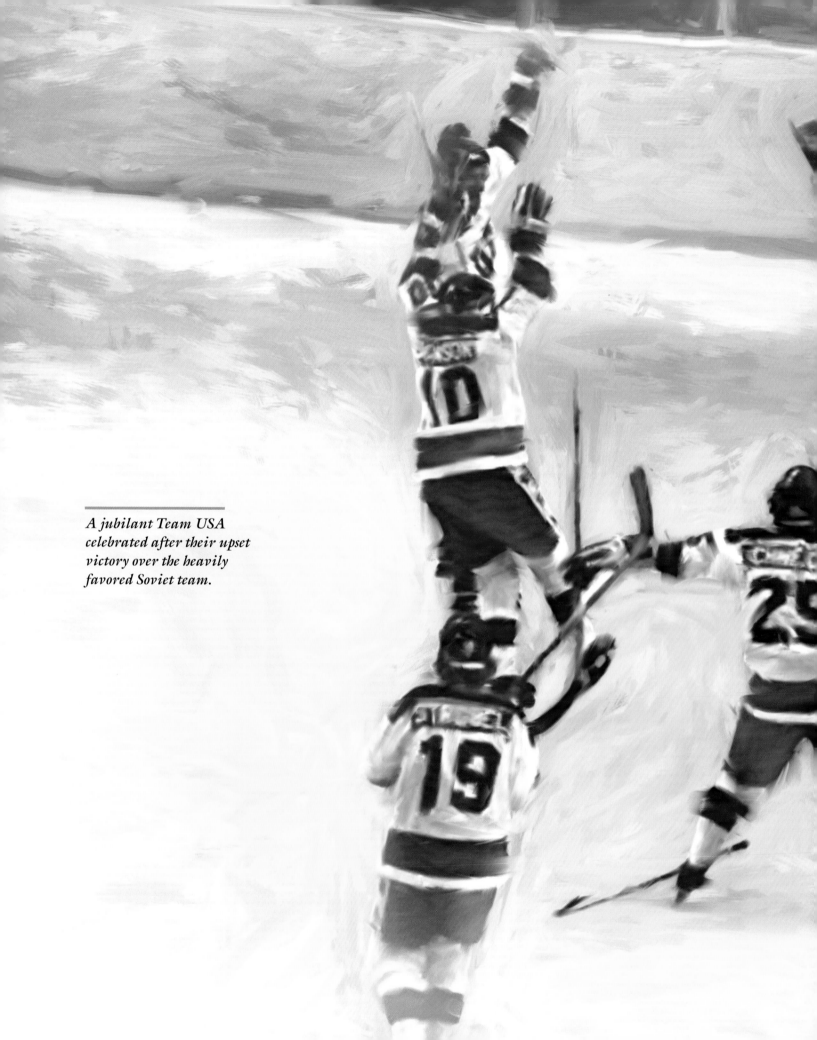

A jubilant Team USA celebrated after their upset victory over the heavily favored Soviet team.

Chapter Two

Broadway Joe and the Jets

Super Bowl III, New York Jets vs. Baltimore Colts
Miami, Florida, January 12, 1969

Three days before Super Bowl III in 1969 the Miami Touchdown Club was hosting the ceremonies for the Player of the Year award. Besides the usual bevy of crewcut-sporting jocks, the building was dominated by cigar-chewing sports reporters and button-down league executives. They were here to honor one of their own, sort of.

The man of the hour—a sore thumb, by all visual accounts—strode to the podium to collect his due. He looked more like a Slavic version of one of the Beatles than a quarterback. As he swaggered his way to the podium, his hair bouncing off his collar, a diehard NFL fan shouted, "Hey Namath, we're gonna kick your butt!"

Joe Namath had heard such arrogance all week and was sick of it. "Wait a minute, pal. I've got news for you," Namath yelled back, his tone venomous and serious as hell. "We're going to win this game." Namath then pointed his finger, dagger style. "I guarantee it!"

Cocky? Hell yes. This was Broadway Joe Namath. He was, after all, the former prince of Alabama and for years the most eligible bachelor in New York City. And, some said, the coolest guy around, a regular Frank Sinatra in a football jersey.

Though his team, the New York Jets, had just won the AFL championship game, they were an 18- to 23-point underdog against the Baltimore Colts of the NFL, the well-established league that had boasted easy victories in the first two Super Bowls. However, the hotshot quarterback thumbed his nose at his detractors. Remember, this was Broadway Joe, not Johnny Unitas or Bart Starr.

The next day, Namath's prediction made bold headlines nationwide. An AFL team beating an NFL club? The notion offended not just old-school football fans but flag-waving Americans as well. To many, the Baltimore Colts, led by quarterbacks Johnny Unitas and Earl Morrall, represented America's traditional values. Conversely, the upstart AFL, personified by the long-haired playboy quarterback of the Jets, reflected the rebellious youth of the late sixties. Within this context, the matchup became the most anticipated Super Bowl to date. Namath's outlandish prediction fueled interest even more.

Though the top dog in the AFL in the late 1960s, Joe Willie

Joe Namath completed 17 of 28 passes for 208 yards to earn Super Bowl III MVP honors.

Namath was used to overcoming odds. He grew up in Beaver Falls, Pennsylvania, a steel-mill town about 30 miles from Pittsburgh. His family lived in a poor, predominantly African-American neighborhood—an unusual situation for a white youth in the fifties.

A high school star in baseball, basketball, and football, Namath turned down pro baseball offers to play quarterback at the University of Alabama. Though he broke curfew and injured his knee three times as a senior, Namath earned All-America honors for his golden arm and swashbuckling leadership. The day after earning MVP honors at the 1965 Orange Bowl, Namath signed the fattest rookie pro football contract ever with the Jets: $400,000 and a green Lincoln convertible.

Namath's presence suddenly made the AFL glamorous and intriguing. He was the real deal at quarterback, winning AFL Rookie of the Year honors in 1965. In 1967

Jets coach Weeb Ewbank was among the first to congratulate his quarterback on making a bold prediction a reality.

he became the first professional quarterback to pass for more than 4,000 yards in a season, and the next year he was named league MVP.

Off the field, women gushed over Namath as if he were Elvis. Jets guard Dave Herman remembered one such mob scene in Cleveland, where New York was playing a preseason game. "Most of them were girls, all dolled up like they were waiting for a Hollywood producer," Herman said. "When Joe Namath stepped off the elevator, it was like a stampede. People went crazy, screaming, climbing over each other just to touch him."

Throughout Super Bowl week, Namath maintained his cool image. While oiling himself poolside at the Galt Ocean Mile Hotel, Joe reiterated that the Jets were simply better than the Colts. His teammates agreed. "We were as good as any team in football," recalled Jets receiver Don Maynard. "We had the No. 1

☙☙☙

"We're going to win this game." Namath then pointed his finger, dagger style. "I guarantee it!"

☙☙☙

defense in the league. We had a good field goal kicker. Great quarterback. A great running attack."

Indeed, New York fullback Matt Snell busted through lines like an armored truck. Maynard was the fastest Jet this side of the newly marketed 747. Offensive tackle Winston Hill didn't just block, Snell said, he blew out the defensive line. Even the Jets' secondary, supposedly the team's Achilles' heel, was ready to rumble. Cornerback Johnny Sample said he wanted payback against the NFL for "blackballing" him.

On Sunday, 75,377 fans—including President-elect Richard Nixon, who despised long-haired upstarts like Namath—packed the Orange Bowl for this supercharged showdown. Earl Morrall, Baltimore's starting quarterback because Unitas was out with an elbow injury, marched the Colts downfield on their opening drive. Yet the Jets secondary put the squeeze on Baltimore's receivers. New York kept the Colts off the board on this drive, then picked off a Morrall pass.

Offensively, the Jets were ready to roll, thanks largely to a flaw they discovered in the Baltimore defensive set.

"There was a way to get an early read on their defense," Maynard said. "When I got extremely wide, they had to show their zone defense before they wanted to. So when Joe steps up to the line, he's got five or six extra seconds to see if they're playing zone on my side."

Namath proceeded to outfox the Colts. Mixing it up on an 80-yard drive, he hit George Sauer for two key passes and ran Snell successfully behind tackle Winston Hill. When Baltimore blitzed, Namath adroitly dumped a pass to Bill Mathis out of the backfield. Once the Jets were inside the 10-yard line, Snell rammed his way into the end zone. The score remained 7–0 at halftime.

New York continued to dictate play in the third quarter. Winning the battle of field position, the Jets set up two field goal attempts for Jim Turner, who twice split the uprights. New York led, stunningly, 13–0.

With three minutes left in the third quarter, Colts coach Don Shula turned to the ailing, ancient Unitas, the man who had won the "Greatest Game Ever Played" to capture the 1958 NFL championship. Yet even Unitas couldn't solve the Jets defense, which yielded a paltry 10 yards in the third quarter. When Turner booted a nine-yard field goal early in the fourth period, New York moved ahead 16–0.

In prevent mode, the Jets allowed Johnny U. to lead a slow march to the end zone. But his desperate attempts in the final minutes fell short, and New York shocked the world with an utterly convincing 16–7 victory. On the day, Morrall and Unitas had completed just 17 of 41 passes for 181 yards and four interceptions. Namath, meanwhile, deftly completed 17 of 28 tosses for 206 yards and no interceptions, earning the game's MVP award.

In the glow of victory, Namath maintained his cool, saying the only thing that surprised him was the absence of champagne in the victors' locker room. Yet Broadway Joe's epic performance transformed professional football. The AFL's newfound respect contributed to the merger of the two leagues prior to the 1970 season. Meanwhile the suddenly hip Super Bowl joined the World Series, Indy 500, and Kentucky Derby as American institutions.

Chapter Three

Buster Douglas: I Did That for My Mama

Heavyweight Championship of the World
Mike Tyson vs. Buster Douglas
Tokyo, Japan, February 10, 1990

A mother's love meant everything to James "Buster" Douglas. Lula Pearl Douglas, who reared him in Columbus, Ohio, was the light of her son's life.

A neighborhood bully had been humiliating young Douglas to such an extent he decided to tell his mother. Expecting to be coddled, he was instead told there was something worse than the fear. What that was, he didn't know yet, but Lula Pearl was about to teach him. She grabbed him, forcibly sat him down, then told him to either stand up to his tormentor or be prepared to stand up to *her*. Reluctantly, and still scared, he followed her advice. She was right, the bully backed down.

If ever a boxing bully lived, it was surely Mike Tyson. Short and stocky, he hunted opponents in the ring with the savagery of a shark on the attack. Tyson employed tactics of intimidation in creating an aura of invincibility backed by 37 victories—33 by knockouts. The only question when he stepped into the ring was *when* he'd knock out his opponent, rather than *if*. Nobody gave Douglas a chance. His fight with Tyson would be on free TV, not the usual pay-per-view. Who would

Douglas had been seen as a career underachiever until he sent Tyson to the canvas in a 10th-round knockout.

Some wondered whether Douglas would make it past the first round. He wound up shocking the boxing world.

pay to see a 45-to-1 shot hit the canvas like a sack of potatoes? And so the fight was in Tokyo, where the spendthrift Japanese would pay through the nose to see any title fight, no matter how ridiculous the matchup. Tyson-Douglas was perceived in the U.S. as interesting as a crocheting contest at an old folks' home.

Douglas would be the mouse fed to the pet snake, a mere way station for Tyson to pass through en route to a significant payday against Evander Holyfield. Sure Douglas had size at 6'4", 240 pounds, but his heart and aggression were questionable. He smiled a lot, maybe too much. His sweet face and mild demeanor were in

stark contrast to Tyson's snarl and bulldog bearing.

Douglas became a fighter in 1981 and managed to progress through the heavyweight ranks on athletic ability alone. After he beat name fighters Tex Cobb and Greg Page, an International Boxing Federation title shot against Tony Tucker fell his way in 1987. The fight would reinforce all the doubts about Douglas. For nine rounds Douglas had his way with Tucker, but the tide turned quickly. By the end of the round Douglas's failure to train hard enough showed. In the 10th round, Tucker maneuvered Douglas into a corner and kept punching; no stamina left, Douglas fruitlessly covered himself until the referee stopped the fight. As far as the boxing world was concerned, his place in it would be as no more than a sparring partner for a real contender. Just another flash in the pan whose sizzle was all fizzled.

Outside the ring, more personal setbacks befell Douglas.

He'd seen his kid brother, Artie, die from a gunshot wound. His father, Billy, a fighter of some quality, had been his trainer until the Tucker fight, which so disgusted him that he abandoned his son. His wife walked out on him—prompting him to drink heavily and led to a DWI charge. And the mother of his 11-year-old son was diagnosed with leukemia. But none of these setbacks prepared him for the gut punch he received just 23 days before his fight with Tyson.

Lula Pearl died of a stroke.

Suddenly Douglas had lost his mother, his mentor, his teacher, his best friend, his inspiration. But he had not lost what she taught him about life, that being scared at times was part of it. It was how you dealt with the fear that mattered.

Heading into the Tyson fight, the strategy in the Douglas camp harked back to the lesson Buster learned from Lula Pearl: Stand up to the bully.

To Douglas's way of thinking, his bout with Tyson was all about the sweet science, not merely a head game. He believed the simple philosophy that hitting Tyson would be the best approach. As he saw it, no fighter had ever hit the champ hard enough to gain his respect. He also knew Tyson entered the ring salivating to begin. The champ wanted to start fast and finish off opponents early. And Tyson always got what he wanted, even with quality opponents like Michael Spinks, whom he beat in 91 seconds, and Carl Williams, who lasted 93. Could Douglas even make it into the second round?

From the outset Douglas showed no fear. He kept Tyson from moving inside while using his reach to pepper his head with a constant barrage of rights. Tyson took the fight to Douglas in the third and fourth rounds, but Douglas would not back down and was rewarded for his display of heart when he landed a right to Tyson's head in the fifth—a barn burner even the fans could feel when it made contact with the stunned Tyson.

Douglas continued to score with his right to Tyson's head. The champ's left eye began to swell, fueling Douglas with confidence he could pull off the biggest boxing upset of his generation. In the eighth round Douglas started strong and had the round won until a right uppercut brought him back to earth. Douglas dropped to the canvas with six seconds remaining in the round. Upset at being caught with the punch, Douglas slammed his fist against the mat, then kept his wits while watching the referee count down the seconds. Douglas looked clearheaded but waited until the last second to get to his feet. The bell to end the round sounded before Tyson could exploit any damage. Tyson's contingent later charged the referee of starting the count too late and that Douglas should have been ruled a Tyson KO. The protest would fall on deaf ears.

Though floored, Douglas quickly gained his composure. In the ninth he delivered a barrage of rights that completely shut Tyson's eye. Iron Mike was being punished but good. Douglas had become the bully, using his weight to push Tyson around the ring, positioning him where he could deliver a series of punches that snapped Tyson's head back. The crowd was wild; Tyson appeared as if he would go down, and that had never happened. But the champion survived the round.

Douglas, always accused of lacking the killer instinct, pulled off an uncharacteristic 10th round. Whether it was an aberration or divine intervention from Lula no one knows. He attacked like the Marines on Iwo Jima, putting together a powerful four-punch combination that sent Tyson to the deck for the first time in his career, his mouthpiece skittering across the canvas. Iron Mike was down. And he wasn't getting up.

Somewhere out there, Lula Pearl must have been smiling from ear to ear. Her little boy had remembered his lesson: There *is* something worse than being scared—being scared off. And that didn't happen to her boy that night.

Chapter Four

The Amazin' Miracle Mets

World Series, New York Mets vs. Baltimore Orioles
Shea Stadium, New York, and Memorial Stadium, Baltimore, October 1969

As the summer wound down in 1969, New Yorkers reflected on an amazing year. Joe Namath had led the New York Jets to a monumental upset in the Super Bowl. Astronauts received a ticker-tape parade in New York City after landing on the moon. A half-million young people partied in nearby Woodstock. And the New York Mets, who never before had finished above ninth place, actually developed into a respectable team.

Even though the Mets trailed the Chicago Cubs by nine and a half games on August 14, New Yorkers still were stunned by their team's fine play. Prior to 1969, the club had been called the "Amazin' Mets" only sarcastically. From 1962 through 1968, the team had *averaged* 105 losses.

Entering 1969, the Mets were listed as a 100–1 long shot to win the World Series. Yet manager Gil Hodges, a stern taskmaster, exorcised the losing attitude out of the clubhouse. "He wanted things done right 100 times out of 100," said pitcher Jerry Koosman. "Once the game started, we knew what to do." Hodges milked victories out of a young, potent pitching staff and a hustling bunch of no-name position players.

Offensively, Cleon Jones (.340 average, 92 runs) and Tommie Agee (26 homers, 97 runs) steadily produced. But, due to Hodges's penchant for platooning, no other Met scored even 50 runs. Nonetheless, hitters came through in the clutch. After Donn Clendenon was acquired in a June trade, he drove in a lead run or winning run in his first 16 games.

In truth, it was the Mets' pitching that packed 2,175,373 fans (tops in the league) into Shea Stadium. Led by fireballers Tom Seaver (25-7, 2.21 ERA) and Koosman (17-9, 2.28), the Mets amassed a league-best 28 shutouts. The 24-year-old Seaver, known as "Tom Terrific," earned the Cy Young Award. "Tom was a leader by example for the whole team," said Koosman. "Not just the pitching staff."

The Mets hurlers maintained their vigor throughout the summer. When New York hosted the Cubs on September 9, they were only 1½ games out of first place. In that game, a black cat jumped onto the field and skittered past the Cubs dugout. The furry symbol of bad luck sealed Chicago's doom. New York beat the Cubs in both that game and the next to move into first place. The Mets rocketed like Apollo 11, finishing 38–11 for 100 overall wins and an eight-game cushion over the Cubs.

Because each league splintered into two divisions in 1969, the League Championship Series commenced that year. New York faced the Atlanta Braves, powered by legendary slugger Hank Aaron. Though the Mets were considered underdogs because of their inexperience, they broomed the Braves in three games: 9–5, 11–6, and 7–4.

Mets right-fielder Ron Swoboda made one of the greatest catches in World Series history in Game 4, robbing Brooks Robinson of extra bases in the ninth inning.

Still, the greatest challenge of all loomed in the World Series. The Baltimore Orioles, managed by ingenious strategist Earl Weaver, had amassed a staggering 109 wins. They captured the AL East by 19 games and swept Minnesota in the playoffs.

Baltimore boasted such fearsome sluggers as Boog Powell (37 homers that season) and Frank Robinson (32 for the season, on his way to 586 career longballs). Star pitchers Mike Cuellar, Dave McNally, and Jim Palmer averaged nearly 20 wins apiece, while Gold

Catcher Jerry Grote embraced pitcher Jerry Koosman while teammate Ed Charles joined the party after the Amazin' Mets' 1969 World Series triumph.

Glovers Brooks Robinson, Mark Belanger, and Paul Blair sealed the field. The Orioles seemed unbeatable.

Baltimore showcased its talents at home in Game 1. Don Buford belted Seaver's second pitch for a home run, and the Orioles added three in the fourth. Cuellar cruised to a 4–1 victory.

In Game 2, Koosman actually outdid Cuellar, no-hitting Baltimore until the seventh. In the ninth, the Mets cracked three singles to go up 2–1. When Baltimore put two on with two out in the bottom of the ninth, tension gripped Memorial Stadium. Mets owner Joan Payson couldn't even look, covering her eyes with a scarf. The count went full on Brooks Robinson, who then ripped a shot off third baseman Ed Charles's chest. Charles recovered and nipped Robinson at first for the Mets' first-ever World Series win.

As the series moved to Shea Stadium for Game 3, such celebrities as former First Lady Jackie Kennedy Onassis packed the stands. Powered by an Agee homer and a two-run double by Mets starter Gary Gentry, New York took a five-run lead. Memorably, Agee made two catches that saved at least five runs: a backhanded, off-the-shoetops grab with two men on, and a swan-dive catch in right-center with the bases loaded. New York held on to win 5–0.

Seaver and Cuellar dueled magnificently in Game 4, which New York led 1–0 through eight. In the top of the ninth, however, Baltimore threatened with runners on first and third with one out. From that point on, a series of improbabilities occurred that gave credence to the Mets' "miracle" nickname.

Right-fielder Ron Swoboda, never known for his glovework, made a diving grab of a Brooks Robinson line drive. A runner tagged and scored, but Swoboda likely saved the game. In the 10th, Baltimore's Buford misplayed Jerry Grote's flyball into the sun for a double. After a walk, pinch-hitter J. C. Martin bunted. Pitcher Pete Richert's throw caromed off Martin, scoring pinch-runner Rod Gaspar from first base. Amazingly, the Mets were up three games to one.

Baltimore took a 3–0 lead in Game 5, but the Mets never quit. In the sixth, Cleon Jones was hit by a pitch

From Long Island to Manhattan, people ran into the streets to share congrats and hugs. The new guys from Flushing had finally given fans a reason to forget those previous baseball franchises that had moved west.

on his shoe, earning first base after pointing out the shoe polish on the ball to the umpire. Clendenon then followed with a homer, his third of the series. Al Weis, who had gone deep only twice all season, tied it with a homer in the seventh. By this point, the Orioles seemed ready to succumb to fate. With two doubles and two Baltimore throwing errors in the eighth, New York took a 5–3 lead. When Koosman breezed in the ninth, the Metropolitans, so recently the laughingstock of Major League Baseball, had won the World Series.

In the bowels of Shea Stadium, where a team of nobodies had just achieved the upset of the century, all was quiet. "We stayed in the clubhouse and just talked amongst ourselves about what we had just done, and we got choked up," said Koosman. "It got to the point where it was difficult to speak. It was a very emotional time."

Out on the streets of New York, it was another matter altogether. From Long Island to Manhattan, people ran into the streets to share congrats and hugs. The new guys from Flushing had finally given fans a reason to forget those previous baseball franchises that had moved west. And for a franchise that had yet to reach the ripe old age of 10, this was nothing short of miraculous.

Chapter Five

The Louisville Lip and the Big Ugly Bear

Heavyweight Championship of the World, Sonny Liston vs. Cassius Clay
Miami Beach, Florida, February 25, 1964

"The Black man has been brainwashed. It's time he learned something about himself," the handsome young "liberated Negro" shouted to the crowd in the white-frame meeting hall. Many were not sure who he was. Those who did, came for amusement, just to hear him talk—who could possibly take a lunatic like this as a serious athlete?

"When he goes to the store," he continued, "he sees the Angel food cake is white cake; the devils food cake is black cake." He scowled. "Strong coffee is black coffee, you understand. You make it weak…you integrate it." A smile slowly formed on his face. "Rich dirt is black dirt," he continued, looking at a black man in the crowd. "Don't feel bad" he told him as his smile transformed into an ear-to-ear grin.

Who *is* this guy?

Black people knew exactly who he was—the next heavyweight champion of the world, of that they are sure. So is the speaker, Cassius Clay.

Never shy about flapping his gums, Cassius Clay knew how to use words to get attention. He also knew how to make his words give him a psychological advantage in the ring. Even a fearless brute like Sonny Liston feared a crazy person. Who wouldn't? As Liston saw him, Clay was a bit crazy. But there's something

Clay landed a straight left to Liston's face in the third round.

about crazy that shakes one's bones.

The challenger *was* crazy, but so are foxes, and when they're rabid, they'll attack a bear. And "The Bear," as Liston was known in fight circles, saw the young upstart as more suited for a straitjacket than a pair of boxing gloves.

Clay, who later took the name Muhammad Ali, grew up in Louisville, Kentucky, and didn't step into

༄༅༈

Clay showed a style
like no fighter before him,
"floating like a butterfly and
stinging like a bee."

༄༅༈

the ring until his bicycle got stolen at age 12. Though he weighed just 89 pounds, he wanted to find the thief and teach him a lesson. He told a police officer about the theft and the officer directed him to the ring to learn how to box. You could say he caught on to the sport, winning 100 out of 108 amateur fights, two national Golden Gloves championships while in high school, and a gold medal at the 1960 Rome Olympics three months after graduating from high school. Two months later he won his first professional fight.

Progressing through the fight-for-pay ranks in the heavyweight division, Clay showed a style like no fighter before him, "floating like a butterfly and stinging like a bee." He had his critics due to the loose-lipped shots he took at opponents and he was enamored with his own pulchritude. Back in 1964, a black man was supposed to know his place and Clay's position on the map was light-years ahead of his time.

To his detractors he was uppity, but for his growing legions of fans, he flowed like poetry.

At age 22, Clay had compiled a 20–0 record to earn his first title shot at the heavyweight championship against Liston. If anybody could shut down the "Louisville Lip," Liston was perceived as the one to batten his hatches. Unlike Clay, who enjoyed the relative ease of a middle-class upbringing, Liston had 25 brothers and sisters and grew up in poverty in Arkansas, which led him up the path toward becoming a criminal and eventually prison. Liston learned how to box while serving a five-year sentence for robbery. He had the aura of a thug, complete with alleged mob ties, but aside from these obvious elements making him a character few would care to deal with, he also possessed wonderful talents in the ring. He could slug it out with the best of them, but he also carried a ring knowledge that allowed him to use the tools he possessed like a carpenter does a saw. Liston's toolbox contained a powerful jab and the largest fists in the history of heavyweight champions. Add to the package the steely eyes that showed no emotion and the time he spent in the big house, and it was easy to understand why many of his opponents were beaten before they even stepped into the ring.

For all of Clay's flash, his chances looked remote. Everyone was certain the Bear would teach the Mouth a lesson in respect. So did the oddsmakers, establishing Liston as a 7–1 favorite.

Clay didn't wait until he stepped into the ring to begin waging battle, beginning his mind-play against Liston the day he pulled up in front of his quarters in a bus and yapped nonstop about how he was going to whip the champion. Leading up to the fight he continued to tell reporters and anybody else who would listen how he would defeat "the Big Ugly Bear," as he was now calling Liston.

Once the fight began, Liston looked eager to

His handlers had to hold the boisterous Clay back after a seventh-round TKO of Liston made the 22-year-old the world heavyweight champion.

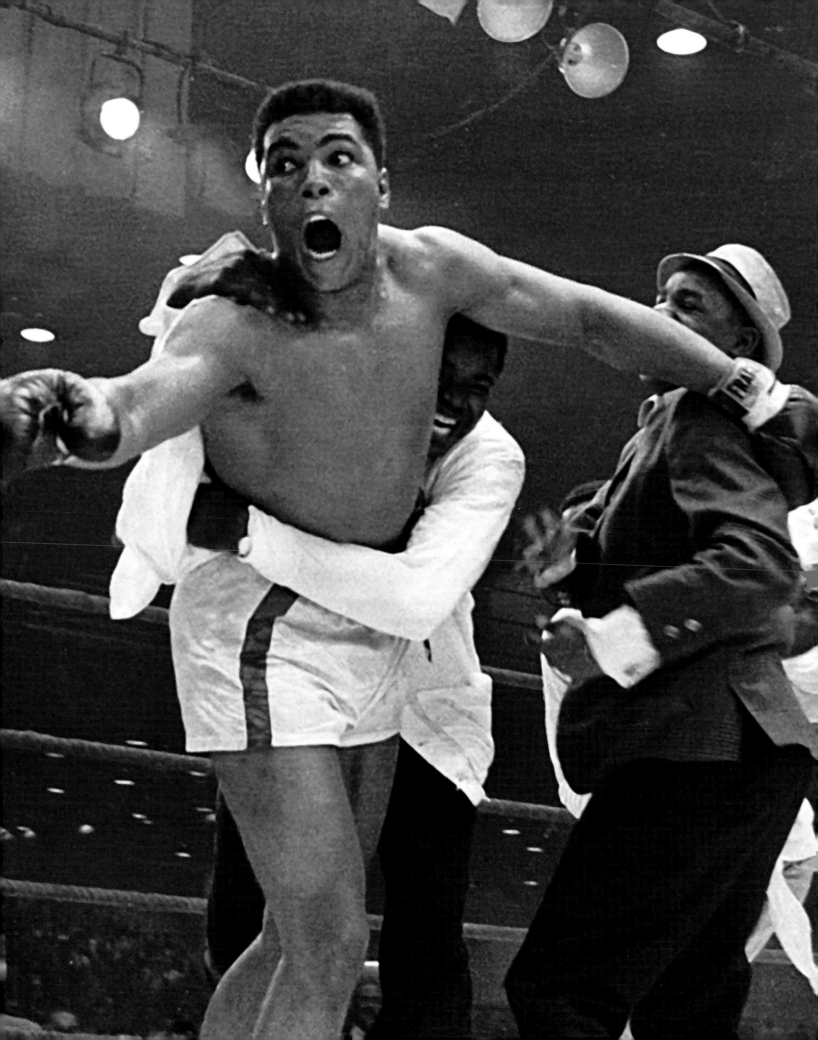

pummel Clay, which was no easy task. The challenger bobbed and weaved around the ring, employing enough fancy footwork and dancing to make Liston feel as though he was swatting at flies. Clay spent much of his time being elusive, dancing merrily, alternately smiling and talking, but when he attacked...the dancer transformed into a warrior. In the second round he split one of Liston's eyebrows. *Everything* went Clay's way, but that was in the early going.

But then the light got fuzzy, and Clay blinked back tears. His eyes began to burn. He was struggling just to see his opponent.

It was later speculated that Liston had put liniment on his gloves to impair Clay's vision. Others, like Clay's trainer, Angelo Dundee, believed it was either Monsel solution, an iron-based coagulant that was put in the cut on Liston's eyebrow, or it was residue from the liniment Liston's corner had been rubbing on their man's shoulders between rounds.

"Either way, it got on my kid's gloves and then into both of his eyes," Dundee told the *Boston Herald*. "I stuck my pinkie in his eye and put some of the stuff in my eye, and I'll tell you, it burned like hell, but I washed his eyes out with water, threw the sponge away, and then I threw the towel away, too."

Dundee pep-talked his fighter as they prepared for the next round, even though Clay could barely make out his hands in front of his eyes. They were burning like scorched meat. For the next three minutes Clay did his best Fred Astaire imitation to stay away from the stalking Liston.

"All I did was give him the perfect instruction—run—and that's what he did," Dundee said.

Until the sixth round, that is. As Clay's vision

PEARLS OF WISDOM FROM THE CHAMP

Cassius Clay, who later took the name Muhammad Ali, was well known for his inclination to speak his mind—no matter how boastful or outrageous. His most famous line, "Float like a butterfly, sting like a bee," was one of many fabulous quotes he contributed to American folk tradition.

Following are some colorful pearls of wisdom spoken both as Cassius Clay and later as Muhammad Ali, proving the champ could also wag his tongue as well as he could maneuver his fists. And occasionally he'd trigger a fabulous retort, like the first item on the list below.

- When a flight attendant told Clay he needed a seatbelt, he replied: "Superman don't need no seatbelt." The flight attendant shot back: "Superman don't need no airplane either."
- "I'm so mean I make medicine sick."
- "A man who has no imagination has no wings."

- "Eat your words. Eat your words. I am the greatest."
- "I'm young, I'm pretty, and I can't be beat."
- "Don't count the days, make the days count."
- "If you can do it you ain't braggin'!"
- "I'm so fast I can turn out the lights and be in bed before it gets dark."
- "The man who views the world at 50 the same as he did at 20 has wasted 30 years of his life."
- "I know where I'm going and I know the truth, and I don't have to be what you want me to be. I'm free to be what I want."
- "I'll beat him so bad he'll need a shoehorn to put his hat on."
- "Hating people because of their color is wrong. And it doesn't matter which color does the hating. It's just plain wrong."
- "It's the repetition of affirmations that leads to belief. And once that belief becomes a deep conviction, things begin to happen."

The former Cassius Clay, with Black Muslim leader Malcolm X after watching a replay of the fight with Sonny Liston, signed his name "Muhammad Ali" after converting to Islam.

returned, so too did his aggression. He attacked relentlessly throughout the round, landing his lightning-quick left jabs with increasing frequency. Midway through the round, Clay opened a cut under Liston's left eye with yet another unblocked jab. The crowd, sensing that the end could be near for the visibly fatigued Liston, buzzed in anticipation of the upset. When the bell sounded to end the round, Liston walked slowly to his corner, refusing at first to take his seat on the corner stool.

The Bear sat down wearily. And he never got up. The fat lady had sung. The Big Ugly Bear didn't answer the opening bell of Round 7. His shoulder was out. There wasn't a punch left in him.

Clay bounded out of his corner to the center of the ring, dancing with raised arms as all fighters do moments after the big victory.

"I'm the greatest!" he shouted. "I'm the king!" Cassius Clay, the 7–1 underdog, shouted for all the world to hear.

Chapter Six

The Greatest College Basketball Upset Ever

College Basketball, Chaminade Silverswords vs. Virginia Cavaliers
Honolulu, Hawaii, December 23, 1982

After a brutal stretch of games in December 1982, the University of Virginia Cavaliers looked forward to their Christmas treat: a cream puff opponent, the Chaminade Silverswords, on the Hawaiian island of Oahu.

The Cavaliers certainly deserved the break. Earlier in the month, they had defeated Duke by 13 points and then trounced Patrick Ewing and Georgetown. They followed up with an 8,000-mile plane ride to Tokyo, where they knocked off mighty Houston (led by future NBA superstars Akeem (later Hakeem) Olajuwon and Clyde Drexler) and then Utah.

As for their next opponent: "They figured it would be a cakewalk," said Chaminade guard Tim Dunham, "and how could you blame them?"

To the East Coast media accompanying the Cavs, Chaminade (pronounced Sha-ma-nod) was little more than a joke. One mainland sportscaster said it sounded like a French perfume. Other announcers pronounced it Cham-in-aid, as in lemonade.

Chaminade, in fact, wasn't even an NCAA school. With a student body of 900, the university was a proud

member of the NAIA. The athletic department's building was so small, locals called it "The Shack." Silverswords coach Merv Lopes, a Charles Bronson look-alike, earned just $10,000 a year. And yet they had to face Virginia, which featured 7'4" center Ralph Sampson and was ranked No. 1 in both the AP and UPI polls.

But the truth was, the Silverswords could play. Despite a loss to 5-9 Wayland Baptist, the club entered the Virginia contest with a 10-1 record. Haenisch, a German import who was new to the game, provided points and boards. Muscular forward Ernest Pettway played bigger than his 6'3" frame. So too did Dunham, who stood 6'0" on his tiptoes but owned a 42-inch vertical leap. Center Tony Randolph, though a mere 6'7", could frustrate opposing centers with his deft perimeter shooting.

Most important, the Swords meshed well, hustled hard, and oozed confidence. And they were psyched for Virginia. "You could tell by our energy level that we were putting everything we had into that one basketball game," Dunham said. "No one was going to leave that floor with one ounce of energy left in their body."

Despite their gung ho attitude, Chaminade seemed

Virginia All-American Ralph Sampson (50), fighting the flu, struggled to keep up with undersized but high-energy Chaminade center Tony Randolph.

no match for Virginia, a Final Four participant nine months earlier. Besides Sampson, who had been named the National Player of the Year the two previous seasons, the Cavaliers boasted a lightning-quick floor general in Othell Wilson and a lights-out shooter in forward Jeff Lamp. Virginia was so powerful that Lopes's goal was to lose by no more than 20 points.

Thirty-five hundred fans attended the game at the University of Hawaii's Blaisdell Arena. True to their character, the Swords busted hard out of the gate. They dove for loose balls, contested every pass, and bellied up on D. They clearly outhustled the Cavaliers, who undoubtedly were suffering the effects of jet lag.

Sampson, also battling the flu, struggled to keep pace with the Swords' energetic center. "I knew I couldn't handle him inside," Randolph said, "so I took him outside." Randolph's hot hand from long range lured Sampson to the perimeter, softening the middle.

Meanwhile, Virginia coach Terry Holland was feeling the heat. "They packed the lanes tight on us," he said. "They made us take perimeter shots, and we missed a lot of easy shots and just couldn't put the ball

Few knew how to pronounce "Chaminade" before the game, but sportscasters around the country were forced to learn after college basketball's biggest upset.

in the hole. They were collapsing and double- and triple-teaming Sampson."

Though Virginia out-rebounded Chaminade in the first half, the Silverswords outshot the Cavs and forced more turnovers. The score was 43–43 at halftime, and the Swords' confidence was sky-high. "When you start executing your plays, you start believing," Haenisch told ESPN.com. "We were tied at halftime and went into the locker room feeling 'they're not any better than us.'"

Virginia regrouped in the second half and began to pull away. After guard Ricky Stokes scored from the right baseline with 11:14 to play, the Cavs led 56–49. Yet the Swords wouldn't roll over. Down 58–56, Chaminade guard Mark Rodrigues lobbed a no-look alley-oop pass to a hard-charging Dunham. The six-foot jumping jack skied above Sampson and threw down an exclamatory jam, rocking the house. The score was tied at 58.

"There was a growing sense that we had a chance to at least take it down to the wire," said Dunham. "And then it was incredible, and loud, when people started to believe that we could actually win the game. People went crazy."

The lead seesawed until the 1:37 mark, when Chaminade guard Mark Wells scored on a baseline drive to give his team a 70–68 edge. The Silverswords maintained the lead, 74–72, with seconds remaining. Virginia had a chance to tie the score, but—with 10 seconds to go—official Giff Johnson whistled Cavs guard Othell Wilson for traveling. Virginia furiously debated the call, but to no avail. Chaminade nailed three free throws and won 77–72.

Blaisdell Arena erupted in euphoria and disbelief. The Silverswords cut down the nets, while Haenisch and Rodrigues actually sat on the rims—like kings on their thrones.

"I must be dreaming," said Coach Lopes. "It's really amazing what human beings can do!"

Back on the mainland, in the wee hours of Christmas Eve, the news arrived of the upset. ESPN anchorman Tom Mees, working the late shift, was handed the result of the game. He refused to report it, insisting that the staff verify the unbelievable score.

Outside the Virginia locker room, reporters asked Coach Holland to explain what had happened. "Greatest college basketball upset ever," he responded. "That's what I call it."

OLD PALS FROM THE HOOD

Chaminade is about 5,000 miles from Virginia, but—wouldn't you know it?—the two teams' centers hailed from the same area. While Chaminade's Tony Randolph starred at Lee–Staunton High School in Virginia, Ralph Sampson toiled for Valley League rival Harrisonburg High.

"Tony and Ralph grew up together," said Chaminade's Tim Dunham. "I think Tony dated Ralph's sister or Ralph dated Tony's sister or something like that. They knew each other real well."

They also had played together in pickup games, and Randolph had learned how to expose the flaws of the towering giant. Prior to the Virginia game, Randolph and Dunham stayed up half the night discussing strategy.

"Tony went outside on him," Dunham recalled. "He made Ralph leave the key. He hit like eight jump shots on him, and Tony could do that to you. He just kept making jump shots and stretching the defense, pulling Ralph outside. Then us little guys could sneak in there for layups." Sampson finished with just 12 points in 38 minutes, while Randolph poured in 19. Sampson went on to star in the NBA, earning the All-Star Game MVP award in 1985 and leading the Houston Rockets to the NBA Finals in 1986. Some may deem Randolph's lifework even more impressive. He worked for the state of Hawaii for 13 years, counseling troubled juveniles.

Chapter Seven

Jim Valvano: Cinderella Is Italian and Lives in North Carolina

NCAA Basketball Final, North Carolina State vs. Houston
Albuquerque, New Mexico, April 4, 1983

On the afternoon of the NCAA championship game, in Albuquerque, New Mexico, NC State Coach Jim Valvano, a hyper Italian-American from New York, battled a hernia and the flu. Prior to that night's game against No. 1–ranked Houston, Jimmy V was shot up with fluids to reduce his 104 degree fever.

Then, just before tipoff, Valvano erased the team's conservative, slow-down game plan from the locker room chalkboard. "He goes, 'If you think we're going to hold the ball in front of 40 million people, you're friggin' crazy,'" NC State guard Mike Warren told ESPN.com.

Valvano's Wolfpack had made the finals despite 10 losses. More amazingly, they had trailed in the final minute in six of their last eight victories. Erase the whole game plan? Why not? For a team riding such an insane streak of luck, or destiny, relying on logic no longer seemed relevant—even against a squad as mighty as Houston.

Coach Guy V. Lewis's Houston Cougars, aka "Phi Slamma Jamma," boasted center Akeem (later Hakeem) Olajuwon and guard Clyde Drexler, future

NBA superstars. They, along with Larry Micheaux, Michael Young, and Benny Anders, dunked their way to victory in their 25 previous games. Included was a 94–81 throw-down of powerhouse Louisville in the national semifinal game, in which the Jammas stuffed 10 dunks in the final 13 minutes.

While the Cougars cruised to the title game, the Wolfpack scratched and clawed for every victory. Inspired by the energetic and bombastic Valvano, the NC State starters were a modestly talented but mentally tough quintet. Bombardier Dereck Whittenburg led the team with 17.5 points per contest, while Thurl Bailey averaged 16.7 points and 7.7 boards per game. Point guard Sidney Lowe distributed the rock and picked pockets defensively. Front-courters Cozell McQueen and Lorenzo Charles, nicknamed Co-zilla and Lo-zilla, battled hard in the paint.

The Wolfpack not only lost 10 games, but two of

Few plays in college basketball history can match Lorenzo Charles' buzzer-beating dunk that gave N.C. State the 1983 national title.

the losses were by 18 points each to unranked teams. To even qualify for the NCAA tournament, NCSU had to win the exceptionally competitive ACC tourney. Shockingly, they did—in dramatic fashion. The Wolfpack squeaked past Wake Forest 71–70, upset Michael Jordan–led North Carolina, and slayed Virginia—led by three-time National College Player of the Year Ralph Sampson.

For this Cinderella team, midnight nearly struck in round one of the NCAAs. NC State trailed Pepperdine by six with just 24 seconds to play. The Wolfpack cut the deficit to two with eight seconds to go and Whittenburg at the line for a one-on-one. In what some might call micro-coaching, Valvano told 6'11" lefty McQueen to move to the left side of the lane in case a missed free throw bounced that way. Sure enough, an errant Whittenburg foul shot caromed to McQueen's dominant left hand, and he tipped it in to tie the game. NC State won in double overtime.

By this time, NCSU players had utter faith in Valvano and themselves. "He treated us with such great respect that everybody on that team wanted to play hard for him," said Whittenburg. "We had complete belief in him…. We were confident that if we stayed close in a game, we were going to win it."

Game after game, the Wolfpack rode their faith to victory. After trailing sixth-ranked UNLV by 12 in the second half, they rallied to win 71–70. NC State then routed Utah and rallied to nip Virginia 63–62, winning a trip to the Final Four in Albuquerque, New Mexico. In the national semi-final game, NCSU breezed past Georgia, whose shooting was as cold as Valvano's fever was hot.

Despite their spectacular run, the Wolfpack were overwhelming underdogs against Phi Slamma Jamma. Valvano, though, saved his greatest

Jim Valvano (right) *and the Wolfpack stood atop the college basketball world after upsetting powerful Houston.*

After North Carolina State's miraculous victory in the 1983 championship game, coach Jim Valvano ran frantically around the floor, looking for someone, anyone, to hug. The moment was pure Jimmy V, the man who not only effused positive energy, but embraced basketball, life, and even his players for all they were worth.

"I'm a very emotional, passionate man," Valvano said in a speech at the ESPYs in 1993. "I can't help it. That's being the son of Rocco and Angelina Valvano. It comes with the territory. We hug, we kiss, we love."

Many credited NCSU's title to Valvano's big heart. "We really took to his personality," said Dereck Whittenburg. "He saw us as people and treated us with such great respect, that everybody on that team wanted to play hard for him."

NCSU's championship shot Valvano to national stardom. And when he was diagnosed with cancer in 1992, he moved millions to tears with his passionate, inspiring speeches. Cancer could destroy his body, he said, but it couldn't touch his mind, his heart, his soul.

At the '93 ESPYs, Valvano announced the creation of the V Foundation for Cancer Research. He died just two and a half months later, but his spirit lived on. By 2004, the V Foundation had raised more than $32 million for cancer research. Even in death, he kept on giving.

coaching magic for the final game. His game plan obliteration before tipoff electrified his players. "We were a fired-up team," recalled Warren. "We didn't need doors; we ran right through them."

Valvano employed a masterful plan. The Wolfpack would wall off the inside to prevent penetration and jams, forcing Houston to beat them from the perimeter. They also—despite Valvano's pregame rhetoric— would slow down the tempo, muddying the track for the racehorse Cougars. In the final minutes, NCSU would foul Houston intentionally and relentlessly, hoping the 61 percent foul-shooting team would dig its own grave.

The first half went according to plan for NC State. Houston, unable to get to the basket, became Phi Shoota Missa. Drexler, normally good for at least 20 a game, struggled with four fouls. Bailey, meanwhile, drained 15 first-half points for NCSU, which led 33–25 at halftime.

In the second half, a determined Olajuwon spurred a 17–2 Cougar run. Up 42–35, with the game seemingly in the bag, Coach Lewis ordered a "spread delay" offense. He hoped to burn the clock while opening the floor for drives and layups. His strategy produced just one layup while letting NC State back in the game. When Whittenburg hit his second straight bucket with 1:59 to play, the score was knotted at 52.

Still tied at 1:05, Valvano boldly ordered his players to foul. They hacked freshman guard Alvin Franklin, who missed his first shot of the one-and-one. NC State rebounded the ball and—with a nation gripped in suspense—worked for the last shot.

With the clock in single digits, Whittenburg recalled, "I was thinking, *I need to get this ball to the basket,* and I put up the shot." His attempt, a 35-foot heave, fell short of the rim. What followed, however, was one of the most replayed moments in sports history. Lorenzo Charles, 6'7", soared high for the airball and, while still in midair, flushed it home.

NC State fans rushed the court, while Phi Slamma Jamma players pounded the floor in anguish. Valvano ran frantically about, looking for someone to hug. Never before had the NCAA tournament staged such high drama.

Chapter Eight

Curse Busters

American League Championship Series, Boston Red Sox vs. New York Yankees
Fenway Park, Boston, and Yankee Stadium, Bronx, New York, October 12–20, 2004

When the Boston Red Sox fell behind the New York Yankees three games to none in the 2004 American League Champion Series, they were given up for dead. No team in 100 years of postseason play had ever pulled itself out of a 3–0 hole to win a series. But more important, the Red Sox were "cursed"—doomed to failure ever since the sale of "The Bambino," Babe Ruth, to the Yankees in 1919.

Bolstered by a young Ruth—a dandy lefty pitcher who was emerging as a prodigious slugger—Boston won world titles in 1915, '16, and '18. However, Red Sox owner Harry Frazee was in debt, and he began to sell his ballplayers to the highest bidders. In December 1919, Frazee sold Ruth to the Yankees for about $100,000 and a loan of $300,000.

Over the next 84 years, it seemed that Frazee had sold his soul to the devil. Ruth became the greatest player of all time and laid the foundation for the best

Boston's David Ortiz (right) *won Game 4 on a 12th-inning home run. Thus began a string of eight straight wins that gave the Red Sox a championship.*

October 27, 1986, George White suffered a Sox-fan breakdown. Boston had blown Game 6 of the World Series on Bill Buckner's error two days earlier, and now they dropped Game 7 to the New York Mets. "I picked up the phone and called home," White said. "My father answered, and I said, 'I'm here all alone, the Red Sox have just lost the Series, and I need my mother.' I was 44 years old."

For generations, Boston boasted the most loyal, intelligent fans in baseball—and also the hardest suffering. After the Buckner game, Red Sox diehards seemed to bear an invisible cross, lugging the burden of the team's misfortunes season after season for another 18 years.

In 2004, however, a new day dawned. Boston players let their hair down and copped a happy-go-lucky attitude, and so did their fans. Out was the serious, fatalistic diehard with a transistor radio in one hand and a scorecard and pencil in the other.

In were the face-painting, wig-wearing yahoos who typified the new Red Sox Nation. One teenage girl, with shoulder-length brown hair, painted a beard on her face to become the female Johnny Damon.

The positive energy electrified Fenway Park. Even when down three games to none in the 2004 ALCS, Sox fans stuck to their new, upbeat motto: "Keep the Faith." What followed was an explosion of euphoria—eight straight wins against the Yankees and Cardinals, followed by a victory parade that drew 3.2 million people (more than five times the population of Boston!).

For the first time in their lives, Red Sox fans could bask in championship glory. And for many, it had been a long life. Said Red Sox chairman Tom Werner, "There have been so many people in their 90s who said, 'I just want to live long enough to see one championship before I die.' This is for them."

dynasty in sports history—26 world titles in all. The Red Sox, stung by the "Curse of the Bambino," couldn't win even one World Series.

Boston came close several times, only to lose in heartbreaking fashion. The Red Sox lost to St. Louis in the 1946 World Series, dropping Game 7 on Enos Slaughter's "mad dash" around the bases. They lost two more Game 7s—to St. Louis in 1967 and Cincinnati in 1975—before the ultimate World Series breakdown in 1986. Up 5–3 in the 10th inning of Game 6 against the New York Mets, with two outs and no one on, Boston actually blew the game. The winning run scored when a grounder skipped through the legs of Boston first baseman Bill Buckner. The Mets, of course, went on to win Game 7.

The Yankees, though, remained Boston's biggest rival. For decades, Yankees fans rubbed their superiority in the faces of Boston diehards. Bad blood surfaced on the field as well, with ugly brawls erupting in 1973 and '76. In 1978, the Yankees beat Boston in a one-game playoff for the division title, winning on a home run

from light-hitting Yankees shortstop Bucky Dent.

In 2003 the curse reached epic proportions. A brawl marred the ALCS, with Boston ace Pedro Martinez throwing 72-year-old Yankees coach Don Zimmer to the ground. The Yankees got revenge in Game 7, rallying in the bottom of the eighth and winning in the 11th on Aaron Boone's walk-off home run.

Years of failure were taking their toll. The Red Sox had become too somber a ballclub: from the solemn voice of their PA announcer to their fatalistic fans to the cleancut players who choked with the title on the line. It was time for the Red Sox to let their hair down, and they did—literally.

When Boston leadoff man Johnny Damon arrived at spring training in 2004, he sported a beard and silky hair down to his shoulders. "We call him Jesus," said outfielder Kevin Millar, "and he's running

Johnny Damon hit two home runs in Game 7, driving in six runs and powering Boston to a 10-3 romp.

around sprinkling water on people to end the curse."

As the season progressed, other Red Sox grew out their hair, including Martinez and superstar slugger Manny Ramirez. Moreover, new manager Terry Francona infused positive energy into the club. Other acquisitions bolstered the team's hopes for success, including big-game pitcher Curt Schilling and closer Keith Foulke. From August 16 through September 11, the Red Sox went 20–2, and they earned a wildcard playoff berth with a 98–64 record. Ramirez (43 homers, 130 RBI) and David Ortiz (41, 139) powered the best offense in the league.

More important, the Red Sox entered the playoffs looking loose and confident. "We're a bunch of grinders—just a bunch of idiots," said Millar. "But we never quit." They proved it in the AL Division Series. Boston swept Anaheim, winning the finale on a 10th-inning, game-ending homer by Ortiz.

Boston next faced New York in the ALCS, and soon the Red Sox crashed from their sugar high. The Yankees won the first two in the Bronx, 10–7 and 3–1, before massacring the Beantowners, 19–8, at Fenway Park. At that point, Red Sox fans called it a season. They knew the reality: No team in major league history—dating back to the 1903 World Series—ever had rallied from an 0–3 deficit to win a postseason series. But remember, this was no ordinary team.

Down 4–3 in the bottom of the ninth of Game 4, Boston's Bill Mueller singled in Dave Roberts to force extra innings. In the 12th, Ortiz belted another walk-off home run, this one at 1:22 A.M. The big fella proved himself again the next night. Boston rallied for two in the eighth, one on an Ortiz homer, to tie the score at 4. The tension remained until the 14th, when Ortiz singled in the game-winning run.

The Red Sox still had to win Games 6 and 7, both in New York, but now the Yankees felt the tug of the choke collar. Schilling, pitching on a dislocated ankle tendon, showed the pride of a champion in Game 6. He yielded just one run in a 4–2 Boston victory. "When I saw blood dripping through the sock and he's giving us seven innings, that was storybook," said Millar.

And it had a happy ending: Boston, thanks to Damon's two homers and six RBI, cruised in Game 7, 10–3. Sox owner John Henry rightfully called it the greatest comeback in baseball history.

But the Red Sox still needed to beat St. Louis—their other old nemesis—in the World Series to break the curse. Once Mark Bellhorn crushed his game-winning homer in the eighth inning of Game 1, however, there was no stopping the Sox. They cruised to four straight over the Cardinals, giving them eight in a row, to secure their first world title since 1918.

Red Sox fans erupted in celebration, culminating in a victory parade that drew nearly three and a half million people. Lifelong Sox fan Anthony Mimichiello, 92, offered perspective: "I stopped going to the games after 1986. I quit. They kept breaking my heart. But we finally won one. It's the greatest thing to ever happen to Boston."

The 2004 Red Sox celebrated a dramatic seven-game win over the rival Yankees, a prelude to their first World Series title since 1918.

Chapter Nine

Rulon Gardner:
The Super-Size Champion

Summer Olympics, Greco-Roman Super Heavyweight Wrestling Final
Sydney, Australia, September 27, 2000

Afton, Wyoming, population 1,818, is considered the jewel of Lincoln County. At greasy spoon diners around the area, farmers mingle to debate the most pressing issues of the day—what to feed an ailing dairy cow, or the practical limits for the cost of a fishing license or other pressing questions local folks need answers to.

But for weeks after local boy Rulon Gardner went to the Olympics, the conversations rarely turned to anything but him, save a few slight digressions—like overeating. "Look at Rulon," they might say. "Didn't do no damage to him."

Today, a couple of weeks after he won the Gold Medal in Sydney, Australia, for beating Russian wrestler Alexander Karelin, the whole town, and then some, are going to throw a little celebration. Rulon's home now and he's coming too.

Gardner drove to town from his family farm on his tractor, complete with his Olympic gold medal dangling from his brawny neck. Bouncing along the side of the highway, he reached the edge of town, where he pulled the tractor to the side of the road and transferred to a fire truck, to be chauffeured into town by the fire department.

Dismounting the truck, he strolled down the entire five blocks of downtown carrying an American flag. Then, the 6'3", 286-pound Gardner was hoisted—with

some difficulty—onto a thronelike chair. Aware he's no lightweight, the Star Valley High School wrestling coach had recruited some former high school wrestlers to get him on top of his royal chariot, cleverly named the "Greco-Roman coach," a homemade job they put together especially for the occasion. It consisted of two poles and a chair. Wobbling along the town streets, the fatigued throne-bearers dropped him off between the car dealership and the gas station convenience store, where they'd built a stage. "This medal is not mine," he said, picking up the gold from his sweaty 54-inch chest. *"This is all of ours!"*

A couple of weeks earlier the hefty farm boy was in the very last place you'd ever expect to see someone who looks like the poster child for the evils of gluttony. As heavy as ever, his ample girth was squeezed into a wrestler's uniform. Off the farm now, this wall of a man was America's hope for a medal in the Super Heavyweight Division of Greco-Roman wrestling at the 2000 Summer Olympics in Sydney, Australia. Gardner would have to wrestle Russian colossus Alexander Karelin for

American Rulon Gardner (right) *held on for dear life—not to mention a gold medal—against the mighty Russian Alexander Karelin.*

the gold before a crowd that included IOC president Juan Antonio Samaranch.

Few, if any, expected Gardner to stop Karelin from easily winning his fourth gold medal: No one had beaten the Russian wrestler in 13 years. Standing 6'3" and weighing 286 pounds, the bald, angular-featured Alexander Karelin looked like some genetically engineered by-product of the Cold War. Rumor had it that Karelin trained by high-stepping at top speed through densely packed, waist-high snow-drifts in Siberia. And that he once carried a huge refrigerator up eight flights of stairs without breaking a sweat. Of course, the more victories Karelin racked up over the course of his 13-year-long winning streak, the more out-landish the stories became about his feats of extraordinary strength and endurance.

The only certainty about the mysterious Karelin was his effortless domination of the mat.

Karelin's mastery of Greco-Roman wrestling was not lost on Gardner, who only took up this style of wrestling in 1993, the year he placed fourth in the NCAA championships. By 1996, Rulon was good enough to make the cut for the Olympic Trials. What should have been a shining moment for him—sweet vindication for the years of being called "Fatso" by classmates and dismissed by neighbors as slow and awkward—sadly dissolved into a very public embarrassment. Through a combination of crossed signals, poor timing, and monumentally bad luck, Gardner missed his weigh-in at the Olympic Trials by 20 seconds. It was a humiliating moment for Gardner, who would later watch U.S. wrestler Matt Ghaffari sob inconsolably after losing to Karelin in the 1996 Atlanta Games.

Nor would Gardner's luck improve when he faced Karelin for the first time in 1997. Three times Karelin simply hoisted his American competitor aloft and tossed him on his head to win the match 5–0. It was an awesome display of Karelin's signature move, the reverse body lift. His massive arms locked around Gardner's waist, Karelin arched his back, lifted Gardner up, and heaved the American feet-first *over his head*. As Gardner later told Jack McCallum of *Sports Illustrated*, "I landed so hard the back of my heels almost came around and touched my head."

As Gardner's ultra-devout Mormon parents and wife watched anxiously from the sidelines in Sydney, the dairy farmer's son stepped onto the mat to face his nemesis. There were no theatrics or acrobatics—just the grim spectacle of two super-heavyweights locked in a sweat-drenched bear hug. Ever the aggressor, Karelin repeatedly tried to swivel Gardner to take him down, but Gardner invariably repelled him. Spectators expecting Karelin to make fast work of Gardner were

Gardner went from rural Wyoming to the top of the wrestling world.

ᖂᖆ

Rumor had it that Karelin trained by high-stepping at top speed through densely packed, waist-high snowdrifts in Siberia.

ᖂᖆ

astonished. Even though he was cited by some for passivity in the match, Gardner more than held his own opposite the Olympic champion.

Then, early in the second round, Gardner scored the coup de grace. Gripped by Karelin for 28 seconds, Rulon suddenly broke free by "squirming like a worm"—he wiggled his hips just enough to settle his stance and surprise Karelin, who released his iron hold for a split second. In that moment, Gardner scored the first and only point of the match. Since neither had scored at least three points, the match went into a mandatory overtime.

Although he appeared noticeably fatigued, Karelin remained formidable. Raging against the inevitable, he kept trying to push Gardner down, but the match had taken a heavy toll on the Russian. With five seconds left on the clock, Karelin wearily conceded defeat by bowing his head in resignation. Jubilant in victory, Gardner executed a cartwheel to thunderous applause: The junk food junkie with the gentle smile had slain the ferocious Russian giant.

A few weeks later when Jay Leno had him on his show, 2,400 folks from the Afton, Wyoming, area—that's 600 more than the local population—congregated at Star Valley High School to watch Rulon on TV. Gardner made a spectacular grand entrance to *The Tonight Show* set, second only to the one he had made back home in Wyoming at the Afton bash. He entered from stage left...doing a cartwheel!

Chapter Ten

Rollie Ain't No Fool

NCAA Basketball Final, Villanova Wildcats vs. Georgetown Hoyas
Lexington, Kentucky, April 1, 1985

On April Fool's Day 1985, Villanova coach Rollie Massimino surprised his players. The Wildcats, upset victors in five NCAA tournament games in March, were about to play the mightiest team of all—the Patrick Ewing–led Georgetown Hoyas—in the championship game. Massimino, the jolly, cigar-chompin' coach, told his players to go sit in their hotel rooms and meditate for 15 minutes.

"It was very powerful," said reserve guard Harold Jensen. "He asked that we picture playing, executing, and winning the game, visualize celebrating and the feeling you would have."

The coach also should have asked them to say 10 Hail Marys, because Villanova—one of three Catholic schools in the Final Four—was a 10-point underdog against Georgetown.

Massimino himself said the Hoyas were as good as any team in NCAA history. The national champion a year earlier, Georgetown entered this game with 16 straight postseason victories. The team was 34–2 in 1984–85, losing the two games by a total of three

points. Led by three-time All-America center Patrick Ewing—and future NBA stars Reggie Williams and David Wingate—Georgetown crushed national power St. John's in the semifinals 77–59.

Villanova, meanwhile, had proven that it couldn't beat Georgetown *or* St. John's, losing to the fellow Big East teams five times during the season (twice to the Hoyas).

Dwayne McClain dunked in front of Georgetown center Patrick Ewing (33) while Villanova teammate Ed Pinckney looked on.

Right: *Villanova's Rollie Massimino made all the right steps in the NCAA's Big Dance.*

The Wildcats had ended their unimpressive 19-10 regular season with a 23-point loss to Pittsburgh, and they made the tournament only because the field was expanded to 64 teams for the first time.

Though Villanova, a school outside Philadelphia, boasted a star player in center "Easy" Ed Pinckney, it lacked offensive firepower. Massimino compensated for his shortage of talent by controlling the tempo and continuously changing defensive sets to confuse opponents. The Wildcats' slow-down game worked better in the tournament than during the regular season because the 48-second shot clock wasn't used in the Big Dance that year.

Seeded eighth in the Southeast Regional, Villanova opened the tournament with a win against ninth-seed Dayton—on Dayton's home floor. 'Nova's reward was a matchup against No. 1 seed Michigan, whom it shocked 59–55 thanks to 20 points from forward Dwayne "D-Train" McClain. Massimino slowed the

pace to a crawl in the next two games, downing ACC powers Maryland (46–43) and North Carolina (56–44). After stunning 31–3 Memphis State in the national semifinal game 52–45, the Wildcats found themselves—for only the second time ever—playing in the NCAA championship game.

After their 15 minutes of meditation, and a pregame meal, the Wildcats arrived at Rupp Arena in Lexington, Kentucky. The bottom line was that no No. 8 seed had ever won the NCAA championship, and as such the Wildcats seemed doomed. Longtime Villanova trainer Jake Nevin, arriving on the floor in a wheelchair, could only hope to see his team accomplish what they'd never been able to accomplish before: go home national champions.

Massimino, whose sideline brilliance had earned him National Coach of the Year honors, rolled out his familiar but hardly renowned starting lineup: Pinckney, a slithery center who led the team in scoring; McClain,

THE STAT SHEET: 1985 NCAA CHAMPIONSHIP GAME

VILLANOVA	FG-A	FT-A	REB	AST	PF	PTS
Harold Pressley	4-6	3-4	4	1	1	11
Dwayne McClain	5-7	7-8	1	3	3	17
Ed Pinckney	5-7	6-7	6	5	3	16
Dwight Wilbur	0-0	0-0	0	1	0	0
Gary McLain	3-3	2-2	2	2	2	8
Harold Jensen	5-5	4-5	1	2	2	14
Mark Plansky	0-0	0-1	0	0	1	0
Chuck Everson	0-0	0-0	0	0	0	0
Totals	22-28	22-27	14	14	12	66

GEORGETOWN	FG-A	FT-A	REB	AST	PF	PTS
Bill Martin	4-6	2-2	5	1	2	10
Reggie Williams	5-9	0-2	4	2	3	10
Patrick Ewing	7-13	0-0	5	2	4	14
Michael Jackson	4-7	0-0	0	9	4	8
David Wingate	8-14	0-0	2	2	4	16
Perry McDonald	0-1	0-0	0	0	0	0
Horace Broadnax	1-2	2-2	1	2	4	4
Ralph Dalton	0-1	2-2	0	0	1	2
Totals	29-53	6-8	17	18	22	64

Turnovers: Villanova 17, Georgetown 11 • Halftime: Villanova 29, Georgetown 28 • Attendance: 23,124

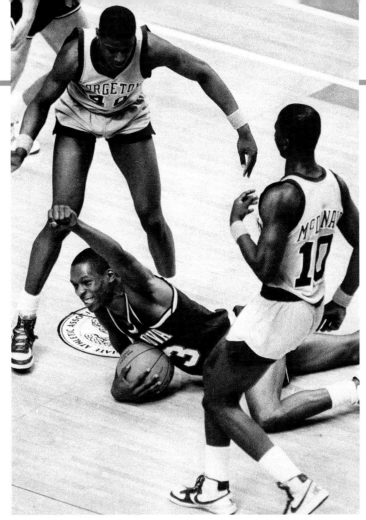

McClain capped a near-perfect game for Villanova by pouncing on the ball as the final seconds expired.

the 'Cats' finest marksman; Harold Pressley, a defensive specialist; Gary McLain, the senior point guard who controlled the tempo; and Dwight Wilbur, a "shooting" guard who had averaged just 1.2 points per game in the tournament.

In the Georgetown seating section, a student sported a sign that read, "Cinderella, Midnight Is Here." As the teams prepared for the tipoff, 'Nova got a good look at Ewing, the "Hoya Destroya," who could intimidate foes with his menacing glare alone. Ewing had won 121 collegiate games and, in the '85 tournament, helped limit opponents to 36 percent shooting from the floor.

The Wildcats needed more than prayers; they needed to play perfect basketball. In the first half, they nearly did. Despite intense defensive pressure, Villanova at one point swished 7-of-8 field goals. How did they

do it? "Patience, good shot selection, and a couple fortunate rolls," said Jensen, 'Nova's sixth man.

The Wildcats' sharpshooting prompted Georgetown coach John Thompson to relieve offensive whiz Williams with defensive specialist Horace Broadnax—a sign that Villanova was controlling the game. With the half winding down, 'Nova trailed by just one, 28–27. Wildcats fans rose to their feet, then roared in delight as a Pressley bucket put his team ahead at halftime.

Oozing confidence, the Wildcats took it right to Ewing in the second half, with Pinckney, Pressley, and Jensen all finding success. On the other end, Ewing and Co. couldn't solve Villanova's matchup zone and its many variations. On the strength of a 9–2 run, 'Nova went up 38–32. Wingate's bull's-eye shooting brought the Hoyas back, though, and they took leads of 42–41, 44–43, 46–45, and 54–53. Not since fictional underdog boxer Rocky Balboa battled Apollo Creed had Philadelphians witnessed such high drama. After milking the clock, Jensen hit the shot of the game—a 16-footer from the right wing. With 2:36 left, 'Nova led 55–54.

Down the stretch, the Wildcats played like champions, forcing turnovers and bad shots and burying free throws with icy consistency. Up 66–64 in the waning moments, McClain pounced on a loose ball, protecting it like a wildcat would its kitten until the clock ran out. "It was euphoric when the buzzer sounded," Jensen recalled, "a rush like no other."

On April Fool's Day 1985, Villanova had become the lowest-seeded team ever to win the national title. The Wildcats' .786 field goal shooting—including 9-of-10 in the second half—set an NCAA tournament single-game record. They had performed so magnificently that the Georgetown players applauded as the Wildcats mounted the victory stand. "You couldn't get much better," Coach Thompson said.

Amid the celebration, Jensen walked up to trainer Jake Nevin, who till now could only dream his beloved school would win a national title. Jensen kissed him on top of the head. "This one's for you, pal."

Chapter Eleven

Black and White and Read All Over

NCAA Basketball Final, Texas Western Miners vs. Kentucky Wildcats
College Park, Maryland, March 19, 1966

The finalists at the 1966 NCAA championship game looked like two pups from the same litter…sort of.

Kentucky was ranked No. 1; Texas Western—now University of Texas–El Paso—ranked No. 3. Incredibly, both boasted a 23-game winning streak during the season. Beyond that, one team was salt, the other was pepper. The Kentucky lineup was nothing but white bread; Texas Western was almost entirely black. That good ol' boy camaraderie that often links southern schools was left back in the Texas Hill Country hollows. This was the Big Dance and, as everyone of that era knew well, blacks don't dance with whites, not in the Southland. Not in 1966.

The two head coaches reflected the dichotomy well. Adolph Rupp, in his 36th season as Kentucky's bench boss, was an old-school disciplinarian. He had won four NCAA titles, more than any other coach at the time, and was honored as National Coach of the Year in 1966. A cantankerous southerner, Rupp had a reputation as a racist. He had never recruited or coached an African-American player. In fact, he had even called newspaper editors asking them to put asterisks next to the names of black high school players so he would know whom *not* to recruit.

Texas Western coach Don Haskins was born in 1930, the year Rupp started coaching at Kentucky. Haskins eschewed a tightly controlled offense for a wide-open attack. Haskins not only welcomed black players, he spat at the notion of the day that said clubs needed at least some white players to maintain team discipline. In 1966 Haskins's top eight players were African-American, and the team became the first in NCAA Finals history to feature an all-black starting lineup.

Entering the championship game, Kentucky garnered seemingly all of the respect. The

---

Tommy Kron (30) made an outlet pass to Kentucky teammate Larry Conley (40) over the head of Lattin, but Texas Western's defense proved too tough for the Wildcats.

Wildcats, known as "Rupp's Runts" because they were so small, had reached the NCAA Finals in College Park, Maryland, by defeating a tough Duke team—a game that many were calling the "real national championship." Texas Western, meanwhile, "sneaked in" by knocking off lightly regarded Utah in the semis.

Rupp seemed smugly confident that he would wear his fifth national crown. After all, he said at a press conference, a team of all-black players could never beat an all-white team.

Haskins, meanwhile, wasn't sure about anything. He couldn't sleep during Final Four week, and he battled throbbing headaches. Perhaps because Texas Western had never challenged for a national championship—in any sport—he repeatedly said that this was his only chance for a title. The night before the championship game, well past midnight, Haskins drank some beer and reflected about life with some friends in his motel room.

Though Haskins battled uncertainty, and the press considered Kentucky's victory a foregone conclusion, the Texas Western players believed they would prevail. "We never doubted we were going to win the game," said David Lattin, the 240-pound center. "Player for player, we were the better team, and we knew it."

The Miners didn't boast any All-America players, or even all-district, but they were one of the best defensive teams in the nation. "Big Daddy D" Lattin and forward Nevil "The Shadow" Shed specialized in shutting down opponents.

Rupp's Runts, featuring future NBA super-coach Pat Riley, were a small, quick, fundamentally sound

Any uncertainty on Don Haskins's part was long gone by the time he shook hands with Kentucky coach Adolph Rupp (center) after steering Texas Western to the NCAA title.

"When that clock started ticking off, it seemed that the whole world just stood still…. Five, four, three…. I could feel my heart beating. We were going to beat Kentucky. We were going to win the national championship."

bunch who could shoot the lights out. Haskins decided to offset their speed by starting a three-guard lineup. Willie Worsley, a 5'6" waterbug, would start alongside 6'1" Orsten Artis and 5'9" Bobby Joe Hill, the Miners' most dynamic player. Other than that change, Haskins would stick to his usual game plan: man-to-man defense and a freelance attack on offense.

Early in the game at Cole Fieldhouse, with the score tied 9–9, Hill beat the Runts at their own game. The lightning-quick point guard stole the ball from Tommy Kron and sped to the bucket for two. Then, on the very next play, Hill swiped Louie Dampier's dribble and stormed the other way for another layup. The one-two punch may not have been a knockout blow, but it stunned and staggered the veteran Wildcats.

Rupp tried to frustrate Texas Western with a 1-3-1 zone, forcing the underdogs to score from the perimeter. However, the Miners made their shots while, ironically, the normally sharp Wildcat shooters did not—largely because of the Miners' tight defense. The stingy D helped Texas Western build an eight-point lead with four minutes to go in the first half. "We tightened the rubber band on 'em," said Lattin, "and never allowed them to feel comfort-

able that they could come back and win."

Throughout the second half, Kentucky tried repeatedly to close the scoring gap, only to see Texas Western pull away each time. After UK moved within one point with three and a half minutes to go, Artis and Hill combined for six straight points. Kentucky now repeatedly fouled the Miners, hoping that the supposedly undisciplined club would choke at the line. No way. Said Lattin: "I remember thinking, 'Okay, you want to keep putting us on the line? We're going to keep making them and stretching this lead.'"

With each free-three attempt, the Miners hammered nails into Kentucky's coffin. During one stretch, they buried 26 foul shots in 27 attempts. Clearly, TW had much greater fortitude than Rupp or the press had given them credit for. "We had that confidence against anybody," Lattin said. "It didn't matter if you were ranked No. 1. We felt like we were bulletproof."

The Miners increased the lead to nine. Then, with the score 72–65, TW's pint-sized ball-handlers dribbled out the clock. "Oh, how I can remember those last seven seconds," said Shed in *And the Walls Came Tumbling Down*. "When that clock started ticking off, it seemed that the whole world just stood still…. Five, four, three…. I could feel my heart beating. We were going to beat Kentucky. We were going to win the national championship."

With Texas Western fans chanting, "We're No. 1," the final horn sounded. Cheerleaders and fans rushed onto the court, and Miners players climbed on each other's shoulders to cut down the net.

Not only did the Miners score a major upset, but they forever exploded the myth that a black team couldn't beat a white team. The victory, Hill told the *St. Petersburg Times,* "was the thing that opened doors in the ACC, the SEC…. Everybody started recruiting blacks after that."

Rupp's old ways had been disproved, and a nation hungry for the highest level of sport took notice. On that day, the squad from Texas Western served decisive proof that athletic ability and team spirit had nothing to do with race.

Chapter Twelve

Seabiscuit: "The Little Guy"

Pimlico Special, Seabiscuit vs. War Admiral
Pimlico Race Course, Baltimore, Maryland, November 1, 1938

Jockey George Woolf surprised Charlie Kurtsinger and War Admiral by taking Seabiscuit to the lead at the first turn.

Seabiscuit, on the rail, led War Admiral as the horses turned into the home stretch of their famous match race at Pimlico.

Extraordinary wealth, eastern establishment social cachet, championship race horses—why is this man not smiling?

Because Samuel D. Riddle, of the Pennsylvania Riddles, owner of the imperious stallion War Admiral, frowns upon uselessness; that is, superficialities like niceties, smiles, warmth, or humility. Even more upsetting to him now is the presence of so many inferiors in his midst, whose ranks include everyone not in his rarefied orbit.

All noblesse, no oblige, the septuagenarian millionaire lords over the common rabble, aka the press. He's now letting them know in no uncertain terms that his cherished horse War Admiral reigns supreme on the eastern racing circuit as 1937's Triple Crown winner. Surely even rubes like them must concede that the four-year-old War Admiral, whose sire was none other than legendary Man o' War, is unbeatable.

As much as they despise Riddle, most sportswriters grudgingly admit that the old crank is probably right. Although he seems to have inherited his owner's nasty streak, War Admiral regularly lays waste the competition. This sleek, powerfully built thoroughbred runs so fast, the track resembles scorched earth in his dusty wake. Any owner harebrained enough to pit their horse against War Admiral invites public failure and Riddle's scathing derision.

Enter Charles Howard. A brash, expansive San Francisco millionaire, nouveau riche by Riddle's blue-blood standards, and the owner of a knock-kneed runt of a horse burning up the racetracks on the West Coast. He's had it up to *here* with Riddle's tedious boasts and thinks his sleep-loving, five-year-old racehorse by the name of Seabiscuit can put that high and mighty War Admiral in his place. After much wrangling and grandstanding, a date is finally set for the California upstart to race the old-guard champion at Maryland's Pimlico Race Course: November 1, 1938.

Oddsmakers give War Admiral a slight edge over Seabiscuit in the 1³/16 of a mile race breathlessly hyped as "the Match Race of the Century."

Riddle still isn't smiling.

At four o'clock that crisp autumn afternoon, jockey George "The Iceman" Woolf rode Seabiscuit past the overflow crowd of 40,000 spectators to the start, where jockey Charley Kurtsinger waited astride the skittish War Admiral. Per Riddle's decree—one of many he had issued before finally agreeing to the race—there was no mechanical starting gate, since the famously temperamental War Admiral hates it. A flagman will instead drop the flag as starter George Cassidy rings the bell.

War Admiral was a jittery mess, twirling in circles and unresponsive to Kurtsinger. Seabiscuit looked like

he's just awakened from a luxurious nap and couldn't care less that 40,000 pairs of eyes are trained on him. Only Woolf can tell that Seabiscuit is fully, electrically alert to what lay ahead.

Howard and Riddle watch from their boxes. Conventional wisdom had it that War Admiral would break first, setting a ferocious pace that Seabiscuit wouldn't be able to match. Seabiscuit may have been the popular favorite—a hero to the Depression-era "little guy" Riddle holds in such contempt—but War Admiral is peerless on the racetrack.

Two false starts prolonged the exquisite agony of horse racing fans, both at Pimlico and across America, where some forty million people sat by their radios, listening to radioman Clem McCarthy's live commentary on NBC.

The flag dropped. Cassidy pressed the button and the bell rang as the horses burst from the starting line. Woolf used his whip to jump-start Seabiscuit, but the horse didn't need much incentive to give it his all. He careened ahead of War Admiral, taking a full-length lead as they zoomed past the first furlough to whoops and yells from spectators wreathing the track.

In his box, Riddle felt a slight pang of doubt before brushing it aside like a mosquito. War Admiral will not—cannot—lose to this flash-in-the-pan refugee from the glue factory.

Meanwhile, Seabiscuit widened his lead to two lengths right before the first quarter. At the pace he's setting, Seabiscuit would undoubtedly tire soon. At least that's what Kurtsinger believed as he pushed War Admiral to narrow the gap. Legs pumping furiously, War Admiral began moving up, closing in on Seabiscuit until the horses were running side by side, almost touching each other as they zoomed past the mile post.

Only three-sixteenths of a mile remained in the race. Any other horse running at Seabiscuit's breakneck pace probably would have collapsed by now. Somehow, though, Seabiscuit always knows to hold something in reserve, and this day was no exception. Woolf leaned over and murmured a few words of encouragement into the horse's ear. In a final, breathtaking surge, Seabiscuit suddenly rocketed ahead of War Admiral, who fell further and further behind, too spent to do anything but trail Seabiscuit by four seconds across the finish line.

Jubilant, Howard screamed and kissed his wife. Not only had Seabiscuit won, he'd also set a track record for Pimlico, running the mile and three-sixteenths in 1:56.

Riddle turned to Howard. Slowly, almost painfully, a feeble smile formed on his thin lips.

"It was a good race," he muttered and exited, as if winded by the strain of appearing magnanimous in defeat.

Down in the Winner's Circle, a flowery wreath of yellow chrysanthemums draped over his powerful neck, Seabiscuit appeared unfazed by the pandemonium. The full import of his achievement means nothing to him. Today was just another race to win and War Admiral another opponent to vanquish. Nibbling at the chrysanthemums, 1938's newly crowned Horse of the Year waits patiently for the adoring crowds to disperse so he can go back to the stable for a nice, long nap.

Seabiscuit, with jockey "Spec" Richardson up, won the Agua Caliente Handicap in March 1938. Entertainers Bing Crosby and Arline Judge joined owner Charles Howard and trainer Tom Smith.

Chapter Thirteen

The Typographical Error

World Cup Soccer Elimination Game
United States vs. England
Belo Horizonte, Brazil, June 29, 1950

S hielding his eyes from the glare, U.S. goalie Frank Borghi surveyed his teammates as they got into position on the field of Belo Horizonte's stadium. The night before, his team had partied in town. But now reality was setting in. The U.S. squad, a bunch of working stiffs, were about to play the legends of the game in the World Cup.

"7–0." That's all Borghi hoped for now—to keep that snotty English soccer team from scoring more than seven goals would be a coup all right. If he and his teammates could keep them to no more than seven goals, then maybe, just maybe, the Americans could hold their heads up reasonably high as they walked off the field in defeat.

It was a story right out of a Frank Capra movie. Eleven men—mostly blue-collar guys who played soccer on the weekends—were representing America in the 1950 World Cup. They had survived a grueling series of elimination games to make it to the qualifying rounds in Brazil, but their remarkable journey had rated no more than a squib in the sports pages, if that. It wasn't just that soccer itself flew well below the radar for most sports fans in America. Even outside the United States, where soccer practically constituted a religion for millions in Europe and South America, the unexpected presence of the U.S. team in the World Cup was considered a non-event. Especially when the stellar English team, reportedly insured for

After a hard-fought defensive battle, only one ball had made it into either team's net.

The American team of amateur and semi-pro players was expected to be a sacrificial lamb against mighty England, but it wound up setting the World Cup on its ear.

$3 million by venerable Lloyds of London, was making its long overdue World Cup debut that year.

For twenty years, ever since Uruguay had hosted the first World Cup in 1930, the English had resisted participating in the international tournament, which is held every four years. Admittedly, World War II had forced the event's organizers to suspend the World Cup for 1942 and 1946, but the English had been conspicuously MIA from the start. At the same time, they loudly and regularly proclaimed England to be the birthplace of modern soccer, so their long-standing refusal to compete struck many as inexplicable.

Could it have been that the English, whose disdain for all things French was legendary, were peeved that a *Frenchman*—World Football Federation president Jules Rimet—had first conceived of the World Cup in the 1920s? Whatever the reason, the English team had finally decided to grace the World Cup with their presence in Belo Horizonte, where they expected to make quick work of those upstart Yanks. In fact, English coach Walter Winterbottom was so confident that victory was assured, he let star player Stanley Matthews sit out this qualifying game. While his teammates made the 500-mile trek from Rio de Janeiro to Belo Horizonte, Matthews dozed on the beach in Rio, like any other pale, sun-starved British tourist on holiday.

Although the English team's dismissive attitude toward the Americans smacked of traditional British snobbery, no one disputed that Winterbottom's team was comprised of superior players who'd played together for years. In contrast, the American team had been virtually cobbled together at the last minute; they'd practiced just once before boarding the plane bound for Rio. Like Borghi, many of them were minor league baseball or football players who played soccer to stay in shape or for the love of the game—because it sure as hell wasn't for glory or profit. Playing for the American Soccer League in the 1940s, Walter Bahr never made more than $50 a game. His teammates took home even less, if they got paid at all, for playing on factory teams in the industrial leagues of the Northeast. Given the outstanding reputation of the English team, none of the American players harbored any illusions about their chances of winning the qualifying round.

Approximately 30,000 spectators gathered in Belo Horizonte's stadium to watch the English rout the Americans on June 29, 1950. As they took to the field, exhausted yet shot full of adrenaline, the Americans eyed their much vaunted opponents warily. With Matthews lolling on the beach in Rio, the English player to watch was inside-forward Stanley Mortenson, a veteran player whose speed was matched by his phenomenal scoring ability.

In the haze of an overcast sky, the game began. After a few minutes, it became stunningly clear that England had vastly underestimated the Americans, whose cracker-jack teamwork surprised everyone, including themselves.

At the 37-minute mark of the first half, the score was 0–0. Several times England, led by Mortenson, had come close to scoring, only to be repelled by Borghi or, worse, overshoot the goal entirely.

Then the unthinkable happened.

Twenty-five yards from the English goal, American midfielder Walter Bahr took a shot. The ball soared through the air, seemingly on course for the out-stretched hands of English goalie Bert Williams. But at the last minute, Bahr's teammate Joe Gaetjens suddenly rose from the throng of players clustered near the goal. In an uncanny display of skill and timing that some observers jokingly attributed to magic—Gaetjens was from Haiti, the land of voodoo—he headed the ball past Williams for the goal. With eight minutes left in the first half, the Americans were actually ahead 1–0, to England's crimson-faced mortification.

U.S. OPPONENTS AT OTHER CUPS

Of the seventeen World Cup competitions held since 1930, the United States soccer team has qualified to participate seven times. After the team's surprise victory over England in 1950, they suffered a humbling defeat to Chile 5–2. That would be the Americans' last appearance in the World Cup for the next *40* years. The team's World Cup drought finally ended in 1990, when they lost all three of their opening round matches.

In 2002, the United States soccer team redeemed itself by making it all the way to the World Cup quarterfinals. It was the best showing by the U.S. in the World Cup since 1930.

Of course, their unexpected lead was certain to evaporate when play resumed in the second half. No doubt England would be on the offensive, with Mortenson leading the ferocious charge to bury those upstart Yanks—or so many of the spectators predicted.

But as the game continued, it appeared that Gaetjens's spectacular goal had indeed put a hex on England. Despite numerous attempts, they were unable to score a single goal off the Americans. When the game ended, it was the Americans, not the English, whom the jubilant spectators hoisted on their shoulders in victory.

According to Associated Press sports columnist Jim Litke, when an interim report of the score was sent out on the AP newswire as 1–0 with only minutes left to play—and no victor yet cited—sportswriters around the world thought it was a typographical error that should have read "10–0, England."

But by the end of the day, AP confirmed the story. And the soccer world was stunned. USA 1, England 0, in what is still considered one of the greatest upsets of all time.

Chapter Fourteen

The Miracle of Milan

State High School Basketball Championship, Milan vs. Muncie Central
Indianapolis, Indiana, March 20, 1954

Milan's Bobby Plump dribbled the ball past the midcourt stripe. Then, as his team trailed 28–26, with 7:52 to go, he stopped and held the ball against his stomach and just stood there. And then, he stood there some more. With all eyes on him, Plump stood there a little more…just holding the ball. Seven minutes to go, six minutes, and now five something. Bobby didn't move.

In basketball-crazed Indiana, 90 percent of the state was tuned in to the battle for the state high school basketball championship that was broadcast on radio *and television*, the latter being almost unheard of in 1954 as a way to watch a *high school* game, much less any sports championship, save the World Series. Even NFL games weren't broadcast on TV back then.

Inside Butler Fieldhouse, all eyes were now transfixed on skinny Bobby Plump, who held the ball for what seemed agonizingly close to eternity. For Indianans, this was the biggest day of the year, save Christmas—the day the high school finalists faced off. And this year, the contest took on mythical proportions. Milan High School, representing a town of just 1,100 people, was facing the state's perennial juggernaut, Muncie Central. David versus Goliath.

Muncie Central, a much larger school that had won eight state titles, had been to the Final Four 17 times.

Muncie's front court players stood 6'5", 6'4", and 6'2". Milan's squad, on the other hand, had only *one* man over six feet, and just barely—Ron Truitt, the center, was 6'2" and everyone else on Milan's team was five-foot something, even Gene White, their second tallest man—a towering 5'11". Little Milan was obviously short on something, but not determination, nor time—there was too much of it left on the clock now. They had to stall some more, if they were to take Muncie down.

Plump continued to hold the ball. He looked over to Marvin Wood, Milan's head coach (actually, its *only* coach). "He was sitting there with his legs crossed, both hands out, palms crossed—the 'cat-and-mouse offense,'" Plump recalled 50 years later. "I figured he knew what he was doing. So I stood there with the ball for four minutes and thirteen seconds. You have to picture the scene." Plump continues: "Fifteen thousand people screaming as I did *nothing*. They had been scalping tickets outside for 50 bucks—and they only cost $2.50—and they're just screaming at us, and there's nothing happening on the floor."

Indiana boasted several bigger cities in 1954, including Indianapolis, the site of the championship tournament. But the lifeblood of Indiana was found in its hundreds of small towns. These wholesome,

Bobby Plump (25) hit the winning shot, but not before a bigger Muncie Central team challenged their every attempt in the state final.

Milan epitomized the state's small-town basketball spirit.
The town was so tiny, it didn't even have a stoplight.
Only 161 kids attended the high school.
Seventy-three of the students were boys, and
58 of them tried out for the basketball team.

tight-knit communities centered around their one church, one school, and one basketball team. From the night of the first frost throughout the long, blustery winter, basketball glory was all anyone dreamed about.

Milan epitomized the state's small-town basketball spirit. The town was so tiny, it didn't even have a stoplight. Only 161 kids attended the high school. Seventy-three of the students were boys, and 58 of them tried out for the basketball team.

Though a small-school team, Milan could compete with anybody—at least since Coach Wood had come on as coach. At that time, there was only one statewide tournament and it didn't recognize the size of the student body; there were no divisions, all schools competed with one another, the big ones, and the little dribblings like Milan.

Two years before Coach Wood took command of the reins, Milan coach Herman "Snort" Grinstead had been fired after purchasing new uniforms for the squad without obtaining permission, thereby blowing the team's minuscule budget. Wood, practically a kid himself at age 26, was a recent varsity player for Butler University. He injected new ideas into the program, including his "cat-and-mouse" attack, which added motion to offense.

"If you drew up your ideal coach, he'd be it," Milan Indians player Gene White told the *Northwest Indiana Times*. "He wasn't boisterous. He didn't try to intimidate people. He just did it by enthusiasm and knowledge of the game."

Wood led Milan to the state semifinal game in 1953 and to a 19-2 regular-

Decades after sinking the winning basket for Milan High, Bobby Plump
remains a household name among fans of Indiana high school basketball.

Fifty years after the Milan Miracle, fans still make a pilgrimage to the small town, whose population has grown little since 1954. "Just the other day there were visitors from Nebraska," said championship game hero Bobby Plump, "and we've had people come from several foreign countries."

Milan resident Roselyn McKittrick turned part of her antiques shop into a shrine for the '54 champions. Main attractions include congratulatory telegrams, the net that Milan players snipped after their historic win, and a blackboard with a diagram of the final play.

The 1986 film *Hoosiers*, starring Gene Hackman as the coach, was based on Milan's run to glory. Fans and critics loved the film's small-town charm and spirit. The movie, like the Milan Miracle itself, captured the simplicity, purity, and nostalgic beauty of rural Indiana in the 1950s.

Wrote *Washington Post* film critic Rita Kempley, "*Hoosiers* scores big by staying small." And when character Jimmy Chitwood hits the last-second shot, added Kempley, "You can't help but feel a catch in your throat."

According to the *Indianapolis Star*, the Milan Miracle was the top sports story in Indiana history. Seemingly every native of the state knows the tale, including those who work for the postal service. One person once sent a letter addressed simply "Plump/Indiana." Days letter, it arrived at Bobby Plump's home.

Actor Gene Hackman (center) *helped put a Hollywood spin on the Milan story in the sports classic* Hoosiers.

season record in 1954. Earlier in the '54 state tournament, they defeated Indianapolis Crispus Attucks, led by future NBA megastar Oscar Robertson. Still, Milan was a pint-sized underdog compared to Muncie Central. A school of 1,200—more than seven times larger than Milan—Muncie had won the state title in 1951 and '52. In fact, eight state championship banners hung from its gym's rafters. Moreover, not since Thorntown prevailed in 1915 had a school as small as Milan won the Indiana state crown.

Plump, after more than four minutes of idle drama, finally called a timeout. Wood later explained the stall by saying he was just trying to think of something to do. With three minutes left and Muncie leading 28–26, the action heated up. At 2:55, Plump attempted a game-tying shot and missed, and Muncie grabbed the rebound. The Bearcats, though, coughed up the ball, and Milan's Ray Craft scored to knot the game at 28.

With 1:42 to play, Muncie's Jimmy Barnes fouled Plump, who willed in both free throws. The crowd, pulling largely for the underdog, went wild. Muncie turned over the ball again, but Milan couldn't capitalize, as Craft's clincher attempt spun off the rim. With 48 seconds remaining, Muncie forward Gene Flowers tied the game 30–30 with a driving one-hander.

After half a century, Bobby Plump vividly recalls what happened next: "During the timeout, Woody says, 'Craft, you throw it to Bob. Bob, you dribble till there's five or six seconds left, and either take it to the basket or pull up for a shot.' Our starting center says, 'We'll get on the left side and clear it out for Bob on the right,' and Woody says okay."

With six seconds to go, Plump made his move. He drove toward the lane, leaned forward, faked a pullback, and then rose for a jumper. In a moment that seemed longer than his four-minute stall, the ball floated peacefully through the air...and then softly through the cotton net. Three seconds later, the game was over. "Everyone just stormed the court," Plump said. "It was exactly like a dream coming true."

What followed was a celebration that rivaled President Eisenhower's inauguration. The next day, the victorious Indians were escorted back to Milan in Cadillacs. "It was 86 miles from Indianapolis back to Milan," said Plump, "and every town of any size that we passed on the way home would come and meet us at the outskirts with signs and police sirens blaring.

ဢ

Thirty thousand people—

almost 30 times more people

than Milan's entire population—

greeted the victors that day.

ဢ

"By the time we got home, there were cars parked on both sides of the road for miles. Police sirens, emergency vehicles, people everywhere. And behind us was about an 18-mile caravan."

It was a triumphant return for the ultimate underdogs. Thirty thousand people—almost 30 times more people than Milan's entire population—greeted the victors that day. Some folks walked 10 miles or more from the nearby farm country. A moment like this in the Hoosier state is something to relish!

Most tellingly, time has not made the Indians' story any less moving. Years later, a museum was erected just to honor the '54 team. In 1986, one of the most critically acclaimed sports movies ever, *Hoosiers*, starring Gene Hackman as the coach, was based on Milan's astonishing story. Hollywood, after all, trades on dreams and miracles...just like they do in Indiana where one happened to nine boys who weren't even tall enough to touch the rim of a basketball hoop.

Chapter Fifteen

Funny Cide

Kentucky Derby, Churchill Downs, Louisville, Kentucky, May 3, 2003

By mid-spring the magnolias of the Southland have withered and fallen to petals, but Louisville is in full bloom. The blue grass of Kentucky that blankets the nearby countryside perfectly complements the blue-blooded aura of its southern aristocracy. At its holy ground, Churchill Downs, button-down gentlemen and flighty belles in full dress sip mint juleps while their thoroughbreds approach the starting gate at the Kentucky Derby.

Funny Cide, a 12–1 underdog, crashed the elegant party at the Derby, complete with his owners, Sackatoga Stable, horse racing's equivalent of Delta House. The motley collection of co-owners were a group of friends who ventured into thoroughbred racing on a whim, coming up with the idea one Memorial Day over some beers at a backyard barbecue. Subsequently, in 1995, they created a racing syndicate,

Funny Cide, with Santos aboard, became the first New York-bred ever to win the Derby.

each of them throwing in $5,000 to buy a horse—a move reminiscent of dumping one's money in the middle of the ocean—but it worked to some degree. By 2002 the group, whose managing partner was Jackson Knowlton, the owner of a small health care consulting firm in Saratoga Springs, New York, paid

∽❧∾

Tagg commanded as much respect from fellow horsemen as a pug club fighter might get from a world champion trainer. He just didn't belong at the Derby, nor did his horse, a gelding owned by a group of working-class stiffs.

∽❧∾

$75,000 for Funny Cide, the great-great-grandson of 1977 Triple Crown winner Seattle Slew.

Horse trainers for such a sanctimonious event as the Derby usually have blood lines similar to the horses they send out on the track, Bob Baffert, D. Wayne Lukas, and the like. The Derby belonged to them. Yet here was Funny Cide, a gelding trained by a guy named Barclay Tagg.

Tagg commanded as much respect from fellow horsemen as a pug club fighter might get from a world champion trainer. He just didn't belong at the Derby,

nor did his horse, a gelding owned by a group of working-class stiffs. And now, these guys had the audacity to line him up with a thoroughbred like Empire Maker, a horse that was everything a Derby winner should be. If any horse had the heart of a champion it was Empire Maker. And the papers too. Sired by former Derby winner Unbridled and born to Toussaud, a highly regarded mare who had earned Broodmare of the Year honors. Oddsmakers knew a sure thing when they saw one and Empire Maker was the chalk for this horse race.

Funny Cide kicked off his season as a three-year-old with a fifth-place finish in the Holy Bull Stakes at Gulfstream Park in Florida on January 18. Several weeks later he finished third in the Louisiana Derby, a race in which he'd lost the lead, then refused to quit, making a late run to the finish. He finished second to Empire Maker in the Wood Memorial on April 12, but to think such a horse could give Empire Maker a run in a race like the Derby was preposterous, even if the favorite had a bruised right front foot. Still, Funny Cide's camp had reason for hope. The horse had continued to improve each time out, showing a decided dislike for losing.

Jose Santos, Funny Cide's jockey, had been in great demand during the 1980s and 1990s before his stock began to plummet. From 1997 to 2002 he no longer consistently landed the marquee mounts in the big races. His last ride in the Derby had been 1999. But Santos still had something left. The previous fall he was entered in the $5 million Breeders' Cup Classic and rode a long shot, Volponi, to victory. After winning the Breeders' Cup, Santos saw Knowlton at a party and spoke to him about Funny Cide, telling him, "I love that horse, that's my Derby horse for next year."

At the Belmont Stakes Funny Cide (second from right), *finished third, behind more heralded horses Empire Maker and Ten Most Wanted.*

Jockey Jose Santos proved he still had what it took to win the big race, piloting Funny Cide to the winner's circle.

In winning the 2003 Kentucky Derby, Funny Cide became the first gelding to win the Run for the Roses since Clyde Van Dusen in 1929, which leads to the follow-up question: What is a gelding?

According to the *American Heritage Dictionary,* a gelding is any castrated animal. However, the term normally refers to a male horse.

Funny Cide was de-sexed shortly after being born with one testicle undescended. Obviously such a procedure made Funny Cide incapable of leading the typical Derby winner's life, which is to spend the remainder of its days in stud.

Funny Cide was the eighth gelding to win the Kentucky Derby. Here's a look at the others:
- 1876—Vagrant
- 1882—Apollo
- 1888—Macbeth II
- 1914—Old Rosebud
- 1918—Exterminator
- 1920—Paul Jones
- 1929—Clyde Van Dusen
- 2003—Funny Cide

The Sackatoga Stable boys arrived at the Derby with all the grace of a bunch of Yankees drinking their way through an all-boys vacation. After Funny Cide's owners were told the cost of hiring a motor coach would be over $3,000, they rented a school bus for considerably less cash, nicknaming it their "big yellow stretch limo." The bus was stocked with beer and Bloody Marys, rather than the usual mint julep fare. Their tip for the driver? Bet Funny Cide.

Positioned in the sixth post, Funny Cide bumped with Offlee Wild out of the gate, but Santos was able to keep his horse in front of the fray that filed into place behind him. This left him free to give chase to the early leaders, Brancusi, Peace Rules, and Eye of the Tiger. Santos pushed Funny Cide into third once the pack hit the backstretch, patiently waiting behind Peace Rules and Brancusi.

"He kept digging and digging," Santos said. "He wasn't accelerating, but he went the same pace."

Brancusi, who led by a head at the far turn until Peace Rules passed, ran out of steam and fell to the back of the pack. Funny Cide moved toward the front in pursuit of Peace Rules while Empire Maker thundered from eighth place into third looking every bit like the favorite. Surely this would be the point when the blue blood rose to its rightful place.

Peace Rules hugged the rail, Funny Cide had the middle, Empire Maker ran outside. As the trio made the turn for home they were dead even.

"I was starting to feel pretty confident there," Tagg said. "He looked like he wasn't going to quit and it didn't look like the other horses were going to gain on him too much."

Blue blood gave way to heart at this point. Funny Cide dug for home and remained strong until the finish, winning by one and three-quarter lengths in a time of 2:01.19, the 10th fastest time in the 129-year history of the Derby.

Funny Cide, the gelding who got no respect, became the first New York–bred horse ever to win the Derby, and the first gelding since Clyde Van Dusen (in 1929) to win the Run for the Roses.

"It's a thrill beyond belief," Knowlton said. "We are the little guys in the game and for me it's just so rewarding that everybody who dreams of owning a horse or two can look at what we've accomplished. It's like the lottery. It's a dollar and a dream."

Cheap enough, but you can wake up in the Winner's Circle, which is what dreams—and horse races too—are all about.

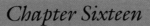
The Comeback-Slash Upset of '98

Temple Owls vs. Virginia Tech Hokies
Blacksburg, Virginia, October 17, 1998

Two minutes before halftime, hordes of fans hit the concession stands. In a game like this a pretzel or a beer was more exciting than the predictable walloping of an opponent who couldn't win a game all season. After undefeated Virginia Tech scored off a touchdown pass by quarterback Nick Sorensen, the Hokies led lowly Temple 17–0 with 2:08 left in the half. Now it was time for a hot dog…maybe even time to go home. Temple was going to lose *another* game and Virginia was going to chalk up another win. So what else is new?

Pity those who packed it up and split. Unbeknown to them as they left the parking lot at the half, they were about to miss one of the most extraordinary moments in American sports—the greatest comeback-slash-upset in the history of college football.

Entering this homecoming game, Virginia Tech owned a record of 5–0, was ranked 14th in the country, and considered itself a contender for the national championship. The Hokies boasted the stingiest defense in the nation, yielding just six points per game. They had not lost to a Big East team at home since their 1995 opener— and they certainly weren't going to lose to the Temple Owls.

The Temple program was in complete disarray. The Owls hadn't won a game all year (0-6), and in fact had dropped eight straight since November of the previous season. Temple had not

Virginia Tech quarterback Nick Sorensen found the
going tough against Temple in the second half.

When Temple, a 35½-point underdog, beat Virginia Tech, reporters checked to see if any other college football team had ever overcome such a large point spread. Only one team had. On October 26, 1985, the University of Texas–El Paso, a 36-point dog, defeated defending national champion Brigham Young.

UTEP entered the game with a record of 0–6, including blowouts by lightly regarded Air Force (48–6) and Kent State (51–24). Meanwhile, BYU (6-1) was ranked No. 7 in the country and had won 24 conference games in a row. A week earlier, Cougars quarterback Robbie Bosco had set an NCAA record with 585 passing yards against New Mexico.

Would he top 600 versus the porous UTEP defense?

Not a chance. After a great week of practice, the Miners were prepared physically and mentally for the reigning champs. Though Bosco was on the verge of breaking a 10–10 tie in the second quarter, UTEP's Danny Taylor made what amounted to a 14-point interception. He picked off Bosco's pass in his own end zone and returned it 103 yards for a touchdown, putting the Miners ahead 17–10.

Texas–El Paso's defense shut down BYU's passing attack in the second half, helping UTEP pull off an epic 23–16 upset. Their fans could be forgiven for tearing down the goalposts: it would be the Miners' *only* victory all year.

---

beaten a ranked team since 1987, and it had not defeated a Big East school on the road in 26 tries.

First-year coach Bobby Wallace, the former head man at North Alabama (Division II), had yet to win a game in Division I. In fact, he found it hard enough just fielding a team. Due mostly to injuries, Wallace suited up 11 players against Virginia Tech who had not started in the opener. Temple played without its best wide receiver, its No. 1 offensive lineman, its two best defensive linemen, and its premier linebacker.

Moreover, Wallace had lost his first- *and* second-string quarterbacks to shoulder injuries a week earlier. Devin Scott, a true freshman, was forced into duty against Virginia Tech. Four other true frosh started on Temple's defense. "I've never seen a more injured, beat-up football team in my life," Wallace said. "We had kids playing positions they had never *practiced* before."

Virginia Tech was so powerful, and Temple so vulnerable, that oddsmakers made the Hokies a 35½-point favorite. When the Owls fell behind 17–0, they in essence had to overcome 52½ points worth of inferiority—and they had only 32 minutes left to do it. Lots of luck, guys.

Yet while Hokies fans waited in line for their pre-halftime snacks, a freak thing happened on the playing field. With 40 seconds remaining, Scott flipped a screen pass to slotback Rahsaan Harrison near the right sideline. With that end of the field clogged, Harrison angled to the left and raced downfield, with a parade of blockers leading the way. His 67-yard romp put Temple on the scoreboard. "I just had to get into the end zone," he explained, "and I wasn't going to settle for less."

VT fans were annoyed but not alarmed—until the Owls' opening drive of the third quarter. With disturbing ease, Temple drove downfield against the vaunted Hokies defense. Owls fullback Jason McKie, another freshman, rambled 13 yards for a touchdown to make the score 17–14. It was the first rushing touchdown that Tech had allowed all year.

Less than four minutes later, lightning struck again. Scott heaved a pass over the Hokies secondary to speedy Carlos Johnson (also a freshman!). The raw QB had tried the pass all week in practice, unsuccessfully, but on this magical Saturday Johnson hauled it in. He left Hokies defenders in the dust en route to an 80-yard touchdown, giving the Owls an unimaginable 21–17 lead.

Tech coach Frank Beamer tried to explain his team's monumental collapse. "It looked like things were going our way and it was going to be a ho-hum day," he said. "Then we started to play ho-hum."

The Hokies still had 24 minutes left to score, but they could not find a way to crack the adrenaline-driven Owls defense. Temple's Leon Gray and Chonn Lacey (again, both freshmen) picked off passes during the game—the first interceptions by Temple all year. VT

Freshman Jason McKie rushed for the first TD given up by Virginia Tech in 1998.

didn't score again until the 10:50 mark of the fourth quarter, when Lamont Pegues crossed the goal line to cap a 69-yard scoring drive. Virginia Tech led, seemingly for good, 24–21.

Undaunted, Scott orchestrated yet another inexplicable drive. With 6:04 remaining, he himself scored on a quarterback sneak, giving Temple a 28–24 lead.

With 1:58 left to play, the Hokies' pride finally returned. With their unblemished record on the line, they were not about to lose this game—especially in their house, on homecoming, against an 0–6 team. Starting on his own 12-yard line, Sorensen marched his troops downfield, taking what Temple's prevent defense would give him. The Hokies drove all the way to the three, where they faced second-and-two.

But after bending for 85 yards, the Temple defense suddenly wouldn't budge. On second down, the Owls stonewalled running back Shyrone Stith for no gain. On the next play, Sorensen found a wide-open Ricky Hall in the end zone—but Hall dropped the ball, falling to the turf in agony.

With one play left, Tech decided to give it to Pegues. The star tailback had rushed for more than 160 yards on the day, but his first-half fumble near Temple's goal line haunted the Hokies the rest of the game. This was his chance to atone for his sin. The Hokies ran Pegues on a sweep, but Temple— having seen the same play earlier—sniffed it out. Linebackers Leon Gray and Ramone Budgetts led a flock of Owls who shoved Pegues out of bounds at the five-yard-line.

"We brought everybody on the team on that last play," Wallace said. "If they had raised up and thrown the ball, there wouldn't have been a person covered. Sometimes you gamble, and we did and we got lucky."

With 19 seconds left, the Owls ran out the clock, kicking off a hoot of a celebration. Temple players were so ecstatic that they dug up grass as a souvenir. It was a fitting symbol for a team that had dug itself out of a 52½-point hole.

Chapter Seventeen

John Daly:
The Ninth Alternate

PGA Championship, Crooked Stick Golf Club
Carmel, Indiana, August 8–11, 1991

Somewhere in Zimbabwe a child is between his feeding and his nap and is screaming at the top of his lungs. That child, the firstborn son of golfer Nick Price, proved to be John Daly's godsend.

Young Gregory entered the world on August 8, 1991—opening day of the PGA Championship. Rather than miss Gregory's arrival, papa-to-be Price withdrew from the 73rd PGA Championship and went home to welcome his son to the world. Had Price been a little less cavalier about the whole thing, John Daly, a chubby unknown golfer from rural Arkansas might still be a hick no one ever heard of. But Price's withdrawal allowed Daly, the tournament's ninth alternate, to take the open spot.

Price's departure left his caddie, Jeff "Squeeky" Medlen, without a gig in the tournament. Nevertheless, he drove to Crooked Stick Golf Club in Carmel, Indiana, believing somebody might need a caddie. He was right. Daly hired him on the spot.

The portly rookie Daly was a former All-America at the University of Arkansas who had found little success in the professional ranks since turning pro in 1987. Still, the 25-year-old known as "Long John" and "Wild Thing" had something special and was eager to see how well it might work in the company of the world's best golfers.

Growing up in the rural community of Dardanelle, Arkansas—population 3,621—Daly learned to play golf on a nine-hole course. And unlike so many of the pedigreed players on tour, Daly didn't hone his game under the watchful eye of some local country club professional. He instead taught himself how to hit the ball by watching Jack Nicklaus's swing on TV, memorizing instructional diagrams in golfing magazines, and just doing what felt right. When he was four years old, his father gave him a starter set consisting of two sawed-off clubs. By the time he was 10, he could beat his father; at 12, Daly could handily vanquish local players twice his age. Four years later, Daly's confidence got another boost after he won his first U.S. junior title. Next stop, PGA Tour glory—or so Daly believed. But while his do-it-yourself approach to golf had propelled him to victory in the 1990 Ben Hogan Utah Classic, he initially seemed like an also-ran on the PGA Tour. After joining the tour in March of 1991, he had little to show for himself, save for a third-place tie in the Chattanooga Classic. In fact, he had only made the cut in 13 of the 24 PGA tournaments he'd played in

"Long John" held nothing back in the final round, attacking his drive on the 14th hole.

Daly and his caddie, Jeff "Squeaky" Medlen, celebrated along with thousands of fans who latched on to the big-hitting underdog.

his six humbling months on the tour.

After receiving the news he'd be filling Price's vacated spot in the PGA Championship, Daly drove all night from his home in Memphis to Indianapolis, covering 500 miles and arriving just in time for the first round. Since he had not played so much as a practice round, Daly approached Crooked Stick like a hacker would the local muni. Wiping the exhaustion from his red-rimmed eyes, he asked a fan where the tough holes were as he made his way to the first tee.

Squeeky watched Daly hit his driver and the caddie offered the best advice he could muster: "Kill." Daly acquiesced and the galleries fell in love with the folksy big swinger. They lined up three and four deep so they could see the burly 25-year-old with just the faintest hint of mustache send the ball hurtling across the green. Daly brought a refreshing new swing to a tour full of swings that all looked the same. He took the club further back, turned through his swing more completely, and followed through more violently than any player—and still managed to keep his balance. This unique swing, coupled with his big shoulders and strong legs, produced epic drives that left bystanders slack-jawed in amazement. Comparisons to Babe Ruth, who brought many of the same qualities to baseball, were inevitable from the outset. Even seasoned veterans like Raymond Floyd were impressed by Daly. In a TV interview, Floyd quipped, "I watched a few of his swings Saturday and I went home with a bad back."

Armed with his trusty Cobra driver—the one with a titanium shaft and a head made of Kevlar (the stuff used to make bulletproof vests)—Daly hit his drives to places others could not reach. They flew over fairway bunkers that were hazardous to the other players and cut off corners to find the far reaches of the dogleg holes. Prior to the tournament, Crooked Stick, a par 72, had been lengthened to 7,295 yards, the

A most unlikely winner, John Daly hoisted the Wanamaker Trophy at the 1991 PGA Championship.

round 69. Others weren't so lucky. Many fell by the wayside, like Curtis Strange, who shot an 81 and didn't show for the second round.

Daly followed his first-round success with a 67 on day two to take the lead. Even he couldn't believe he was leading and called his position a fluke. But he reaffirmed his standing in the third round during a three-hole sequence on the front side. He hit a huge drive, followed by an 8-iron to the 456-yard par-4 fourth hole. The approach shot landed a foot from the pin and stopped. Next up was the 609-yard par-5 fifth, which Daly nearly reached in two shots before flawlessly executing a chip that left him a tap-in birdie. On the sixth hole, a 199-yard par-3, he hit a 5-iron over the water to a difficult pin placement. He then ran in a tricky downhill putt from 12 feet to make his third consecutive birdie.

Despite taking a three-shot lead after three rounds, Daly's swing still had skeptics predicting failure. There was always the chance that Daly would choke in the final rounds. He wouldn't be the first PGA newcomer to dazzle in the opening rounds of a major tournament, only to succumb to nerves and finish at the back of the pack. Doubt could have easily crept into Daly's mind when he bogeyed the first hole of Sunday's round. Instead, he battled any would-be final day demons by throwing up a birdie on the second hole. He then charged to birdies on five, 13, and 15. Kenny Knox and Bruce Lietzke were close enough to pressure Daly, who remained flawless until a double-bogey at 17 reduced his lead to three strokes, sending a bad vibe through the raucous crowd. Would the fan favorite fall apart this close to victory?

The answer was a resounding no. Daly's drive on 18 found the rough, but he hit an 8-iron to the middle of the green and made par to save the day. He shot 71 to finish at 12-under-par 276 to capture the 1991 PGA Championship.

"This is like a miracle," Daly said afterward. "This kind of thing just doesn't happen that often."

Daly wasn't exaggerating. With his victory, he became the first PGA rookie to win a major in 15 years.

second-longest distance in the history of the PGA Championship. Jack Nicklaus called Crooked Stick "the most difficult course I'd ever played."

Daly, however, navigated Crooked Stick with relative ease. Having the ability to reduce much of the yardage to the green with his prodigious drives, Daly could use a 7- or 8-iron in his approaches to Crooked Stick's soft greens, rather than the 3-irons the other pros were forced to hit. As a result, he shot an opening

Chapter Eighteen

Greg LeMond: The Battle of France

Tour de France, Final Stage
Versailles to Paris, July 23, 1989

I t was the 23rd day of the Tour de France and over a third of the competitors had dropped out. It was down to the survivors now, the iron men who survived the grueling Alpine climb and the danger of the descent. Each of them had already raced over 2,000 miles. Today they were rested and would battle it out on the last 24.5-kilometer stage from Versailles to Paris, the final stretch.

Greg LeMond looked a little fidgety. He'd been so close to the front-running Frenchman Laurent Fignon so many times, even ahead in spots, but the Frenchman just kept gaining on him. Right now Fignon was haughtily assuming the posture of the winner, swaggering as he walked, boasting as he talked.

The night before, the *Houston Chronicle* affirmed what everyone thought was a foregone conclusion: "Fignon," they wrote, "looks set to become only the sixth rider to win the Tour de France three times, and the sixth to win the tours of Italy and France the same year."

LeMond's former coach shared the same sentiment. With Fignon having a 50-second lead, coach Paul Koechli assessed LeMond's chances of beating him this way: "Unthinkable!"

A 50-second gap was far too much; anyone who was familiar with bicycle racing knew it. A win for the American would require that he make up a two-second gap on Fignon each kilometer. No one could do that! And there were other reasons LeMond couldn't win: for starters, the 28-year-old American cyclist hadn't won an event for three years. Why would he win one

LeMond donned a Phrygian revolutionary cap on the eve of the French Revolution's bicentennial anniversary.

now? Last year a shin injury ended his season early, and there was that appendectomy too. But they were small liabilities in relation to something else.

That something else was reason enough, some thought, for LeMond not to be even competing, not now, not ever. In LeMond's own words it went like this: "It's a miracle I'm even racing. Two years ago I was almost dead."

In April of 1987 he was on the wrong end of a shotgun. LeMond and his brother-in-law were hunting turkeys near Lincoln, California. Like most shooting victims he didn't remember much, just the pain and waking up in the emergency room. The only good news was that the doctors thought he had a reasonable chance to live, even though his vital signs had been touch-and-go the first few hours he was on the respirator. Before that, no one was sure he'd make it, especially when his lung collapsed.

The impact of 60 shotgun pellets traumatized his very being. His kidney and liver were hit, so were his diaphram and intestines. His heart sustained fewer injuries—only two pellets were lodged in it—and it continued to beat, even as he lay unconscious, having passed out from loss of blood. Even today, he carries 30 shotgun pellets in his body, with the two still lodged in his heart.

But LeMond's heart is a big one, not just a strong one. However, he had his own doubts about his chances of winning the Tour de France now. The only thing he could say that eve of the final stretch was, "Possible." But how possible was it…really?

Not very. Months before, he had been diagnosed as anemic. And his team had lost confidence in him too. LeMond relates: "They were trying to claim that maybe my liver was bad, my lung was shot up, maybe I had lead poisoning. That's why I wasn't riding well."

Casting a bigger shadow of doubt was Fignon, the

LeMond raised his arms as he crossed the finish line to win the 19th stage of the Tour, yet he still chased Frenchman Laurent Fignon in the final days.

cocky Frenchman who was thought to be a shoo-in. Hours before the final race, he went up to LeMond and told him: "You raced a great race, Greg. I have to tell you, my coach, Guimard, predicted that this is the way it would finish, me winning and you second."

Truth be told, LeMond later admitted he would have been happy just to be in the top 20. Twenty-three days ago, a second-place finish was unthinkably good, but now there was at least a remote chance of a victory, but it involved the "impossible"—closing a two-second gap each kilometer, 50 seconds in all. He'd have to pedal the fastest race in the history of the Tour. No one had ever done anything like it and no one probably ever could, even he knew it.

"There's little chance," LeMond told the press. "But I'm going for it."

Was it false bravado, or was he impossibly out of touch with reality? It would be doubly hard since this last and final race of the Tour's 21 was a race against the clock, not an open road race with competitors starting simultaneously. A rider had to know how to pace himself, and that's not easy. Lots of heart was needed, and a strategy to go with it.

LeMond would forge a three-pronged attack against the clock. First, there was a special aerodynamic helmet that might cut the wind. He would also ride a bike with the frame slanted forward, another American innovation, one the Europeans weren't using yet. Lastly, what many thought was a disadvantage: He waived the right for his handlers to be in a support vehicle and shout out his time along the course. He preferred not to have his concentration broken. Perhaps he thought anything they might tell him would be bad news, so he would just put his head down and sprint like a son of a bike.

While some might call it pressure, most thought it was folly: closing a two-second gap each kilometer— winning a short race by 50 seconds. Impossible! Ironically, LeMond didn't feel pressure. Quite the contrary. Just before the race, he felt terrific, the best he'd felt since the Tour began 23 days ago.

His rival, Fignon, felt the same way. Who wouldn't

He'd have to pedal the fastest race in the history of the Tour. No one had ever done anything like it and no one probably ever could, even he knew it.

feel good a few minutes before the victory? To the Frenchman, this last and shortest leg was just a formality.

Fignon started his time trial after LeMond had already completed his. The American averaged a record 34 miles an hour, and was now eight seconds ahead of Fignon. His time was 26 minutes, 27 seconds. He had done the "impossible," pedaling the final stage faster than anyone in the history of the Tour.

Fignon would have to turn in the second fastest time in the Tour's history, 26 minutes, 49 seconds, to keep his lead to the end. But Fignon was one of the greatest champions of bike racing and if anyone could do it, he could. After five kilometers Fignon lost 10 seconds to LeMond. He cranked up his pace. Another five kilometers later, he was 19 seconds behind. By the 14th kilometer he had fallen 24 seconds behind; his lead over LeMond was now only 26 seconds, still comfortable, but would it be enough? At 18 kilometers, he was 34 seconds behind LeMond. Incredibly, Fignon ran the race in an inconceivable 27 minutes, 55 seconds... but it was 58 seconds slower than LeMond.

The American had beaten the Frenchman's total time for the Tour's 21 events by only eight seconds to win the 1989 Tour de France, LeMond's second win of what would be three Tour victories in his career (1986, 1989, and 1990).

Buffalo cornerback Nate Odoms got a lift from team-mate Henry Jones after intercepting a Warren Moon pass in overtime, setting up the winning kick.

Opposite: *Andre Reed (83) and Keith McKeller celebrated Reed's third touchdown as Buffalo rallied for an improbable 38–35 fourth-quarter lead over Houston.*

The Mother of All Comebacks

NFL Wildcard Game, Buffalo Bills vs. Houston Oilers
Rich Stadium, Buffalo, New York, January 3, 1993

t was halftime of the 1992–93 AFC wildcard game, and Buffalo coach Marv Levy dressed down his players like a vice principal during after-school detention. His Bills had let down the city of Buffalo, trailing the Houston Oilers 28–3. "Whatever happens," Levy scolded, "you guys have to live with yourselves after today."

Though the Bills had represented the AFC in the previous two Super Bowls, Houston owned Buffalo's

number. The Oilers, in fact, had humiliated the Bills 27–3 in the season finale, meaning they had pounded them 55–6 over their last one and a half games.

In the first half of this contest, at Buffalo's Rich Stadium, the Bills were totally eclipsed by Warren Moon. The Houston quarterback completed 19-of-22 passes for four touchdowns. When the Oilers returned an interception for a score early in the third quarter, making it 35–3, even diehard Bills fans threw in the towel. At that point, "We had a chance," said Levy. "About the same chance a guy has of winning the New York Lottery."

If this were a lottery, quarterback Frank Reich would have to pick a string of lucky numbers to get his team back in the game. A career-long backup, Reich had started this contest in place of injured star quarterback Jim Kelly. Nevertheless, the calm and methodical Reich possessed the right mind-set to orchestrate a comeback. In fact, he once had led the University of Maryland to victory over the University of Miami after trailing 31–0.

In the third quarter, Reich drove Buffalo 50 yards on 10 plays. Running back Kenneth Davis, playing in place of injured superstar Thurman Thomas, capped the drive with a rushing touchdown. Still down 35–10, the Bills squibbed an onside kick and recovered it after Houston retreated into deep coverage. Just four plays later, Reich arced a 38-yard touchdown pass to wideout Don Beebe: 35–17.

A roused Bills defense forced Houston to punt, and again field general Reich marched his troops down the field. His linemen gave him time to relax and throw, and he routinely beat the single coverage on his receivers, Beebe and perennial All-Pro Andre Reed. In the fifth play of this drive, he hit Reed for a 26-yard TD—Buffalo's third in less than five minutes.

Many of the 75,141 fans in attendance had left at halftime, and even more had bolted after Houston went up 35–3. But with the score now 35–24, fans actually returned to the stadium. They begged ticket-takers, in vain, to let them back in. Some fans were so desperate to reenter that they tried to climb the fences around the stadium.

Moon, meanwhile, felt the heat of the Bills' aggressive 3-4 defense, which Buffalo reverted to in the second half. Safety Henry Jones picked off Moon and returned the ball to the Houston 23. On a fourth-and-five play, Reich connected with Reed at the goal line. With 2:00 left in the third quarter, the Miracle Bills had pulled within a touchdown, 35–31.

Moon finally ended Buffalo's momentum, draining half of the fourth-quarter clock with a sustained drive. The Oilers' 31-yard field goal try, however, went awry, as a sudden rain (yes, rain in Buffalo in January) and a gust of wind forced the holder to blow the snap.

The Bills took over with 6:53 to play and, on third-and-four, surprised Houston with a running play. Davis burst through a hole for 35 yards to the Houston 33. After moving to the 17, Reich reunited with Reed for yet another touchdown. The Bills now led 38–35, which—if it stood—would be the greatest comeback in NFL history.

The Oilers, suddenly the underdog, maintained their composure and marched down to the Buffalo nine-yard line. With 12 ticks remaining, Al Del Greco booted a chip-shot field goal. Physically and emotionally sapped, both teams headed for overtime.

The football gods had played head games with the Oilers all day, and the overtime coin toss was no excep-

tion. Though Houston won the toss, it turned out to be their demise. Three plays into overtime, Moon fired over the middle for Ernest Givins, who was virtually tackled before the ball arrived. No flag was thrown; instead, cornerback Nate Odomes picked off the pass and returned it two yards to the Houston 35. Moreover, a facemask penalty on the play moved the ball to the 20.

Coach Levy didn't fool around. After two running plays netted six yards, kicker Steve Christie—playing in his first-ever NFL playoff game—entered to try

a 32-yard field goal. Christie split the uprights, completing the National Football League's mother of all comebacks.

With the crowd in a frenzy, Bills players pranced up the runway to the locker room. Along the way, elated on-duty state troopers whacked Levy with congratulatory pats. Upon reaching the clubhouse, Levy promised everyone on the team a game ball.

Riding an emotional high, Buffalo proceeded to romp to the Super Bowl, trampling Pittsburgh (24–3)

No team in NFL history had a bigger comeback win to celebrate than the Bills did when Steve Christie's overtime field goal beat the Oilers 41–38.

and Miami (29–10) on the road. And although the Bills lost to Dallas in the big game 52–17—their third straight loss in the Super Bowl—fans could take solace. They had witnessed one of the greatest playoff victories in the history of sports.

Chapter Twenty

An Old Dog in Paradise

World Series, New York Yankees vs. Florida Marlins

Yankee Stadium, Bronx, New York, and Pro Player Stadium, Florida, October 18–25, 2003

Jack McKeon felt a rush of emotion watching Game 7 of the 2003 American League Championship Series between the Boston Red Sox and New York Yankees. Having grown up in New Jersey he'd made many a trip here, to Yankee Stadium, the place where baseball gods were minted.

But now, being the manager of the Florida Marlins, McKeon felt compelled to feign indifference when asked which team he'd rather play in the World Series. Yet deep in his heart he knew the truth: he wanted the Yankees. Because to be the best you have to beat the best, and for a baseball guy, it doesn't get any better than playing at Yankee Stadium. And for an alien team—literally and figuratively in a different league—*winning a World Series at Yankee Stadium*...well, have you ever heard of a stranger in paradise?

Aaron Boone eventually punched the Marlins' ticket for a trip to New York with his game-winning home run in the 11th inning to advance the Yankees to the World Series. Thus, McKeon would manage in his first World Series at age 72—making him the oldest manager in the history of the Fall Classic—and he would do so in the House That Ruth Built, where Joe DiMaggio and Mickey Mantle once roamed center field and where baseball's most storied franchise had written much of the game's history.

A full baseball life had passed since McKeon's halcyon days of youth. Along the way he'd managed 15 years in the minors, filling out lineup cards in places like Missoula and Fox Cities, before getting his first major league opportunity with the Kansas City Royals in 1973; later he managed the Oakland A's, San Diego Padres, and Cincinnati Reds. His résumé also included scouting, front office advisor, and general manager—a stint that earned him the nickname "Trader Jack" for his willingness to deal. In May of 2003, after spending two summers at home in North Carolina, McKeon interviewed with the Marlins hoping to land a scouting job or a position as a special assistant to the general manager. He came away as the Marlins manager.

In five months—less time than a Hollywood marriage—McKeon led the Marlins from 10 games under .500 to the National League playoffs. A cigar-smoker with a wrinkled face resembling a well-worn catcher's mitt, McKeon relied on a managing philosophy based on hunches and the playing of "little baseball," which called for quality pitching, solid defense, and coveting each run like a rare artifact. Perhaps his greatest asset was an ability to relate to the youngsters playing for the Marlins. Routinely he traded good-natured insults with the kids while pushing the old-school baseball resonating within him.

Alex Gonzalez, who stepped to the plate in the 12th inning of Game 4 batting .094 for the postseason, hit a game-winning homer that pulled Florida even in the Series.

McKeon settled the team, invigorated it, and then sold the idea they were good enough to be playing in October. McKeon wasn't blowing smoke, either. He saw quality middle defense in shortstop Alex Gonzalez, second baseman Luis Castillo, center-fielder Juan Pierre, and strong-armed catcher Pudge Rodriguez. Add to the equation a quality staff of young starters in Josh Beckett, Brad Penny, Carl Pavano, and Dontrelle Willis, and it wasn't a stretch to envision great things. They just needed to believe and play loose. To this end McKeon constantly touted his philosophy.

"From the start I talked up the idea of arriving at the ballpark prepared to play hard and to have fun," McKeon said.

No team in baseball had as much fun as the Marlins. Their dugout became a raucous playground where even the reserves couldn't muster reason to pout. Mimicking McKeon was half the fun.

But the World Series brought forth a seemingly unbeatable foe for the Marlins, a team so young most of its players barely shaved. The Yankees were the Tiffany's of baseball, complete with a $185 million payroll and a manager considered baseball's best in Joe Torre. Added baggage for the Marlins came in the fact that the American League had won the All-Star Game, which, for

the first time, gave the winning league home-field advantage in the World Series. Translated, the Marlins might have to play as many as four games at Yankee Stadium, where the Yankees routinely treated their

Jack McKeon, the 72-year-old manager who pushed all the right buttons, enjoyed a victory cigar as the Marlins paraded through downtown Miami.

McKeon looked as vulnerable
as a carcass on the side of the road
with vultures circling overhead.

opposition like the Washington Generals, the Harlem Globetrotters' hapless foils.

In trying to counter these great odds, McKeon convinced his team that World Series games were no different from any other games. He also told them nobody expected them to be there, so why not let the pressure be on the Yankees?

The Marlins responded by continuing to play loose as they had throughout the regular season and playoffs. McKeon stood in the background, paying little attention to the statistics and relying on his lengthy baseball experience to push all the right buttons. He'd already plugged into the lineup 20-year-old Miguel Cabrera, which put All-Star third baseman Mike Lowell on the bench during September and most of the postseason, and he masterfully handled starting pitchers and relievers.

McKeon made moves that seemed to make no sense other than the fact they worked.

Trailing the Series two games to one, the Marlins manager stuck with Gonzalez in the 12th inning of Game 4 even though Gonzalez carried to the plate a .094 postseason batting average. He responded with a game-winning home run to tie the Series.

The Marlins then closed out Game 5 when first baseman Derrek Lee nabbed Hideki Matsui's drive after being repositioned from— you guessed it—the Marlins dugout.

Looking to close out the Yankees in Game 6, McKeon acted like a magician removing an imaginary cape prior to reveal one last hunch.

Beckett had pitched masterfully in Game 3, but took the loss. Conventional wisdom said not to start his 23-year-old ace on three days rest. McKeon went with his gut instead, announcing Beckett as the Game 6 starter even if it left him susceptible to criticism. He didn't care one iota that playoff starters pitching on short rest had gone 6–20 with a 5.93 ERA in 37 starts the previous five seasons. Instead McKeon saw in Beckett a young Bob Gibson during the 1967 World Series mowing down the Red Sox on short days. He had chided Beckett during the season to work harder, and the finished product was just now rolling out of the showroom. Young, talented, and cocksure, Beckett would be McKeon's perfect choice for Game 6—critics be damned!

On the morning of Game 6, McKeon went about his daily ritual by attending Catholic Mass, hiding his ever-present cigar outside the church, a practice adhering to his philosophy of never wasting a good working cigar. After the Mass he plunked his cigar back into his mouth and told the New York fans who had engaged him in conversation: "We're going to win tonight."

Prior to the singing of "The Star-Spangled Banner," McKeon looked as vulnerable as a carcass on the side of the road with vultures circling overhead. If Beckett flopped that night, the second-guessing would have reached a fever pitch. But his starter responded by dominating the Yankees with a 2–0 Gibson-like complete game effort. Beckett even got the final out of the Series when he fielded Jorge Posada's grounder and tagged the Yankees' catcher.

McKeon's eyes filled with tears behind the round lens of his glasses during the traditional playing of Sinatra's "New York, New York" at Yankee Stadium. The Marlins were world champions and McKeon proved that even an old dog could learn a new trick when he popped the cork from a bottle of champagne and sipped the nectar of champions for the first time...and at Yankee Stadium!

Chapter Twenty-one

Subway Series: Sandy Amoros

World Series, Brooklyn Dodgers vs. New York Yankees
Ebbets Field, Brooklyn, New York and
Yankee Stadium, Bronx, New York, September 28—October 4, 1955

I n Brooklyn they were known as "Dem Bums." In the Bronx they were known as also-rans. Heading into the 1955 World Series, there was no reason to expect the Brooklyn Dodgers would change the status quo, nor that a little known outfielder by the name of Sandy Amoros would become a household name.

Dating back to Brooklyn's first World Series in 1916 when the team was known as the Robins, they had never managed to win a World Series. By 1955 the team had appeared in seven Fall Classics only to fail in each. Five of the losses had come against the New York Yankees, their crosstown rival who boasted baseball immortals such as Mickey Mantle, Joe DiMaggio, Babe Ruth, and Lou Gehrig. Defeating the Yankees just wasn't something the Dodgers were supposed to do.

The 1955 Brooklyn Dodgers had a few of the game's best in well-seasoned Pee Wee Reese and Jackie Robinson. But the prospect of even reaching the World Series looked more remote than in previous years. After winning four pennants in six years from 1947 to 1953, the New York Giants interrupted the postseason party by winning the 1954 pennant and going on to accomplish what the Dodgers could not by capturing the World Series. Nevertheless, the Dodgers' talent level remained high with center-fielder Duke Snider, who hit 42 home runs and led the league in RBI in 1955; first baseman Gil Hodges hit 27 home runs; and Don Newcombe led the pitching staff with a 20–5 mark. Their collective effort proved enough to get the team to yet another World Series,

Brooklyn's Jackie Robinson stole home in the opener, sliding
under the tag of Yankee catcher Yogi Berra.

earning yet another shot at beating the Yankees.

Sitting on the bench for the Dodgers was a player of little note: Sandy Amoros. The 25-year-old native of Havana, Cuba, had hit .247 in 1955 and primarily was known for being a good glove to have available for late-inning outfield defense.

Amoros, whose full name was Edmundo Amoros, grew up in Matanzas, a suburb of Havana, where his father worked as a laborer. He played ball in the sugar-cane fields and was accomplished enough to leave Cuba in 1950 to play for the New York Cubans of the Negro Leagues. Dodgers scout Al Campanis discovered Amoros playing for La Habana during the Cuban winter league in 1951 and signed the youngster. By 1952 Amoros had worked his way up the Dodgers' chain to a spot on the St. Paul roster. That's where he earned the nickname "Sandy" from teammates, who thought he resembled featherweight boxing champion Sandy Sandler, and it's the place where he hit .337 to earn accolades as a can't-miss prospect. But basically, he did miss. He spent the next couple of years bouncing back and forth between Brooklyn and Montreal, the Dodgers' Triple-A farm team. Though he led the International League in hitting with .353 in 1953, he never found consistency at the plate in the majors. This inconsistency resulted in his never earning an everyday position in the majors.

Amoros cast an anonymous shadow among the many outspoken and popular personalities on the Dodgers. One had to be a real fan to even know Amoros was on the roster.

The Dodgers lost the first two games of the 1955 Series by scores of 6–5 and 4–2 to put the Yankees up 2–0. Johnny Podres then put on a pitching clinic in an 8–3 Dodgers win in Game 3, and Brooklyn then took Games 4 and 5. Suddenly Dem Bums were one game away from accomplishing the feat that had eluded them

Dodger left-fielder Sandy Amoros's sixth-inning catch near the wall robbed Yogi Berra of extra bases and started a key double play in the deciding game.

for so long. One win and the Dodgers would have their first World Series championship. But the Yankees were a team that died hard. Yankees southpaw Whitey Ford silenced the Dodgers' bats in Game 6 in a 5–1 Yankees victory to force a deciding Game 7.

Postseason play brings about a different brand of baseball. Managers are prone to make changes more quickly than during the then 154-game regular season.

Amoros cast an anonymous shadow among the many outspoken and popular personalities on the Dodgers. One had to be a real fan to even know Amoros was on the roster.

Each game of a World Series is a precious commodity. In Game 7 these changes become even more magnified and the deciding game can turn into a diamond-sized chess match.

The Dodgers took a 2–0 lead in Game 7 with a sixth-inning rally that ended when Dodgers manager Walter Alston pinch hit George Shuba for second baseman Don Zimmer. Shuba grounded out to end the inning, but the move set in motion a switch in the field. Junior Gilliam moved from left field to second base and Amoros was inserted in the game as the left-fielder. While all of Cuba cheered the move to use Amoros, who was a national hero, Dodgers fans viewed Amoros joining the contest with indifference.

Podres had been masterful in the early innings, but the Dodgers left-hander began to tire in the bottom of the sixth, walking leadoff hitter Billy Martin before yielding a bunt single to Gil McDougald. Suddenly the Dodgers' hopes of claiming their first World Series looked grim as the always dangerous Yogi Berra stepped to the plate.

With the left-handed-hitting Berra at bat the Dodgers outfielders were positioned toward right field—a move that appeared to backfire when Berra reached out to direct an outside pitch toward the left field line.

UNEXPECTED SUPERMEN OF THE FALL CLASSIC

Sandy Amoros's 15 minutes of fame came during the 1955 World Series when he made his game-saving catch, but the speedy outfielder is only one of many unlikely heroes who have distinguished themselves during the Fall Classic. Here's a look at some others:

Craig Counsell
The slight but scrappy Florida Marlins rookie was a constant pest to the Cleveland Indians' side during the 1997 Series. In Game 7, his sacrifice fly sent Game 7 into extra innings, then the Marlins won in the bottom of the 11th after Counsell reached on an error and scored on Edgar Renteria's two-out single.

Bucky Dent
Yes, he's Bucky "@#$%^*%" Dent in Boston, but the light-hitting New York Yankees shortstop proved to be a bigger threat against the Dodgers in the 1978 World Series. Dent led the Yankees with 10 hits in compiling a .417 average and seven RBI to earn MVP honors.

Moe Drabowsky
In Game 1 of the 1966 Series, the journeyman pitcher gave the Orioles $6\frac{2}{3}$ innings of superb relief, surrendering just one hit and striking out 11 in a 5–2 victory over the Los Angeles Dodgers. The performance by Drabowsky, whom Baltimore had acquired for $25,000 in 1965, set the tone as the

Orioles swept the heavily favored Dodgers.

Al Gionfriddo
Gionfriddo, who went into Game 6 of the '47 Series as a defensive replacement, made a leaping grab of a Joe DiMaggio drive to rob him of a three-run homer in the sixth inning and preserve an 8–6 Dodgers victory. Gionfriddo was back on the bench for Game 7, which the Yankees won. He never played another game in the major leagues.

Darrell Porter
After batting .231 for the St. Louis Cardinals during the regular season in 1982, the catcher was the National League Championship Series MVP and World Series MVP. In the World Series against the Brewers, he had eight hits, including two doubles.

Donn Clendenon
Clendenon did not play in the 1969 National League Championship Series after the right-handed-hitting Mets first baseman platooned with Ed Kranepool during the regular season, hitting just .258 for the Mets after coming over from Montreal. But he started four of the five games against Baltimore in the World Series and hit solo home runs in Games 2 and 4, both of which were 2–1 victories for the Mets. Clendenon added a two-run shot when the Mets won the fifth and deciding game 5–3. He hit .357 for the Series, scored four of the Mets' 15 runs, and had four of their 13 RBI.

Duke Snider (left), *Don Newcombe, and the Dodgers finally got to
celebrate a World Series victory over their crosstown nemesis.*

McDougald tore off around second base while Martin cautiously held at third to check the outcome of Berra's drive.

Amoros, who hit and threw left-handed, took off after the ball, which was slicing away from him toward the left field foul pole. With a full head of steam, Amoros stretched out his gloved right hand approximately five feet from the stands to make the catch. Miraculously he managed to put on the brakes and had the presence of mind to throw to the cutoff man, Reese. Martin hustled safely back to second, but Reese's relay beat McDougald to first.

Instead of facing a tied game with the go-ahead run on second base and no outs, the Dodgers maintained a 2–0 lead with two outs and a runner at second. Podres got out of the inning without allowing Martin to score, then gave up just one more hit during the final three innings. The Dodgers had won their first World Series.

Afterward, Gilliam confessed he would never have caught Berra's drive. Amoros, who spoke little English, grinned at reporters and repeated over and over, "Lucky, lucky. I'm so lucky."

Little-known Sandy Amoros had been the difference in the biggest game in Brooklyn Dodgers history. Podres put the play in proper perspective when he told reporters:

"If that ball had fallen for a hit, the Dodgers might never have won a World Series in Brooklyn."

Chapter Twenty-two

David and His Left-Footed Slingshot

College Football, Boston College vs. Notre Dame
South Bend, Indiana, November 20, 1993

With one play left in Boston College's 1993 season, walk-on kicker David Gordon stood at the center of the football universe. The scoreboard at Notre Dame Stadium told the story: ND 39, BC 38, 0:05 remaining. Fighting Irish faithful stood as one, huddled together, praying that the rookie kicker would choke under the heavy pressure.

Above the goalposts, towering over the stadium, stood a 14-story mosaic of Jesus with his arms raised high; it was none other than "Touchdown Jesus" as he came to be known. Fighting Irish fans believed that the Lord always sided with Notre Dame, but Boston College was a Catholic school too. Who said the most Hail Marys, the Massachusetts boys or the Indianans?

Considering the pressure of the situation, Gordon—a former soccer player at the University of Vermont—deserved credit for just lining up. Everything was at stake for the Irish. They were riding a 17-game win streak and—after their much ballyhooed 31–24 victory a week earlier over undefeated Florida State—were ranked No. 1 in the country. They needed

a victory in this contest to go to the Fiesta Bowl and play for the national championship. Their manic comeback so far in this game, scoring 22 points in the fourth quarter to overcome a 38–17 hole, was a testimony to how desperate they were for victory.

But Boston College was just as determined. A year earlier, Notre Dame had plucked the Eagles bald 54–7. BC quarterback Glenn Foley said he thought the Irish had "rubbed it in a little bit last year." And though Boston College was riding a seven-game winning streak after opening the season at 0-3, they entered the Notre Dame game as an 18-point underdog. "The comments some people made, especially in the Boston media, never even gave us a chance to play the football game," Foley said.

After toppling mighty Florida State, the Irish may have felt they could phone it in against Boston College. No way.

Foley, blessed with great pass protection throughout the game, riddled the Irish secondary in the first quarter. His four-yard touchdown pass to Ivan Boyd put BC up 10–0. Following a Notre Dame TD, Foley hit Boyd for a 36-yard scoring strike for a 17–7 lead. After two long

---

Walk-on kicker David Gordon stood at the center of the football universe when he attempted a 41-yard field goal, which would go down in gridiron history.

scoring drives by both clubs, the Eagles trotted off at halftime with a 24–14 lead.

Irish coach Lou Holtz tried to make adjustments at the half, but to no avail. BC's Darnell Campbell, the nation's leading scorer, blew through a hole on the right side for a 21-yard touchdown romp. Going for the jugular, Eagles coach Tom Coughlin ordered an onside kick. BC recovered but couldn't capitalize.

However, after an Irish field goal, Foley tossed a one-yard scoring pass to Pete Mitchell to extend the lead to 38–17.

In the fourth quarter, however, Notre Dame quarterback Kevin McDougal staged one of the greatest comebacks in the storied history of Irish football. With 11:03 remaining, running back Lee Becton scored from 29 yards out. Then, in a bit of Lou Holtz trickery, Becton hit McDougal with a pass for a two-point conversion.

After Foley lost a fumbled snap, Notre Dame drove 67 yards on six

---

The previous year, Notre Dame Coach Lou Holtz had plucked the Boston College Eagles bald, 54–7. When the 1993 game was played, the pundits gave Holtz and his Fighting Irish an 18-point advantage before the game.

David Gordon didn't just beat Notre Dame on November 20, 1993—he ended one of the great eras of Fighting Irish football.

Notre Dame, which had boasted the greatest winning percentage in college football history but floundered in the 1980s, returned to prominence late in the decade. Coach Lou Holtz, a brilliant motivator and recruiter, stockpiled the team with blue-chip talent. The Irish not only were undefeated national champions in 1988, but the school became the first ever to sign its own television deal with a network: NBC became the home of Notre Dame football.

The Irish remained a title contender for several more years, peaking in 1992 (seven straight wins to close the season) and '93 (opening 10-0). But the loss to Boston College cost them the national championship. Though Notre Dame beat Texas A&M in the Cotton Bowl, the Irish finished No. 2 in the final AP poll behind Florida State, which had defeated Nebraska in the Orange Bowl. Notre Dame fans protested in vain that their team should have been voted No. 1 since the Irish had beaten FSU in November.

As it turned out, the 1993 season was the Domers' last year of glory to date. Notre Dame fell to 6-5-1 in 1994, then lost three to seven games a year, every year, from 1995 through 2004. Ironically, Boston College kept coming back to haunt the Irish. When the Eagles upset Notre Dame 24–23 in 2004, it was their fourth straight win over the Irish. The curse of David Gordon lives on…

plays, culminating in a Ray Zellars four-yard touchdown run. Now trailing 38–32, the Irish forced Boston College to punt. On Notre Dame's first play from scrimmage, McDougal rocked the house with a 46-yard pass play to Derrick Mayes. The Eagles defense hung tough, forcing a fourth-and-goal from the four. But, with possibly the national championship on the line, McDougal hit Lake Dawson with a game-tying touchdown pass. The extra point made it 39–38 Notre Dame with just 1:01 remaining.

Foley, determined to avenge the previous year's humiliation, kept his cool. In just 42 seconds, he marched the Eagles from their own 25 to the Notre Dame 33. He followed with a nine-yard screen pass to Boyd, setting the stage for Gordon's do-or-die field goal.

Gordon sauntered onto the field. The young kicker had been chided as being a rich kid; his father was managing partner of the NHL's Hartford Whalers. But all the money in the world couldn't help him on the football field. Earlier in the season, Gordon had missed a potential game-winning 40-yard field goal in a 22–21 loss to lowly Northwestern. He admitted his sensitivity, saying he had never felt worse in life. This field goal attempt would be 41 yards, a distance from which he had never succeeded in a college game.

As the two teams lined up for the kick, Touchdown Jesus stared Gordon in the face, while David's parents fretted in the stands. *"Make that kick,"* Gordon said afterward. "That's all I was thinking."

The ball was placed in the middle of the field. The snap was high, but Foley, the holder, snatched it and laid it down nicely. The left-footed Gordon booted the pigskin, kicking what he later termed a "knuckleball." As the ball wobbled skyward, it appeared that it had enough leg but that it might drift too far to the right. Somehow, the ball straightened itself and sailed to the left of the right goalpost.

Touchdown Jesus may have blessed the Irish with their late TDs, but now He raised his arms for Gordon's successful field goal. Boston College had prevailed 41–39. As Notre Dame fans gnashed their teeth, the Eagles mobbed their lefty walk-on kicker.

It was the greatest moment in the 100-year history of Boston College football—and sweet revenge for those players humiliated by Notre Dame a year earlier. "Who are they laughing at now?" shouted Eagles lineman Pete Kendall after the epic battle. "They're not laughing at us, baby!"

Chapter Twenty-three

The War That Will Not End

College Football, Army vs. Navy
Municipal Stadium, Philadelphia, Pennsylvania, December 2, 1950

ven though it was five years since the Japanese had surrendered in World War II, in the hearts of millions of American men in 1950, the war had practically ended just last week. For this great generation, there are only three kinds of men: those who didn't serve in the military, Army men, and Navy men.

In 1950 almost every American family had recent and very powerful connections with either the Army or the Navy. The rivalry between the two branches of the military went to the core. It wasn't the preppy type of rivalry like between Harvard and Yale that involves only an elite few, or the Dodgers-Giants rivalry, which is strictly New York stuff. The Army-Navy annual football game is serious business, even more serious than football itself.

The football rivalry dates back to 1890 when the Midshipmen won 24–0 at West Point. Down through the years, both military academies enjoyed fine football teams and combined to form one of college football's great rivalries.

In this meeting in Philadelphia's Municipal Stadium, Navy carried a meager 2-6 record into the contest, while Army thundered in undefeated and ranked No. 2 in the country. Army also held a 28-game undefeated streak—dating back to 1947—and had not lost to their beleaguered rival since 1943, though the Midshipmen managed to tie the Cadets 21–21 in 1948.

Both teams had been especially adept during the World War II years, but while Army had continued to be strong, Navy embarked on a 7-34-3 drought since 1946. In short, Navy didn't belong on the same field as Army, which was favored by three touchdowns. A massacre looked inevitable.

In the interior of the United States that same day, No. 1 Oklahoma took its 30-game winning streak into Stillwater, home of the Oklahoma State Cowboys. Army had to be thinking about the possibility of the Sooners getting upset in the hostile environment. All Cadets had to do was take care of business that afternoon with Navy and they might find themselves ranked No. 1 at the end of the day. A national championship looked like a possibility if Army could finish off its third successive undefeated season and sixth undefeated season in seven years.

President Harry Truman, an ex-Army enlisted man, arrived with his wife, Bess, to join the crowd of 101,000. He posed for pictures with team captains Tom Bakke of Navy and Dan Foldberg of Army, then parked himself on the Navy side since the Midshipmen were the home team. President Truman had begun

President Harry S. Truman flipped the coin for the team captains, Army's Dan Foldberg (left) and Navy's Tom Bakke.

the practice of sitting on the home side in 1948; having the leader of the free world on one's side seemed to bode well for the home team.

In '48 underdog Navy had mustered a tie with Truman on their side, then in 1949 Army blasted Navy 38–0—the most lopsided score in the rivalry's history—when the president sat on the Cadets' side.

As if having the president on their side of the stadium wasn't enough, a good luck telegram signed

by 824 Midshipmen that measured 813 feet was delivered to the Navy locker room prior to the start of the game.

Bakke won the coin toss and elected to receive, which only delayed the potent Army offense taking over and ramming the ball down their rival's throat. But Navy didn't cower in the first quarter. Though their offense failed to perform, the Navy defense stopped Army's offense four times—once at the Navy 15—to keep the game scoreless through the first quarter.

In the second quarter, Navy defensive back Frank Hauff intercepted a pass from Army quarterback Bob Blaik—son of famed Army coach Earl "Red" Blaik—early in the second quarter. Soon Navy began to show signs of life.

With Bob "Zag" Zastrow leading their attack, Navy then took a 7–0 lead. Just before the half, Zastrow struck again, finding Jim Baldinger in the end zone and putting Navy up 14–0 at the half.

The first-half statistics painted an unflattering portrait of Army. They had accrued just one first down and three yards of total offense, which could be partially attributed to a special 6-2-2-1 defense Navy coach Eddie Erdelatz chose to employ. From the unconventional alignment the Navy defense found odd angles in Army's line to shoot their linebackers. Army was caught off guard and couldn't find any suitable countermeasure from their straight T formation.

On the other side of the ball, Navy also used the T formation, choosing to stray from their customary single wing, and used a variety of plays that seemed to keep the Army defense off balance.

Army finally got on the scoreboard in the third quarter when Zastrow was dropped for a 14-yard loss in his own end zone for a safety, making the score 14–2 and setting the stage for a crazed final period.

With Navy protecting their lead in the fourth quarter, Army was on their heels. The Cadets moved

Quarterback Bob Zastrow helped Navy end Army's 28-game streak.

The annual Army-Navy game has been so huge in American history that it has often engendered odd exceptions to accommodate fans who just had to follow the action no matter what.

In World War II General Douglas McArthur—who was leading the Army's war effort in the Pacific—sent a radiogram to the men from West Point following their victory over Navy in the 1944 game: "We have stopped the war to celebrate your magnificent success."

The initial Army-Navy game was played in 1890 at West Point, New York—Army's home. Since then the game has been an annual tradition save for several exceptions. The 1909 game was not played after an Army player incurred injuries in a game against Harvard and died; this was prior to the advent of adequate padding for the players. And the game was not played during the Spanish-American War or during World War I. In the late 1920s the game was canceled due to the Depression.

The policy for future cancellations due to war was set during World War II. Though advisors told President Franklin D. Roosevelt that playing the game would be frivolous, Roosevelt gave the executive order that the game should be played, noting that all athletic events should go on as planned to boost morale. He did put several restrictions on the 1942 contest by canceling the traditional bonfire to save firewood and he declared that the game could only be viewed by fans living within a 10-mile radius of Thompson Stadium in Annapolis in order to conserve gasoline. This restriction kept Army from having much of a following, but created one of the more interesting circumstances from the rivalry as third- and fourth-year Midshipmen were ordered to cheer for Army. Included in this mandate was a required singing of Army fight songs.

While the game was not canceled in 1963 in the aftermath of President John F. Kennedy's assassination, it was postponed for a week.

the ball to the Midshipmen's 21, but failed to score. Again the Army Cadets ran and passed their way to Navy's 15, but failed to bring home any bacon. In yet another Army drive, they reached the six-yard line, again producing no results on the scoreboard.

The Navy crowd was raucous now as Army was being humiliated, but soon the Cadets got a well-deserved break. They moved the ball to the Navy three-yard line and could smell pay dirt in the end zone. Adrenaline fueled the Cadets now—not only were they within striking distance, there was enough time left for another goal-producing possession. Army quarterback Blaik decided to go for the TD with a pass and the crowd was hushed as they came out of the huddle. He hurled a bullet toward the Navy end zone. From nowhere Navy's John Gurski snatched it. The dreams

of an Army come-from-behind victory had been dashed. Now all Navy had to do was run out the clock. As the final seconds ticked down, approximately 3,700 Midshipmen charged the field as the final gun sounded. Army was defeated.

The stadium became bedlam. Navy had broken the Cadets' 28-game winning streak with its 14–2 victory. The celebratory atmosphere on the Navy side hadn't been this big since the Japanese surrendered. The radio sportscasters were frantically calling it the football upset of the century.

Arthur Daley of the *New York Times* wrote: "It was one of those things that strain credulity. You had to see it to believe it."

And Bill Corum of the *New York Journal American* added: "Somebody must have mixed up the uniforms."

Chapter Twenty-four

Hitler and the Brown Bomber

Heavyweight Boxing, Max Schmeling vs. Joe Louis

Yankee Stadium, Bronx, New York, June 19, 1936

Hamburg, Germany, is a port city where roughneck seamen carouse in the bars and indigent Europeans come to earn passage to America, or any other port that will take them. Scrubbing the holds of ships, washing dishes, and prostitution are the harbor town's main industries. Anyplace is better than here, pre-Hitler Germany, where bread is scarce and beer and whiskey flow like a raging river after a downpour.

Nonetheless, this is still Germany, a nation its citizens regard as the most civilized place on earth, where order is everything and at least some pride still prevails. But this nation was beaten down by war, the Great War, the one they said would end all wars, but didn't.

Boxing is almost unknown here, in a nation where violence is considered uncivilized. Hamburg, with all its bars and backrooms, is one of the few places in pre–World War II Europe to find a boxing match, but they are well hidden, practically out of sight. With "colored men" in the sport now, it's even more alien to Germany, where white is its only color, and civility is its second language.

Not until the returning German prisoners from World War I found their way back home did the sport get reintroduced to the country. It was an import from Britain, where their capturers spoke of the glories of "fisticuffs" and provided gloves for the German

prisoners to while away their long days in captivity.

Amid this backdrop a 14-year-old boy wandered into a Hamburg movie parlor. There he saw a newsreel that changed his life forever. It featured an American, a rangy, barroom-brawling ex-hobo, whose stock-in-trade was terror; his name was Jack Dempsey.

In him young Max Schmeling saw not just a prizefighter, but a conqueror of mythic proportions, a knight in armor cast from sweat and calluses. Onscreen he witnessed Dempsey's savage attack on George Carpentier, a Frenchman he cut down like a tree. To him it was more than a sporting event; it was an inspiration, a veritable call to arms. It was the French, at least as the Germans saw it, who were responsible for the desolation in Germany. For three brutalizing rounds he watched Dempsey humiliate the Frenchman, then put him down to stay in the fourth. If only he could do that too.

Well, he could!

The German teenager was tall and built like the Greek god Adonis. His dark features defied his German heritage as much as his pugilistic instinct did.

The film so captivated the youthful Schmeling, an

Schmeling (on scale) *and Louis shook hands at the weigh-in for their heavyweight bout at New York's Yankee Stadium.*

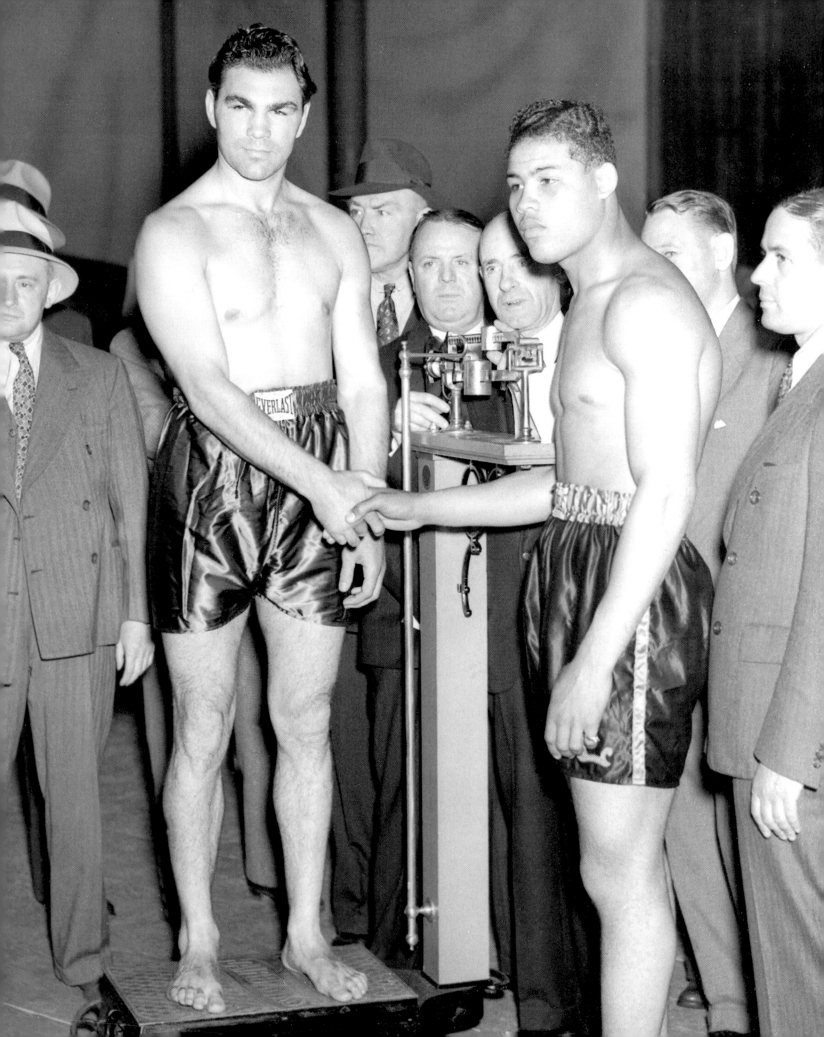

apprentice at an ad placement agency, that he spent most of his earnings to make repeat visits to the theater. Soon he filled everyone's ears with boxing talk to the point where his family became sick of hearing about it. Days later, and with the approval of his father, a ship's navigator, the boy bought his first boxing gloves—a used set from a secondhand store—and a career in boxing had begun.

Having found a passion, Schmeling progressed to a point where he fought Jack Sharkey in 1930 in the final bout of an elimination tournament for the heavyweight championship of the world. Over 80,000 fans at Yankee Stadium watched as Sharkey led on points before landing a low blow to Schmeling in the fourth round. Schmeling fell to the canvas in agony. When he could not continue,

---

Schmeling hit Louis with powerful rights all through the fight, before scoring a knockout in the 12th. He raised his fists in exultation after referee Arthur Donovan had counted out the Brown Bomber.

the judges awarded Schmeling the championship. It was the only heavyweight championship ever won by a foul.

Schmeling managed to hold his title for just one defense before losing the belt to Sharkey in a rematch. In the ensuing years the heavyweight title would bounce around, with Primo Carnera getting it in 1933, then Max Baer defeating him in '34 and James Braddock taking Baer's title in a startling upset in 1935. While Braddock reigned as champion, everyone was watching a new, young fighter named Joe Louis, whose legend was growing as the Brown Bomber.

Braddock, the new champ, was not a big draw, so fight promoters wanted to milk as many fights as they could out of Louis. Cassius Clay (later known as Muhammad Ali) experienced the same thing with myriad nontitle bouts between his Olympic gold medal in 1960 and his first title shot in 1964.

Louis's promoters decided on matching him with Schmeling in a nontitle bout, fully convinced Louis's record of 27-0 with 24 knockouts and Schmeling's notoriety would be a fabulous draw, and it proved to

be, thanks in part to German chancellor Adolf Hitler.

Hitler's infamous message about "the master race" echoed around the world. And now, months before the 1936 Berlin Olympics, Schmeling would face a black opponent, and soon—at least as Hitler saw it—another black man, Jesse Owens, would be humiliated by Aryans in Berlin. But Schmeling vs. Louis came first, and Germany and the world were watching. What a contest this was going to be!

Schmeling had made a modest comeback by knocking out several top contenders. His fame now, however, was as "Hilter's boy," Germany's favorite son and the Nazis' pride. He had to win, for Deutschland, for Hitler, and for the Aryan race. And Schmeling knew it.

With the pressure on him, he went to incredible lengths looking for Louis's weaknesses, watching films of Louis's fights again and again. After a careful analysis of the films, Schmeling felt that he had devised a solid plan to win the fight. The key was to anticipate when Louis would throw his right power punch and to counterattack with his own right.

A raucous crowd greeted the fight at Yankee Stadium. True to his word, Schmeling went to his right hand from the outset and to everyone's surprise, the rights landed. After losing the first three rounds, in the fourth Schmeling landed a right hook to Louis and followed with a second shot that sent Louis pivoting backward. Schmeling then unleashed a flurry of blows that culminated with Louis finding the canvas. He remained down for a count of three before rising.

Louis looked lethargic after the fourth, but Schmeling was not home free just yet. Louis continued to land blows to Schmeling's left eye—which swelled until almost completely closed shut—and to his body, taking away Schmeling's wind along with some of his resolve.

Schmeling continued to attack and his edge grew with each round. When the fight reached the 12th round, Schmeling turned loose a series of rights to Louis's jaw, sending him to the canvas for a second time. Louis failed in an attempt to hold on to the ropes and wilted to the mat, exhausted and wrought with pain. When the referee called out the final 10 of the count, Louis rolled onto his stomach. He was so dazed and beaten, he could not move. Hitler's boy had demolished the Brown Bomber.

The reputed darling of the Nazis then did something unexpected and amazing as the world watched. *Instantly*, even before the referee had time to declare him the winner, Schmeling rushed over to the vanquished and crumpled Louis. Schmeling then reached down to him with his hands, and gently helped him to his feet. The Germans' best example of the Master Race then looked at his shaken black opponent and threw his arms around him.

The world would eventually learn that Max Schmeling was no Nazi; he was a gentleman who possessed a rare grace and compassion for all men. Though he had just won one of the biggest fights of the era—though a nontitle bout—he proved to the crowd he was a champion, whose unexpected, compassionate gesture to Louis won the hearts and minds of all—except for Hitler and his henchmen, who would later admonish him for his behavior.

Chapter Twenty-five

Boris Becker:
The Student Prince
Holds Court

Wimbledon Men's Singles Final, London, England, July 4, 1985

Kevin Curren looked like destiny's darling, the veteran whose time had come. That was the story line accompanying the well-seasoned Curren's run through the men's field at Wimbledon in 1985.

Just one slight obstacle stood in Curren's way before claiming tennis's greatest prize, some 17-year-old kid from Heidelberg, Germany, named Boris Becker.

To the untrained eye, Becker barely registered as a blip on the radar given the sizable storms Curren had weathered.

In his previous two matches leading to the final, Curren needed to pass through former Wimbledon champions John McEnroe and Jimmy Connors if he wanted to become the first player from South Africa since Brian Norton lost in 1921 to have a chance at winning Wimbledon. Curren took care of McEnroe and Connors in a fashion suggesting he would finally hoist the winner's trophy at Centre Court.

Becker was unseeded in his second Wimbledon appearance. Only a year before the 6'2", 175-pound Becker had to drop out of Wimbledon after tearing two ligaments in his left ankle. Yet there was something special about the youngster, even if he did flop around the court like a large dog avoiding bath day. Energy

Becker triumphed over Sweden's Anders Jarryd in a four-set semifinal, but the best was yet to come.

There was plenty of power in Boom-Boom's 175-pound frame, as Kevin Curren learned during a Wimbledon singles final match in 1985.

Boris Becker captivated crowds at Wimbledon by throwing his
17-year-old body all over the famed grass courts during a stunning title run.

and power often accompany such youngsters and Becker had both.

Curren hardly took the youngster for granted.

Fact was, what Becker lacked in experience he more than made up for with a serve that had earned him all kinds of nicknames stemming from its power—the most lasting being "Boom-Boom"—and he'd shown flashes of brilliance during the past year. In December he reached the quarter-finals of the Australian Open and he reached the semifinals of the Italian Open in May. A week before Wimbledon he dismantled Johan Kriek in Queens, prompting Kriek to predict Becker would win Wimbledon. Becker's first-round opponent, Hank Pfister, heralded Becker as better than Bjorn Borg or John McEnroe at the same age and even dared to suggest he might win Wimbledon.

Kriek and Pfister looked prophetic when Becker defeated Tim Mayotte in five sets to advance to the semifinals against Anders Jarryd, the fifth seed of the tournament. Jarryd took the first set 6–2 before losing the next three 7–6, 6–3, 6–3.

While most of the world had no idea who this Becker kid was, Germany reveled in his glory, canceling all regularly scheduled television programming to show his matches once he reached the quarterfinals. The London tabloids had a field day, making World War II references by noting how Germany now wanted to watch a tournament in an area they once riddled with bombs.

Athletes know athletes when they see them. Curren recognized Becker's ability and understood the kid was playing with nothing to lose, and why not, he was a wildcard. Curren secretly wished Jarryd had been his opponent in the finals.

From the first serve of the final, Becker played with reckless abandon, while Curren looked cautious.

Becker's youth shone through in the first set. His footwork and reactions were clearly faster than his opponent's and when he hit, the resulting thunder made jaws drop in awe. Contrasted to Curren, who seemed to be

BOOM-BOOM BORIS

When Boris Becker won Wimbledon in 1985, he became the youngest champion in the history of the men's singles at the storied event. He also became the only unseeded player and the only German ever to win the title, as well as the youngest person to ever win any Grand Slam title in men's singles.

"I was just 17 years and 227 days old," Becker said in *The Player*. "I couldn't legally drive in Germany. I cut my own hair; and my mother sent me toothpaste because she was worried about my teeth."

While the legend of "Boom-Boom" essentially was born at Wimbledon at a stage of life in which he barely shaved, Becker had been around the block where tennis was concerned. He was born on November 22, 1967, in Leimen, West Germany, a small town of barely 20,000 just outside Heidelberg. Becker's father, Karl-Heinz Becker, worked in Leimen as an architect and built the hometown tennis club, Blau-Weiss Tennisklub. No doubt, the connection, along with his father's love of the sport, contributed to his early beginning with a racquet in his hand. To Becker's father's credit, he let the Baden Tennis Association handle his son's tennis education.

He began training to be a tennis player at age three. By age nine he was competing in tournaments. And at 13 he was the youngest player in the German Youth Championships, playing against competition four and five years older. In 1984 he turned professional and two years later the aggressive youngster with the big serve rose to second in the Association of Tennis Professionals (ATP) rankings.

guiding the ball in a tentative fashion, Becker resembled flowing electricity en route to the 6–3 first-set win.

Curren woke up in the second set to remind Becker this indeed was Wimbledon. A particularly telling moment came when Curren rallied from a 0–40 service deficit to take a 4–3 set lead. The set went to a tie-breaker that Curren won by virtue of a backhand that disarmed the youngster on several points.

Curren had grabbed the momentum and stubbornly refused to let it slip away in the third set, taking a 4–3 lead. So Becker took matters into his own hands.

Serving to Curren, Becker used three overpowering aces to make the set even at 4. So dominating were his serves that the ball ripped the grass and diminished the white lines, prompting a broom crew to find Centre Court for an impromptu maintenance detail. Becker took the third set 7–6 and was beginning to become a crowd favorite for his all-out manner of play. No ball looked too far away to take a dive at reaching before it hit the ground. Grass stains decorated Becker's shorts and shirts like the tough-to-eliminate examples portrayed in laundry detergent commercials.

Becker broke Curren in the first game of the fourth set. Curren fought back in the second game to reach two break points before Boom-Boom hit a service winner and an ace to end the threat. Curren simply couldn't keep up with Becker, but the youngster began to feel the pressure when all he needed was to win a game in which he served to close out the match.

"My opponent piles on the pressure, 0-15, 15 all, 30-15, 40-15," Becker said in his book, *The Player*. "I want, want, want victory. I look only at my feet, at my racket. I don't hear a thing. I'm trying to keep control. Breathe in. Serve like a parachute jump. Double fault, 40–30. How on earth can I place the ball in that shrinking box over there on the other side of the net? I focus on throwing the ball and then I hit it."

Becker responded to the challenge, finishing off Curren with a service winner to take a 6–4 set win. He had 21 aces for the match, which lasted three hours and 18 minutes. Becker had become the youngest-ever winner of the Wimbledon men's final at 17 years, 227 days.

Chapter Twenty-six

Dusty Did It

World Series, Cleveland Indians vs. New York Giants
Polo Grounds, New York City, and Municipal Stadium, Cleveland, Ohio
September 29–October 2, 1954

Y ou've heard about the early bird. Apparently so had James "Dusty" Rhodes. The pinch-hitter extraordinaire saw no point fooling around till the pitcher was in a jam. He knew it was much more effective to just put the guy in a pickle right away and sock one out of the park with as little fanfare as possible.

You've probably also heard about the relationship between nice guys and winning ballgames. But Leo "the Lip" Durocher never said that. Not exactly. He said they "finish last," and in '54, Leo and his Giants finished first. So you know where he's at in the nice guy department.

The Fall Classic of '54 was as much about Dusty and Durocher as it was about baseball.

True to the early-bird tradition, Rhodes, a native of Rock Hill, South Carolina, was not in the habit of taking his time analyzing the situation. He just liked to hit the ball and keep things simple. Even though he batted left-handed, he didn't put much stock in whether the pitcher was left-handed or right-handed. His mind wasn't cluttered with trivia; he just wanted to get things over with. Maybe that's why he and Durocher got along so well.

The combination of Durocher and his auxiliary

weapon, Rhodes, hardly swayed the opinion of the baseball pundits as the Giants headed into the 1954 World Series. Everyone knew the Cleveland Indians were going to cream them.

Managed by "El Señor" Al Lopez, the Indians earned their trip to the World Series by beating out a quality New York Yankees team and winning a record 111 games during the 154-game regular season. Pitching fueled the Indians, who boasted of a starting staff that included Bob Lemon, Early Wynn, Mike Garcia, Bob Feller, and Art Houtteman. All were experienced and talented and combined to post a team ERA of 2.78. The trio of Lemon, Wynn, and Garcia posted 65 of the staff's wins.

"That was an All-Star staff," Lopez said. "You can go a long way when you have starting pitching like that."

If the Indians' pitching wasn't enough, they had Bobby Avila, who led the American League with a .341 batting average, and Larry Doby, who led the league in home runs with 32 and RBI with 126.

Meanwhile, the Giants scratched and clawed their way to the pennant, finally outdistancing the second-place Brooklyn Dodgers by five games en route to the World Series. They had won 14 fewer games than the

---

Giants center-fielder Willie Mays made one of the most memorable catches in World Series history when he ran down a Vic Wertz blast at the 440-foot mark.

Indians during the regular season and their pitching looked suspect. In short, the Giants appeared to have an uphill battle just to avoid being embarrassed in the Fall Classic.

The Giants' home field, the Polo Grounds, played host to Game 1 on September 29, 1954, which meant the contest would be won or lost on a field with the oddest of dimensions. Center field was somewhere near

ॐॐ

Rhodes watched Mays's catch from the bench, wondering if they were really going to need him in this game.

ॐॐ

Timbuktu—its deepest point rested 483 feet from home plate, while homers to right field were the cheapest in the major leagues, at 257 feet down the line. Would this quirky geometry be an advantage for one team?

The answer to this question came quickly during the top of the eighth inning in a 2–2 tie when Cleveland first baseman Vic Wertz hit a 440-foot blast to center field. The drive would have been a home run in virtually any other park in the major leagues. Instead Willie Mays ran down the ball to make a spectacular and still famous over-the-shoulder catch.

Rhodes watched Mays's catch from the bench, wondering if they were really going to need him in this game. During the regular season Durocher had inserted Dusty as a pinch-hitter 45 times and 15 times Rhodes had validated his faith by delivering a base hit. Rhodes hit .341 for the season with 15 home runs and 50 RBI in 164 official at-bats.

Durocher was well known for playing hunches, and Rhodes looked like a hunch he could bank on in the 10th inning with two runners aboard and the score still tied at 2. Rhodes pinch-hit for Monte Irvin.

Lemon threw a high curveball on the first pitch, but it was eventually headed right down the middle. Lemon obviously was one of the few people who never heard about early birds and worms. "I liked the looks of it real fine," the early bird told reporters afterward. "So I went after it. The next thing I knew the ball was sailing out toward the promised land," which is what Dusty called the right field line.

Mays and Henry Thompson, the Giants' base runners, stood frozen near their respective bases, unsure of the drive's final resting spot. "The minute I hit it, I knew it was going to drop in or be caught," Rhodes said. When the ball landed in the first row, approximately seven feet inside the right field foul line, the Giants bagged a 5–2 victory.

The scouting report on Rhodes described him as a first-pitch hitter. Well, they got that one right! "Can't understand why a guy would come off the bench and take one down the middle," Dusty told the *Bergen Record* in a 1994 interview. "I remember Bob Lemon was so mad, he threw his glove over my head. I think the glove went farther than the ball."

Fifty years later Lopez remained frustrated about the cruel fate of the Polo Grounds. In Cleveland's Municipal Stadium, Rhodes's hit would have been a flyout, and Wertz's drive would have been a home run. "The longest out and the shortest home run of the season beat us," Lopez said. *Cleveland News* sports writer Geoffrey Fisher wrote: "They'll be talking about Dusty Rhodes' Fu Manchu home run as long as chop suey is served with rice and bean cakes. It was as oriental as a chop stick and as painful as an infected bunion."

Durocher liked Dusty Rhodes's approach. Nothing

Pinch-hitter Dusty Rhodes earned a hero's welcome at the plate after his three-run, 10th-inning homer gave the Giants a 5–2 opening victory.

Mays (left) *and Rhodes were all smiles after the latter's pinch-hit homer won Game 1.*

seemed to bother him, particularly pressure.

"The only thing I knew was, you hit the ball or you didn't, so there was no reason to get excited," Rhodes said. "The pitcher was the one in trouble. Not me."

Durocher went to the bench again in Game 2 to give Rhodes the nod with the Giants trailing 1–0 in the fifth. This time Rhodes delivered a bloop single to center field to tie the game. Rhodes remained in the game and batted again in the seventh inning.

Not pleased with Rhodes's "cheap" hits, Wynn, the Indians' Game 2 starter, buzzed one past Rhodes's head on the first pitch in the seventh.

"I can still feel the ball going by the top of my head," Rhodes said.

Wynn followed with a knuckleball. This time there

was nothing cheap about the result. Rhodes drove the ball off the roof 150 feet up from the right field line. The Giants won 3–1. The early bird had just won the first two games for his teammates...practically single-handedly...with homers.

The Series moved to Cleveland for the third game and once again Rhodes was called upon to pinch-hit. He responded with a third-inning single that ignited a Giants rally in a 6–2 win, putting them up 3–0 in the Series. The Giants completed their sweep the next day, taking a 7–4 win—a victory that saw Rhodes remain on the bench. The Series' unlikely hero finished with four hits in six at-bats and hit the only two Giants home runs of the entire Series.

The Jints had swept one of the great teams in

FIRST TIME UP AND OUT OF THE PARK

Dusty Rhodes homered in his first-ever World Series at-bat when he hit the game-winning home run for the Giants in Game 1 of the 1954 World Series. Here's a list of the other players in baseball history to have hit a home run in their first-ever World Series at-bat.

- David Ortiz, Boston Red Sox, 2004
- Troy Glaus, Anaheim Angels, 2002
- Barry Bonds, San Francisco Giants, 2003
- Andruw Jones, Atlanta Braves, 1996*
- Fred McGriff, Atlanta Braves, 1995
- Ed Sprague, Toronto Blue Jays, 1992
- Eric Davis, Cincinnati Reds, 1990
- Bill Bathe, San Francisco Giants, 1989
- Jose Canseco, Oakland A's, 1988
- Mickey Hatcher, Los Angeles Dodgers, 1988
- Jim Dwyer, Baltimore Orioles, 1983
- Bob Watson, New York Yankees, 1981
- Amos Otis, Kansas City Royals, 1980
- Doug DeCinces, Baltimore Orioles, 1979
- Jim Mason, New York Yankees, 1976
- Gene Tenace, Oakland A's, 1972*
- Don Buford, Baltimore Orioles, 1969
- Mickey Lolich, Detroit Tigers, 1968
- Jose Santiago, Boston Red Sox, 1967
- Brooks Robinson, Baltimore Orioles, 1966
- Don Mincher, Minnesota Twins, 1965
- Roger Maris, New York Yankees, 1960
- Elston Howard, New York Yankees, 1955
- Dusty Rhodes, New York Giants, 1954
- George Selkirk, New York Yankees, 1936
- Mel Ott, New York Giants, 1933
- George Watkins, St. Louis Cardinals, 1930
- Joe Harris, Washington Senators, 1925

*Hit a home run in his first two Series at-bats.

baseball history and Rhodes stood front and center the hero of the huge accomplishment. In line with the southern boy who liked to keep things simple, Rhodes couldn't understand the magnitude of what he'd done, nor was he that impressed. He even told reporters he'd gotten a bigger thrill three years earlier from watching his first World Series game on television rather than playing in it.

When asked what he thought about Dusty's take on the World Series, Al Lopez chuckled: "I wish he would have been watching the 1954 World Series on TV too."

A headdress and pregame war chant by Cleveland manager Al Lopez were not enough to keep the Indians from dropping a 3–1 decision to the Giants in Game 2.

Chapter Twenty-seven

Billy Mills: Billy Who?

Summer Olympics, Men's 10,000 Meters Final
Tokyo, Japan, October 14, 1964

There's an old saying that "To know a man, you must first walk a mile in his shoes." Whoever coined that probably never considered what it would *literally* mean to run six miles in someone else's shoes. But on the night of October 14, 1964, under the glare of spotlights in Tokyo's Olympic Stadium, Billy Mills was just about to do that very thing—run the grueling 10,000-meter race in a pair of borrowed track shoes.

Not that anyone outside the U.S. Olympic Committee knew or remotely cared about Mills's predicament. Here he was, a 26-year-old Marine Corps lieutenant, poised to compete in the biggest event of his athletic career opposite the world's top runners, and none of the reporters had bothered to learn his name. Why waste ink on a nobody destined to finish at the back of the pack? Besides, no American had ever won gold in the 10,000-meter race. And with a qualifying time nearly a full minute behind the favorite, Australia's Ron Clarke, the track and field star from South Dakota's Black Hills wasn't expected to finish anywhere near the top three. Even the U.S. Olympic Committee, Mills's ostensible supporters, had dismissed his request for shoes with brutal candor: "We only have enough for those we expect to do well."

Stung by their callous indifference, Mills had never-

The little-known Mills (722) proved too tough down the stretch for Gammoudi and the other favorites.

theless swallowed his hurt and borrowed some shoes. It wasn't as if he were a stranger to insult. Born to a white mother and an Oglala Sioux Indian father on the Pine Ridge Reservation, Mills had always been a pariah, caught in a limbo between two cultures perpetually at odds. Growing up in one of the country's poorest areas, where there was little except the horrific memories of the 1890 massacre of 300 Sioux Indians at Wounded Knee Creek and rampant alcoholism, Mills had already experienced much pain in his life. Orphaned at 12, he had briefly contemplated suicide before finding solace in long-distance running. The Olympic Committee slight was therefore just another in a long line of setbacks that Mills had learned to absorb with hard-earned grace.

Breathing evenly, Mills took his starting position on the wet track. It was an atypically warm October evening for Tokyo. As he waited for the starting pistol to fire, Mills thought back to what he'd written in his journal three weeks earlier: "GOLD MEDAL." If he had shown his scribbled prediction to his coach or fellow athletes, they would have either rolled their eyes or perhaps laughed outright. Surely he must know that Clarke, the current world record holder in the 10,000-meter race, was virtually guaranteed to finish first, barring a fall or late surge from the 1960 gold medalist, Pyotr Bolotnikov of the Soviet Union.

The starting pistol fired. Mills propelled himself off the block and disappeared into the pack as Clarke immediately took the lead. Eight years earlier, Clarke

With his landmark victory in the 10,000-meter race in Tokyo, Billy Mills became the first American in 52 years to earn a medal in this event. His gold medal also granted the track and field star of the Oglala Sioux tribe membership in the pantheon of Native American Olympic medalists. Since the first Modern Olympics were held in 1896, seven Native American athletes have won medals in events ranging from basketball to hockey to track and field.

Of all the Native American Olympians, the most famous is unquestionably the legendary Jim Thorpe of the Sac and Fox and Potawatomi tribes. At the 1912 Summer Olympics in Stockholm, the all-around athlete won the gold in both the decathlon and pentathlon. Never one to rest on his laurels, Thorpe also placed fourth in the high jump and seventh in the long jump. Following his Olympic victories, Thorpe went on to play major league baseball from 1913 to 1919. In 1950, the nation's top sportswriters named Thorpe, albeit rather prematurely, the greatest athlete of the 20th century.

Here are the seven Native American Olympic medalists to date, in chronological order:

NAME/TRIBE	OLYMPICS/YEAR	EVENT(S)	MEDAL
Louis Tewanima/Hopi	Summer Olympics/1912	10,000 Meters	Silver
Jim Thorpe/Sac and Fox and Potawatomi	Summer Olympics/1912	Decathlon/Pentathlon	Gold
Clarence "Taffy" Abel/Sault Ste. Marie Chippewa	Winter Olympics/1924	Hockey	Silver
Jesse "Cab" Renick*/Choctaw	Summer Olympics/1948	Basketball	Gold
Billy Mills/Oglala Sioux	Summer Olympics/1964	10,000 Meters	Gold
Henry Boucha/Ojibwa	Winter Olympics/1972	Hockey	Silver
Cheri Becerra/Omaha	Summer Olympics/1996	800-meters wheelchair	Bronze

*Renick was captain of the 1948 U.S. Olympic basketball team

had literally gotten burned while carrying the Olympic torch at the 1956 summer games in Melbourne. It had been an inauspicious debut on the world stage for the dark-haired, sinewy runner, then nineteen and something of a track and field wunderkind in his native Australia. In the Olympics of antiquity, such an injury, no matter how minor, would have been seen as an evil omen. Tonight, however, with a pace-setting lead that showed no sign of shrinking, Clarke appeared to be running a charmed race.

Then, as the runners began their final lap, Mills burst free of the pack, along with Tunisia's Mohamed Gammoudi, to match Clarke's ferocious pace. The three jostled for position in the thick of the race's stragglers, i.e., sore losers who refused to let them pass on the inside.

Suddenly, Clarke's victory was no longer a foregone conclusion. Gammoudi had been expected to fight him for the gold, but who was this Yank upstart, number 722? Clearly rattled by Mills's surprise appearance at his side and feeling crowded, Clarke pushed him to the outside lane. With the finish line just 50 meters away, the narrow gap between Mills and the two front-runners began to widen, to the point that Mills trailed them by nearly five meters.

Every muscle in Mills's 150-pound frame ached, yet still he pushed himself, fueled by the same will that had sustained him through the worst of times. The bronze medal, or the silver, wouldn't do; he was fixated now on only one thing, what he'd written in capital letters in his notebook: "GOLD MEDAL." No longer was it a million-to-one chance; there were three and only three things left between him and the gold—

Clarke, Gammoudi, and three yards to the finish line between which he had to catch—and beat—them.

Ignoring the constant pain from his ill-fitting shoes, Mills leaped mightily. He flew past Clarke. Another leap, he rocketed past Gammoudi. He had the lead! Only one meter to go now. A nanosecond later, his arms flew up in the proverbial gesture of victory. He had done it, what no other American had done before—won the 10,000 Meters and set an Olympic record with a winning time of 28 minutes and 24 seconds.

Not a bad accomplishment, considering he had won the race in borrowed shoes.

Mills crossed the finish line in 28:24.4, an Olympic record.

Cool Hand Tom

Super Bowl XXXVI, New England Patriots vs. St. Louis Rams
New Orleans, Louisiana, February 3, 2002

Soldiers surrounded the stadium in case of a terrorist attack, while sharpshooters manned the roof. With all the security, the more than 72,000 fans at the Superdome in New Orleans didn't feel much more secure than the 800 million fans around the world who would watch Super Bowl XXXVI on television. After all, there was a war going on, but a new and more palatable one would erupt on the field any minute.

And yet, after pregame warmups, New England Patriots starting quarterback Tom Brady went back to his locker room and took a nap on the floor.

"I was relaxed…calm and confident," he said. "The locker room was quiet, so I just put my head back and had a little snooze."

Had Brady been a Super Bowl regular, his siesta may have been less surprising. But as a Patriots rookie in 2000, the former University of Michigan quarterback had completed just one pass. He began 2001 as a fourth-string quarterback, even though most teams didn't even *have* four QBs. However, after superstar signal-caller Drew Bledsoe fell to injury in week 2, a game the Pats lost to go 0-2, Brady sparked an extraordinary team turnaround. With the kid at the helm, New England won 11 of its last 14 games.

On the season, Brady completed 264 of 413 passes for a 63.9 percentage—a new Patriots record. He set an NFL record for most passes without an interception to start a career (162), and he finished with the sixth best passer rating (86.5) in the NFL. More important, said

wide receiver David Patten, "The kid knows how to win. He knows how to motivate other players."

Brady was so effective, in fact, that he maintained the starting job even when Bledsoe healed in November. Brady spearheaded the Patriots to an 11-5 regular-season record and a 16–13 overtime win against the Oakland Raiders in the playoffs.

Brady's glory run seemed to end in the AFC Championship Game, when he left with a twisted ankle. Bledsoe came in to key a 24–17 triumph over Pittsburgh. Yet, in a gutsy decision, head coach Bill Belichick selected Brady instead of his three-time Pro Bowler to start against the St. Louis Rams in the Super Bowl.

Actually, a team-first attitude characterized this Patriots squad. They made it to the big game despite being shockingly lean on talent. Besides Brady, only one Patriot was named to the Pro Bowl, defensive back Lawyer Milloy. Antowain Smith rushed for 1,157 yards, but only 4.0 per carry. Wideout Troy Brown amassed 1,199 receiving yards, but he scored only five touchdowns. In fact, New England ranked 19th in the NFL in total offense and 24th in defense. The Pats actually gave up more yards (5,586) than they gained (5,119)!

Besides Brady and coach Belichick, a brilliant game strategist, New England succeeded through exceptional team unity. Bledsoe, for example, took his demotion

Adam Vinatieri was the center of attention on the game's final play.

graciously, helping Brady in meetings and on the practice field. The Patriots even chose not to be introduced individually in the Super Bowl's pregame ceremony.

New England entered the game as an enormous underdog. St. Louis, known as the "Greatest Show on Turf" because of its powerhouse offense, was a 14-point favorite. The Rams had gone 14-2 on the season, finishing first in the NFL in points (503), first in offense (6,930 yards), and third in defense (4,733). Four offensive starters made the Pro Bowl, including quarterback Kurt Warner, the NFL's MVP.

Belichick developed a smart strategy to defuse the Rams' passing game. He would employ five, six, even seven defensive backs. They would drop back in coverage to prevent the big play, then make receivers pay with bone-jarring hits. "They're the greatest track team in history," Patriots cornerback Ty Law said, "but I've never seen a guy run 100 yards with someone in front of them."

Sure enough, New England's defense bent but didn't crack, allowing just a 50-yard field goal through the first 21 minutes. Then, with 8:49 left in the half, the Patriots got the break of the game. Kurt Warner, feeling the heat of a linebacker blitz, fired a pass right to Law, who returned not 100 yards but 47 for a score.

After the two-minute warning, with the Rams threatening to score, Antwan Harris jarred the ball from St. Louis receiver Ricky Proehl. Terrell Buckley picked it up and returned it to the St. Louis 40. With the clock ticking down, Brady calmly orchestrated a five-play drive, hitting David Patten in the corner of the end zone. Incredibly, New England led 14–3 at the half.

Rams coach Mike Martz, frustrated by New England's nickel-and-dime defenses, ran the ball in the third quarter. But when Warner was forced to throw on third down, cornerback Otis Smith picked it off and returned it 30 yards to the St. Louis 33. An Adam Vinatieiri field goal made it 17–3.

New England held the NFL's best offense without a touchdown until 9:31 of the fourth quarter, when Warner snuck into the end zone to punctuate a 73-yard drive. The Patriots still led 17–10, but the momentum

had shifted to the Rams. Then, with 1:51 remaining, St. Louis took over the ball on their own 45. This time, Warner went for the jugular, hitting Proehl for a 26-yard touchdown pass with 1:30 remaining. The point after made it 17–17.

Brady had risen to the challenge all season, but could he orchestrate the ultimate two-minute drive—without any timeouts? Sure enough, Brady completed three short passes to running back J. R. Redmond to reach the Patriots' 41 with 33 seconds to go. Despite a

MVP Brady never let the hype of the big game get to him.

Coach Bill Belichick's defensive game plan slowed the high-powered St. Louis attack, allowing the Pats to win the Lombardi Trophy.

crowded secondary, Brady hit Troy Brown for 23 yards and Jermaine Wiggins for six before spiking the ball at the Rams' 30 with seven seconds left.

Enter Vinatieri for a 48-yard field goal attempt. A distant cousin of daredevil Evil Knievel, Vinatieri proved just as courageous, splitting the uprights for a monumental 20–17 triumph. For the first time in Super Bowl history, a game was won on the final play.

In the postgame bedlam, confetti fell from the Superdome ceiling while players and media mobbed Brady. Not only had he become the youngest field general ever to win a Super Bowl, but he was named the game's MVP. "I always say a quarterback is as good as the team around him," said Brady. And they're only as good as their fourth-string quarterback.

Chapter Twenty-nine

The Has-Been and the Hebrew

Heavyweight Championship of the World
James J. Braddock vs. Max Baer
Madison Square Garden Bowl
Long Island City, New York
June 13, 1935

A cacophony of Irish brogues fused with Italian, Yiddish, Spanglish, and a dozen other odd tongues bellowed from the crowd as they gave voice to their cheers and insults on fight night. During the Depression much of America spoke as if they had just punched in at Ellis Island. With the fervor of a religion, cigar-chomping fight fans flocked to ring venues from the Garden to local fight clubs to watch "*their* boys" take a licking or give one.

In the 1930s, part of the romance of the ring was hearing the announcer introduce the fighters:

"In this corner, the challenger, an Irishman hailing from New York City..." A few Bronx cheers later: "In the opposite corner, defending his title, an Italian on both sides..."

And so it went.

Promoters were convinced an ethnic identity helped build a gate, especially in New York City. There were fighters billed as "the French Hammer," "the Black Wonder" (Bob Travis), "the Irish Champion" (Jack Langan), "the Wild Bull of the Pampas" (Luis Firpo of Argentina), and many others who could draw a crowd based on their ethnicity.

But what's a pug like Max Baer to do, an umpteenth-generation German-Scotch-Irish-American from Omaha, Nebraska? God knows his German side wouldn't be much help; just ask Max Schmeling, the German national who was portrayed as a Nazi, right up there with Hitler.

*When Baer entered the ring,
he clowned around,
entertaining the crowd with
comical antics.*

Baer's answer was to bill himself as a Jew, though his only connection to Judaism was his paternal grandfather who didn't pass on the religion or the ethnic heritage to his Nebraska-born ancestors. Nonetheless, Baer flagged his Jewishness as much as he could, wearing a Mogen David, the Jewish Star, emblazoned on his trunks. It must have worked. Baer, who harbored a playboy image, was not only a huge drawing card, he also fought his way to winning the heavyweight crown, knocking out Primo Carnera of Italy in 1934. The Italian was an incredible 6'6", 260 pounds. Baer could handle anybody!

James J. Braddock, who would soon after challenge Baer for the heavyweight championship, was thoroughly Irish. Born in 1906 in Hell's Kitchen, New York City's Irish ghetto, where the hardscrabble existence could corrupt even the holiest of choirboys, his parents moved their family of seven children to West New York, New Jersey, when James was an infant. Hailing from a notch or two below poverty, Braddock worked in a printer's shop and as a messenger before embarking on an amateur boxing career.

Eventually turning pro in 1928, Braddock fought Tuffy Griffith, an up-and-comer from Chicago who needed a few climb-the-ladder fights before challenging for the title. A substantial underdog, Braddock knocked

*Baer, at 210, had Braddock
outweighed by nearly 20 pounds.*

out Griffith in two rounds. The next year he defeated tough Jimmy Slattery of Buffalo and appeared to be on his way toward a successful run as a fighter.

Then his luck changed.

The losses mounted in such a rapid fashion that Braddock could not land a fight. In his short career, he had already broken his right hand, his ankle became temporarily nonfunctional, and his eyes had suffered severe cuts and scarring. By 1933 he decided to leave the ring to work as a longshoreman to feed his wife and their three children. Even that went badly. There was a depression going on and not much work on the docks. He eventually went on relief, getting $24 a month.

All the while he hungered for a return to the ring, but his reputation as a has-been was firmly established. Nonetheless, his former manager, Joe Gould, found Braddock a fight in June of 1934 when a fresh up-and-comer, Corn Griffin, needed a punching bag to work out the kinks. Griffin hammered Braddock in the first round, sending him to the canvas, only to have Braddock return the favor by knocking out Griffin in the third.

The win led Braddock toward a reversal of fortune from easy mark to challenger. After winning a 15-round decision over highly regarded Art Lasky in March of 1935, Braddock earned the New York Athletic Commission's ranking as the No. 1 contender, though there was some disagreement about how well deserved the ranking was. The commission thus ordered champion Max Baer to either defend his title against Braddock or be stripped of the right to fight in the state of New York.

On fight night, Braddock entered the ring as a 10–1 underdog. Standing 6'3", 191 pounds, the challenger looked lean and vulnerable next to Baer, who measured 6'2½", 210. Many viewed the fight as a joke. Baer had a record of 37-10 with 30 knockouts, while Braddock had fought 81 times, winning 49—26 by knockout. When Baer entered the ring, he clowned around, entertaining the crowd with comical antics.

Just to make sure no one thought the uneven match was a sham, the announcer introduced challenger Braddock as "a man who in the last year made the 'greatest comeback' in ring history." The obvious exaggeration may have been offered to assuage any feelings the fans harbored about whether this was a fight at all, instead of a formality so Baer wouldn't lose his crown for failure to comply with the commission's demand to defend it in timely fashion.

Braddock's plan was to keep going to his right to avoid Baer's long rights. He understood the firepower of his opponent and proceeded cautiously in the beginning, like an accountant kicking the tires of a used car before deciding to buy. In the first round Braddock landed a left to Baer's head and body, but neither fighter landed any significant blows.

In the third Baer landed a punch to Braddock's chin. "Then I was able to come back and smash him with a left in the next breath. I no longer had any doubt," Braddock said.

While taking Baer's best shot, Braddock came to the realization the champ would not be able to land his right. "After the seventh round I felt I was safe," Braddock said. "I just had to keep out of danger."

Aiding Braddock's cause was Baer's carelessness, specifically backhanded punches. He drew cautions for fouls in the fifth, ninth, and 12th rounds, which were recorded as lost rounds. The crowd smelled an upset and began to cheer every time Braddock scored.

Baer began to tire during the middle rounds as Braddock continued to pepper him with left hooks and jabs, racking up points with the judges. Nevertheless, Baer would come right back and pummel Braddock with power shots. But Baer just could not put away Braddock, which haunted the champion. When the combatants came out for the start of the 15th round, they shook hands, and a lethargic round began, ending shortly after Braddock landed a right to Baer's jaw, making Braddock's finish impressive in the eyes of the judges.

Both fighters ended the fight on their feet, leaving the outcome to the judges. When the tallying was done, there was no room for doubt—Braddock won a 9–6 decision, beating one of the best power punchers in the ring.

"I have no alibi to offer," Baer told the *New York Times*. "Jimmy won, and no better fellow deserves a

break. He didn't hurt me in the fight, but my trouble was that I couldn't hurt him."

In addition to making $25,500 for his win—a little over 1,000 times his $24-a-month relief check—

Braddock also made an honest man of the ring announcer by affirming—just as the announcer said before the fight—that he "made the greatest comeback in ring history."

Baer took advantage of a Jewish grandfather to play up his Judaism, to the point where he wore a Star of David on his trunks.

Chapter Thirty

One Ell of an Upset

Big 12 Football Championship, Kansas State Wildcats vs. Oklahoma Sooners
Kansas City, Missouri, December 6, 2003

The Oklahoma Sooners felt pretty good about themselves as they sauntered up to the line of scrimmage—and deservedly so. Here they were in the Big 12 championship game ranked No. 1 in the country, with a record of 12–0. They had steamrolled their opponents so badly, winning by an average of 35 points, that some pundits touted them as the greatest team in the history of college football.

At today's contest the stakes couldn't be any higher. If KSU won, it was off to the Fiesta Bowl. If Oklahoma was the victor, it would guarantee them a spot in the Sugar Bowl to play for the national championship.

Lining up on defense at Arrowhead Stadium in Kansas City were the Kansas State Wildcats—or Pussycats, in the eyes of Sooners fans. Sure, KSU boasted a fine record of 10-3 and were ranked 13th in the nation. But the 'Cats hadn't won a conference title since Franklin Roosevelt's first term (compared to seven national championships for Oklahoma since 1950). On this frigid Saturday in early December, Kansas State was a full two-touchdown underdog.

After a three-and-out for KSU to start the game, the Sooners now had the ball on their own 35. Superstar quarterback Jason White, the Heisman Trophy favorite, hit Lance Donley for 11 yards. On the next snap, Mark Clayton found daylight on the left side for 12 more yards. Then, on the very next play, Kejuan Jones blasted through a hole for a 42-yard touchdown romp. Just like that it was 7–0, and with Oklahoma boasting the nation's No. 1 defense, KSU appeared doomed.

Was a predictable blowout about to erupt? Anyone who thought so wasn't thinking about one man in the lineup—Kansas State quarterback Ell Roberson, who didn't like losing and had a way of getting what he wanted.

Since three straight Wildcats losses in September-October, Roberson had led his team to seven straight victories—despite, said KSU head coach Bill Snyder, "a list of ailments that would cover an entire football team." "I don't make a lot of major statements," Snyder added, "but Ell Roberson is the toughest quarterback playing the game, maybe the toughest football player."

The score remained 7–0 entering the second quarter, but then Roberson and the Wildcats broke loose. Tailback Darren Sproles (a 5'7" All America) spun out of cornerback Derrick Strait's arms and rocketed 55 yards downfield. Three plays later, Roberson connected with tight end Brian Casey for a 19-yard touchdown.

After a three-and-out by Oklahoma, Roberson stuck it to the Sooners again. On the first snap of the

Korey Klein (93), Byron Garvin and the rest of the Wildcat defense were too much for Kejuan Jones and top-ranked Oklahoma.

More than anyone else, Darren Sproles repre-sented the underdog spirit of the KSU football team. As a senior at Olathe North High School in

Kansas State's diminutive Darren Sproles came up huge against the Sooners, carrying 22 times for 235 yards and adding 88 yards on three receptions.

Kansas, Sproles had rushed for 2,845 yards and scored 49 touchdowns. Yet all the major football programs in the region, including Oklahoma, weren't interested in him. The reason: He stood only 5'7"—on his tiptoes.

Sproles decided to sign with Kansas State, the only school that gave him a firm offer from the beginning. Besides his small frame, Darren had other concerns; he was shy and quiet, the result of a slight speech impediment. Moreover, for much of his career at K-State, he worried about his ill mother, who would die of cancer in 2004.

Yet Sproles overcame all of these obstacles. Despite his short stature, he earned the nickname "Tank" for his incredible strength. He could bench-press more than 400 pounds and safe-squat more than 800. Also blessed with 4.4 speed in the 40-yard dash, Sproles developed into an explosive rusher. As a junior in 2003, he ran for 1,986 yards—tops in the nation.

Sproles saved his greatest performance for the Big 12 title game. While Oklahoma's Jason White, the Heisman Trophy favorite, was expected to shine, Sproles stole the show. His 235 rushing yards were the most ever against Oklahoma. "I'm excited about Darren Sproles," KSU coach Bill Snyder said afterward. "You want to vote for a Heisman? There's your Heisman."

While White wound up winning the Heisman, Sproles finished an impressive fifth in the voting— the best showing ever for a Kansas State player.

drive, he connected with James Terry on a perfect hitch-and-go for a 63-yard touchdown play. For only the second time all year, Oklahoma found itself behind. Eight minutes later, Roberson flipped a screen pass to Sproles, who sprinted 60 yards for another touchdown.

'Cats fans went wild, spurred on by the pumped-up K-State band.

By halftime, the Sooners were dazed and confused. After never trailing for more than six minutes all year, they now found themselves down 21–7. Commentators opined that the Sooners looked flat and uninspired.

Undoubtedly, OU players underestimated the skill and determination of the K-State Wildcats. Since taking over in 1989, coach Snyder had transformed the program from a national laughingstock to one of the

Ell Roberson's four-touchdown performance earned Kansas State a Big 12 championship trophy.

finest in the country. In the first half and into the second, KSU shut down Oklahoma's running game. Moreover, with defensive end Thomas Houchin leading the way, the defense hammered White repeatedly.

Oklahoma fans expected a second-half comeback—and Sooner rather than later. But after OU missed a field goal on its first possession of the third quarter, Roberson went for the jugular. He drove K-State 89 yards, capping the drive with a 10-yard touchdown strike to Antoine Polite. The rout was on.

Down 28–7 early in the fourth quarter, White desperately tried to dig out of his own territory. But when he passed over the middle, linebacker Ted Sims picked him off and raced 27 yards for a touchdown. In its last two possessions, Oklahoma turned it over on downs and then, as if to raise a white flag, punted away. After a 63-yard run by Sproles, Kansas State ran out the clock, clinching a 35–7 blowout.

For the first time ever, Kansas State defeated a top-three team—let alone a No. 1–ranked juggernaut. Incredibly, KSU beat the point spread by a whopping 42 points. The Wildcats amassed 519 yards against the most esteemed defense in the nation. The diminutive Sproles ran wild, rushing for 235 yards on just 22 carries—and catching three passes for 88 yards. While the vaunted White threw zero TD passes and was picked off twice, Roberson went 10-for-17 for 227 yards, four touchdowns, and no interceptions.

After the game, as the K-State band belted out "Wildcat Victory," some fans made mental preparations for a New Year's Day vacation: Kansas State was going to the Fiesta Bowl, the school's first trip ever to a Bowl championship series game.

Oklahoma coach Bob Stoops, humbled and awed by KSU's performance, stood outside the OU locker room congratulating K-State coaches and players as they walked past. Roberson, meanwhile, was the last player off the field. The senior quarterback, battered and abused in his three years as a starter, savored every last drop of this extraordinary victory. It was, experts would deem, one of the most monumental upsets in college football history.

Chapter Thirty-one

Where in the World Is Senegal?

*World Cup Soccer Final, Senegal vs. France
Seoul, South Korea, May 31, 2002*

There was no bloodshed. No guns fired. But a revolution occurred south of the infamous DMZ that divides the two Koreas. And when it was over, the only casualty was the French soccer team, whose seven-game winning streak was broken.

In 1960, the impoverished West African country of Senegal had peacefully gained independence from France. Forty-two years later, in the opening game of the 2002 World Cup finals, the Senegalese team, nicknamed the "Lions of Teranga," dealt colonialism another blow: they defeated France, the reigning World Cup champions, 1–0.

It was a stunner that had many veteran soccer observers reaching all the way back to 1950, when the United States defeated Great Britain in a World Cup qualifying game, to find a surprise victory of comparable magnitude. If you had asked any of the commentators or spectators before the game about Senegal's chances for beating the tournament favorite, everyone would have scoffed or rolled their eyes—except for Senegal's president, Abdoulaye Wade. With a conviction that struck many as borderline delusional, Wade had gone on the radio earlier that day to predict victory for the Lions of Teranga.

The Senegalese are renowned for being exceptionally gracious. In their Wolof language, *teranga* means "hospitality." Yet there was nothing remotely hospitable about the aggressive play of Senegal's team

Senegal's Moussa Ndiaye (right) dribbled past France's Bixente Lizarazu during his team's 1-0 upset in the 2002 World Cup in Seoul, South Korea.

that Friday evening in Seoul's World Cup Stadium. But civility had no place on the field against France's formidable "Les Bleus," whose team roster included such stars as Thierry Henry, David Trezeguet, and Lilian Thuram, arguably the best defensive player in soccer. Although France's superstar Zinedine Zidane was sidelined by a thigh injury, the defending World Cup champions were still the hands-down favorites of the 32 teams competing in Seoul.

France's reputation was certainly not lost on the Senegalese players. How could it be, when almost all of them now lived in France, where they played for French soccer clubs? For Senegal had paid a steep price for independence from their colonial occupiers—this country of nearly nine million people on Africa's Atlantic coast was mired in grinding poverty. Playing soccer in France had given Senegalese athletes the chance to make more money in a season than their parents could in a lifetime. But when the opportunity to play for Senegal in the 2002 World Cup had arisen, they had eagerly returned home to practice under Bruno Metsu, a top-notch coach—a top-notch *French* coach.

The night of the Final match, as 65,000 spectators crowded into the stadium, the Lions of Teranga reviewed Metsu's strategies one last time. Since the French players were known for their extraordinary resilience, the Senegalese team's aim was twofold: exhaust them and overpower them. Luckily for Senegal, French powerhouse Zidane, the two-time world Player of the Year, wouldn't be on

Amara Traore gave Senegal's flag a World Cup victory lap no one saw coming.

Pape Bouba Diop traded his jersey for a French one after helping Senegal to an upset win against the defending World Cup champions.

the field that night. And while his replacement Youri Djorkaeff was no slouch, he lacked Zidane's intimidating brilliance.

To no one's surprise, the French came on strong, but something besides Zidane appeared to be missing from their game—namely focus. Perhaps they were too flummoxed by the Senegalese team's unexpected ferocity. Around the 20-minute mark, France's Trezeguet managed to take a shot at the goal, only to see the ball bounce off the goalpost.

Just ten minutes later, it was Senegal's turn, thanks in part to Djorkaeff. Zidane's stand-in didn't just give up the ball to Senegal's Salif Diao at midfield; he practically sent it to Diao with a pretty bow on top. Diao passed the ball to teammate Khalilou Fadiga, who nimbly evaded a tackle attempt by France's Frank Leboeuf to close in on France's goal.

At the same time, Senegalese midfielder Pape Bouba Diop was racing up the field to meet Fadiga.

What happened next was astounding.

As Fadiga attempted to pass the ball to Diop, it collided with the foot of French captain Marcel Desailly. Glancing off Desailly's foot, the ball landed before Emmanuel Petit, who then tried to pass it back to midfield. Unfortunately, Petit's clearance attempt fell short—fatally short—as the ball instead ricocheted off the hands of French goalie Fabien Barthez to the ground where Diop had fallen, well within scoring range. Literally sitting on the field, Diop kicked the ball past Barthez for the goal. Senegal took the lead 1–0.

Although they were deliriously happy, the Senegalese knew it was still way too early in the game to drape themselves in their homeland's red, green, and yellow flag and parade around the field in triumph. The French would never live it down if they actually *lost* the opening game of the 2002 World Cup—to their former colony, of all opponents! The colossal embarrassment would be too much to bear for Les Bleus, who would undoubtedly come back with renewed vigor. But the French team failed to score a single goal off the Senegalese, and the Lions of Teranga roared their way to an unanticipated 1–0 victory that is regarded as one of the greatest upsets in soccer history.

Chapter Thirty-two

Spud Webb: No Small Feat!

NBA Slam Dunk Championship, Dallas, Texas, February 8, 1986

S pud Webb's agent must be a hell of a good salesman. And his client wasn't too bad at what he did either—playing hoops. But all that being said, it was no slam dunk to sell *this* bill of goods to the NBA.

With Michael Jordan injured, the NBA needed a replacement for the 1986 Slam Dunk Contest. At the persistent urging of Spud Webb's agent, Bill Blakeley, the league accepted the Atlanta Hawks rookie as MJ's fill-in. Though only 5'7"—in sneakers with a thick pair of socks—Webb could actually dunk a basketball.

Prior to the big event, Webb's teammates teased him about the dunks he should perform. Spud was only half-amused. "I remember thinking to myself, 'These guys are making a big joke out of this, but it isn't a joke,'" Webb wrote in his autobiography, *Flying High.* "I can do things they don't know about. None of these guys know what I can do."

All his life, Webb had been overlooked, disrespected, and laughed at because he was so short. And he *was* short. When he was 12, Webb

Webb (left), *standing beside teammate Moses Malone, was the shortest man in the NBA when he won the Star Slam Dunk contest.*

Opposite: *Webb of the Atlanta Hawks goes up for a reverse slam dunk during the NBA All-Star Slam Dunk contest at Reunion Arena in Dallas.*

Webb mixed well with the big boys, but this shot was blocked by Bill Laimbeer and Isiah Thomas of the Detroit Pistons.

and his buddy played one-on-one basketball *inside* the garage.

Yet from an early age, Webb learned to overcome adversity. As a young child in Dallas in the 1960s, Anthony Webb was slapped with the nickname "Sputnik" by a family friend, who thought his head resembled the famous Soviet satellite. Webb's young siblings shortened the name to the equally inelegant "Spud."

All six Webb children learned to overcome odds from their parents. Their father, David Webb, was a for-

mer Negro Leagues baseball player who worked two jobs to support his family. Mom Katie Webb had been her high school's valedictorian. Several of their children excelled in sports, but Spud stood out as extra special.

In boxing and football, Spud hit harder than those who towered over him. Told initially to sit in the stands by his junior high basketball coach, Webb scored 20 points in the first game he was allowed to play. At Wilmer–Hutchins High School, the varsity head coach initially didn't pick Webb for his team because fellow coaches had warned that he'd be a "fool" to play a "midget." Webb shut them up by making all-state his senior season.

Passed over by Division I schools, Webb attended Midland Junior College and led the team to the 1982 JuCo national title. Moving on to North Carolina State, Webb sparked the Wolfpack to the Sweet 16 in the 1985 NCAA tournament. The Detroit Pistons selected him in the fourth round in that year's NBA draft, but they cut him from the team. Spud finally landed with the Atlanta Hawks, for whom he was a key contributor off the bench in 1985–86.

In a league dominated by giants, Webb—at 5'7", over a foot shorter than the average NBA player—sparked America's curiosity. The day before the dunk contest, Webb appeared on *The Tonight Show with Johnny Carson*. That same night, he jetted to his home-town of Dallas for the big event.

Teammates Rollins and Cliff Levingston showed up for moral support, as did Wilkins—the reigning Slam Dunk Contest champion and the man to beat in this event. Just prior to the contest, at the suggestion of Hawks PR director Bill Needle, Webb stood under the net, showing the judges just how high he'd have to soar to slam.

In front of 17,000 people, including the Webb family, and millions of television viewers, Spud felt exceptionally nervous. Yet, with a 42-inch vertical leap and more dunking flair than his teammates had ever witnessed, Webb was ready to rumble. For his first dunk, he threw down a double-pump reverse jam. The five judges gave him a 46 out of 50, the best score among the eight participants in the first round.

Spud followed with a 360-degree flush and a double-pump straight-ahead jam, giving him a first-round total of 141—again, tops among all contestants. He advanced to round two along with Wilkins, the New York Knicks' Gerald Wilkins (Dominique's little brother), and the Indiana Pacers' Terence Stansbury.

As a teenager, while practicing jams for hours in neighborhood rec centers, Webb had fantasized about unleashing a spectacularly perfect dunk for all the world

to see. Leading off round two, he went for the gold. Webb tossed the ball ahead on a high arc. It bounced up toward the bucket. He caught it, twirled around, and converted a reverse slam behind his head. Rollins and Levingston were dumbfounded, and all five judges held up their "10" cards. A perfect 50.

Dominique Wilkins kept the crowd in a frenzy with a "nuclear roundhouse tomahawk" jam. He and Webb—Mutt and Jeff—advanced to the final round, where each would display two dunks apiece.

Because his life was turning around that afternoon, Webb wrote, he chose a 360-degree one-handed jam for his first finals attempt. The shot was significant because Spud's hand was too small to palm the ball. He threw it down anyway, prompting hysterical fans to wave their own "10" cards. The judges gave Spud another perfect 50.

Wilkins matched Webb's perfect score with a spectacular 360 windmill slam, meaning it all came down to the final dunk. The crowd hushed in anticipation of Webb's historic attempt. Surging with confidence, he chose another difficult timing dunk. He lobbed the ball off the backboard, rocketed off the floor, caught it with one hand, and rammed it home. Webb burst into a smile as the crowd went wild. He earned yet another score of 50.

Needing perfection to tie, Wilkins uncorked a double-pump, two-handed jackknife. *It was classy!* But it had to be the best, a perfect 10, otherwise Webb would win. The judges flashed their cards: 10, 10, 10, 9, and 9. *Not good enough!* Spud Webb had won. The little man was the NBA's new slam dunk champion. The crowd went bonkers! The press stormed the court! The bench rushed him and hoisted him to the rim. There was an ovation the likes of which MJ, Babe Ruth, and Muhammad Ali never heard.

Everyone was astonished, except the little man himself. After all, he'd been dunking the ball since age 17, though it took over 100 tries before he finally dunked the first one. And, oh yeah, he was only 5'4" then. Now that he's a little taller, it's easier for him...practically a slam dunk.

Chapter Thirty-three

Willis Reed:
The Heart of New York

Game 7, NBA Final, New York Knicks vs. Los Angeles Lakers
New York City, May 8, 1970

All Willis Reed could do was watch. In Game 6 of the 1970 NBA Finals, Los Angeles Lakers center Wilt Chamberlain was stuffing the stat sheet and flushing the New York Knicks' dreams down the toilet. Reed sat on the bench wearing a suit and a solemn expression, with his damaged right leg fully extended.

Earlier in the series, Reed had neutralized "Wilt the Stilt" with explosive low-post scoring, yeoman rebounding, and ferocious defense. But Reed suffered a thigh injury in Game 5 and had to skip Game 6, which L.A. needed to win to avoid elimination. Willis watched the mighty Chamberlain, the NBA's most dominating player ever, amass 45 points in a 135–113 Lakers rout. Afterward, Reed realized the dilemma that lay before him: He could barely walk, yet the Knicks desperately needed him for Game 7 in New York. What was he to do?

As a boy, life was difficult but simpler for Willis Reed. He grew up on a farm in Bernice, Louisiana, where he dreamed of football glory. But as a teenager, he became too big for even football, and reluctantly traded in his shoulder pads for short pants. On the hardwood, Reed combined his great size with a football

Chamberlain, defending, called Reed (19)
his greatest NBA playoff opponent.

player's ferocity to become a dominating force. He then starred at Grambling State, where he averaged 26.6 points and 21.3 rebounds during his senior year.

In 1964 the Knicks wasted their first pick on Jim "Bad News" Barnes, then took Reed in the second round. Willis first impressed New York GM Eddie Donovan in training camp when he asked for a copy of the NBA rulebook. From then on, he proved to be a working-class hero and an eventual team captain. Reed battled relentlessly in the paint and frustrated opposing centers with his buttery left-handed jumpers. He was named NBA Rookie of the Year in 1965 and made the All-Star Game his first seven seasons.

In 1969–70, the native Louisianan averaged 21.7 points and 13.9 rebounds per game, earning MVP honors for the season and the All-Star Game. The Knicks, who went 60-22 that season, brimmed with talent. Guard Walt Frazier averaged 20.9 points and 8.2 assists per game. Dave DeBusschere pounded the boards, while future U.S. senator "Dollar" Bill Bradley was the ultimate team player. All four of them were stars destined for the Basketball Hall of Fame.

In the 1970 playoffs, New York dodged the Baltimore Bullets in seven games, then breezed past the Milwaukee Bucks in five. The NBA Finals, however, would be a monumental challenge. The Los Angeles Lakers boasted three of the greatest players who ever

New York's Dave DeBusschere was surrounded by the Lakers' Wilt Chamberlain, Jerry West, and Elgin Baylor.

played the game: Chamberlain, shooting guard Jerry West, and a small man, forward Elgin Baylor, who averaged 13 NBA All-Star Game appearances apiece.

In the marquee matchup of the Finals, Reed was able to contain Chamberlain, walling him off on defense. Moreover, Reed netted 37, 29, 38, and 23 points over the first four games while pulling down an average of 15 rebounds. The Lakers and Knicks split the first four games, but New York would play Games 5 and 7 at home.

In the first quarter of Game 5, however, disaster struck for New York. Reed, while turning to drive the lane, strained two muscles in his right thigh and fell to the floor like a toppled giant. "Oh, my God!" cried DeBusschere. With Willis out for the game, the Knicks somehow managed to eke out a 107–100 victory. Reed flew to Los Angeles for the next game, but it was

Willis Reed made only two baskets in Game 7, but they were enough to put his Knicks teammates on the road to a championship.

painfully obvious he couldn't play. After the Lakers' cakewalk in Game 6, Chamberlain credited his 45-point eruption to the absence of Reed, whom Wilt called his greatest opponent ever in playoff competition.

Reed flew back that night to New York, where he worked to rehabilitate his leg the next morning, Thursday. By 6:00 P.M. on Friday, 1 hour and 35 minutes before tipoff of Game 7, tensions peaked in America's two largest cities. Thousands of L.A. businesses closed early so fans could get home to watch the game. New Yorkers, who had witnessed the Mets win the World Series seven months earlier, were praying for another miracle.

At 6:03, with Madison Square Garden mostly empty, Reed walked slowly and determinedly onto the court for warmups. He practiced a few moves and shots, while Chamberlain—perhaps playing psychological games—commented about how great Willis looked. After returning to the locker room, Reed informed his teammates that he would indeed play. Knick teammate Cazzie Russell was ecstatic. "It's like getting your left arm sewed back on," he said.

Fans, meanwhile, still didn't know if their big man would play. At 7:30, five minutes before tipoff, all the players were on the court except Reed. Little did fans know that his doctor was waiting for the last possible instant to inject his thigh with cortisone and carbocaine.

Finally, at 7:34 Reed emerged from the entrance-way. Spectators from the opposite side of the court, seeing him first, stood en masse and cheered. Like a wave, fans all throughout the Garden rose to their feet, showering their hero with deafening applause. The feeling was electric, and the Knicks players—Reed included—experienced a jolt of energy.

On New York's first play, the ball went to Reed, who buried a 16-foot jumper. A minute later, he drained another shot from 17 feet. The place went nuts. Willis wouldn't score another point, but he contributed tremendously. The first 17 times Chamberlain received the ball in the post, Reed held him to just two baskets. Meanwhile, Reed's presence inspired the Knicks to play their best ball of the year, with Frazier scoring 23 points in the first half alone. When Reed left the game for good with 3:05 left in the first half, New York led 61–37.

The Knicks breezed to a 113–99 victory, clinching the city's first-ever NBA championship. Reed, after receiving a big thank-you hug from DeBusschere, accepted the award as NBA Finals MVP—making him the first to receive the NBA's MVP trifecta. ABC's Howard Cosell, in a postgame interview with Reed, summed up the feeling of the day: "You have offered, I think, the best that the human spirit can offer."

Chapter Thirty-four

Ed Furgol's Real "Handicap"

U.S. Open Golf, Baltusrol Golf Club
Springfield, New Jersey, June 17–19, 1954

E d Furgol addressed the ball on the tee at the 72nd hole. Neither he nor the gallery of onlookers could believe where he was—on the last hole of the U.S. Open and on the cusp of winning it. It wasn't the usual place to find a disabled man. But right now there was a much more important issue than his physical disability—namely, parring this hole and getting the win. If he could do it, he would be the most unlikely champion of the storied tournament's history.

But there was that fairway; he'd have to hit it solid in the middle. And it was at Baltusrol, on the 18th, a deadly combination of a historically dreaded course…and one of its touchiest fairways, one you had to hit *just* right.

Pressure can do funny things to a golfer's head. Get too tight and you might push or pull the ball into trouble. Intellectually Furgol knew what to do—relax, pull the club back, and send the clubface through the ball in a smooth fashion. But he was at the base of the mountain now and pressure was changing the appearance of the fairway. The lushy grass was a fire-breathing dragon and the beast was mad as hell now, blowing back flames toward the teebox. Furgol felt the heat. All he could do was concentrate as best as he could. A mighty backswing now and he let go. The ball flew off the tee. A vicious hook flew right into the trees that separate Baltusrol's Lower and Upper Courses.

Cary Middlecoff (left) was among the greats who were unable to catch Furgol in the final round.

How could the golf gods be so cruel. He'd come so far and endured so much. Now this.

Some would say that being able to even play golf was achievement enough for the unknown competitor. Growing up in New York Mills, New York, Furgol was one of five children. At age eight, his brother, Hank, introduced him to golf and he fell in love with everything about the sport from the way his hands fit the club to the fluid motion required to strike the ball in proper fashion. And there was the beauty and solitude of the course. Fate would test just how much this boy wanted to be out on the golf course.

The same year Furgol caught the golf bug, he experienced another life-changing event. While on the playground, he watched another youngster going through his paces on the monkey bars and elected to

A packed gallery at Baltusrol, including hundreds on the clubhouse terrace, watched Ed Furgol par the 18th hole to win the U.S. Open.

follow suit. Only he didn't successfully travel the horizontal ladder and fell to the ground, fracturing his left elbow. When the cast was removed five weeks later the idea of playing golf was a pipe dream.

The arm had not been set well, causing the biceps to atrophy. Subsequent operations to repair the damage never took, leaving him with restricted use of his left arm. Imagine being a right-handed golfer with a

withered left arm. Most would not even try to play again. Furgol proved to be the exception. Rather than give up the idea of playing the game he loved, he

wasn't pretty, but it worked for him."

Furgol joined the professional ranks in 1945, but quit in 1952 to take a job at Westwood Country Club in Clayton, Missouri, where he met Helen, who worked in the pro shop. He taught golf and practiced after hours when time allowed. If an opportunity presented itself, he would play in a professional event.

"He liked the stability," said Helen, whom Ed referred to as his "left arm." "Working at a country

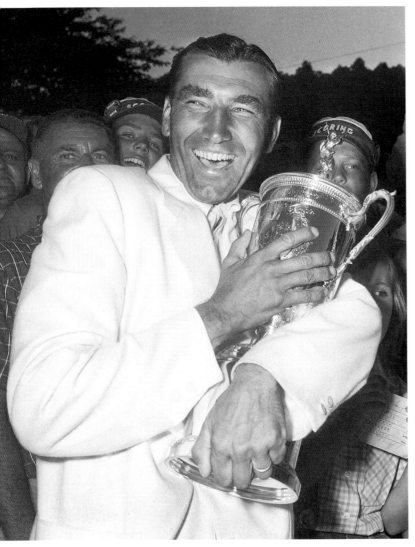

*Though he had restricted use of his left arm,
Furgol had no trouble cradling the trophy
he'd worked so hard to attain.*

𝕊𝕠

*While Furgol lacked the résumé
of most on the PGA Tour,
he didn't lack the confidence.*

𝕊𝕠

club isn't as glamorous, but you always get a paycheck."

While Furgol lacked the résumé of most on the PGA Tour, he didn't lack the confidence. Prior to the 1954 U.S. Open he felt confident enough to tell a wire service reporter he would win. The reporter laughed. Like everyone else, the reporter believed this would be the year when 41-year-old Masters champion Sam Snead finally would capture his first U.S. Open.

After three rounds Furgol held a one-shot lead. In the rearview mirror were the likes of Snead, Cary Middlecoff, Gene Littler, Lloyd Mangrum, Tommy Bolt, and Ben Hogan.

Furgol wasn't long off the tee, but his unorthodox swing produced accurate drives that had an uncanny knack for finding Baltusrol's tight fairways. His precision played a large part in the one-shot lead he carried to the final hole. But his accuracy left him on the teebox at the worst possible time. His hooked tee shot settled in a position making it impossible to

continued to practice, developing other parts of his body such as his hands, wrists, fingers, and shoulders. Hatched through his persistence was a unique swing that worked despite having a left arm six inches shorter than his right. He compensated for his shortcoming through an emphasis on shoulder and hip rotation.

"He had to develop his own style of golf," said Helen Furgol of her late husband's swing. "It

advance the ball to the Lower Course's 18th fairway.

Looking at the trees blocking his route back to the fairway, Furgol didn't lose his cool. The situation called for creativity and imagination, necessary tools for any golfer to win a U.S. Open. How could he best escape the trees so he could have a chance at the green with his third shot? After intense deliberation it came to him. Why not try the adjacent Upper Course? Since it wasn't out of bounds, he elected to play to the Upper Course's 18th fairway. Improvising with a long iron, he successfully curled his second shot through an opening to the desired target. He hit a 7-iron to the fringe of the 18th green, then kept his wits even though his chip left him with a nasty downhill putt to save par. Again he came through to post a total of 284.

Furgol had escaped the woods—but he wasn't out of the woods just yet. If Littler made birdie he would tie for the lead. U.S. Opens are settled with an 18-hole playoff rather than a sudden-death format. When Littler reached the green in three shots, leaving him a four-foot birdie putt, an extra day of golf looked inevitable.

However, with thousands of spectators watching in silent anticipation, Littler failed to sink what should have been an easy putt. The gallery, aware that the U.S. Open had just been won by golf's ultimate underdog, applauded enthusiastically. So in Furgol's rearview mirror at the end of the day stood not only Littler, who finished second, but also golf immortals such as Ben Hogan and Sam Snead.

The man described by some as "the handicapped golfer" had not only won his first prestigious tournament—he had done it in style. Of his $6,000 winner's check, Furgol immediately gave $1,000 to his caddie. He had successfully overcome all obstacles, both lifelong and those encountered on the 18th hole that day at Baltusrol, to become one of the greatest underdog triumphs in the history of professional golf.

BALTUSROL, A FAMILIAR U.S. OPEN SITE

Baltusrol Golf Club played host to the 1954 U.S. Open when Ed Furgol came from nowhere to win the coveted title. Furgol's victory is only a part of the lore for the historic course located in Springfield, New Jersey, which has played a major role in shaping the history of the U.S. Open.

In addition to the 1954 Open, Baltusrol has hosted the event six other times.

In 1903 Baltusrol kicked off its incredible run of hosting the national championship with Willie Anderson capturing the title at what was the ninth Open ever held. Compared to today's standards, the outcome of that one was comical. Anderson had a playoff with David Brown, shooting an 82 to Brown's 84 to capture the title. He went on to win the Open in 1904 and 1905.

Jerome Travers became the second amateur to win the Open—one of only five amateurs ever to win the title so far—when he captured the event at Baltusrol during the 1915 Open. However, Travers was no surprise given the fact he'd already won four U.S. Amateurs.

Tony Manero won in 1936 followed by Furgol in 1954.

Jack Nicklaus, "The Golden Bear," captured two of his record 18 PGA Tour major titles at Baltusrol, winning by four shots over Arnold Palmer in 1967 and in 1980 by two shots over Isao Aoki.

Finally, in 1993 Lee Janzen warded off Payne Stewart's challenge to win his first-ever major. Janzen shot four consecutive rounds in the 60s for a 272 total that tied Nicklaus's record for the lowest score in U.S. Open history.

Chapter Thirty-five

Kerri Strug: Past the Pain

*Summer Olympics, U.S. Women's Gymnastics Team Final
Atlanta, Georgia, July 23, 1996*

What looked like the figure of a little girl stood at the end of the runway. She appeared frail, helpless, and scared to death. A fierce, immobilizing pain throbbed in her left ankle. Virtually everyone in Atlanta's Olympic Stadium could tell that the pint-sized gymnast, Kerri Strug, was in agony. Yet there on the sidelines was her coach, the famously autocratic Romanian émigré Bela Karolyi, urging her to perform a *second* vault at the risk of further damage to her ankle.

Would she really be crazy enough to do it?

Strug wasn't crazy. There wasn't a reckless or masochistic bone in her body. But at tonight's event she was sure she could live with the pain much better than she could stomach being the one who made America lose to the Russians. Pain didn't matter to the Tucson native now; but Team USA's standing did and it was just a hair behind Russia. Strug was the only one who could change that now.

When she was just three years old, Strug had toddled onto the mat after watching her older sister, Lisa, compete in gymnastics. Although the intensive, daily training schedule made free time a luxury, she still had a life away from the gym. She watched her favorite TV show, *Beverly Hills 90210,* and followed the career of basketball great Michael Jordan. But unlike many of her peers, the 4'8", 88-pound gymnast nicknamed "Care Bear" had a thing about the Olympics—she wanted to compete in them someday...and win a gold medal.

At age 14, Strug had been the youngest American at the 1992 Olympics; she had finished 14th overall. Precociously confident, she had declared on national television that she was actually a better gymnast than her more experienced teammate, Kim Zmeskal.

Her best events were the uneven bars and floor exercises, so Strug had worked even

---

Kerri Strug's pain was obvious when she landed on her injured left leg, but her vault earned a 9.712 score, enough for Team USA to win the gold.

harder on the other events, executing as many as 50 vaults in a single practice session to improve her technique. She had been no stranger to pain either; in 1993, a torn abdominal muscle had kept her from competing for eight months.

All of this was just the proverbial warmup act for the 1996 Summer Olympics, where Strug would take center stage in one of the most dramatic competitions for the team medal in recent history.

That Tuesday evening in Atlanta found the U.S. women's team on track for the team gold medal—a historic pursuit, given the Russians' dominance of the sport. The Soviet Union had won every Olympic gold medal since 1952, except for the boycotted 1984 Games, when Romania had won the gold. Team USA had entered the final night of competition in second place behind the Russians, but took the lead after flawless performances on the uneven bars and balance beam.

A USA gold medal looked to be a lock—until the vault competition, when Strug's teammate Dominique Moceanu fell on her first attempt. Fighting off the Russians had appeared to be a forgone conclusion up to that point, but Moceanu's fall clearly marked a shift in momentum.

The shift became more pronounced after Moceanu's second vault—her final attempt—showed the dire effects of her previous fall. The resulting vault, laced with an ample dose of caution, seemed to take the life out of the Americans. In short, the U.S. team's hopes for a gold medal rested squarely on Strug's narrow shoulders.

At 18, Strug was older than most competing in a sport riddled with prepubescent little girls. If there was ever a perfect anchor, the poised veteran looked to be the one.

However, Moceanu's insecurity seemed to be contagious. Strug followed with her first vault and repeated her teammate's mistake by falling and rolling her left ankle when she landed. A sharp pain ripped

Coach Bela Karolyi gave the injured Strug a lift to the gold medal platform.

through it. When she stood and tried to walk, it was evident to both the spectators and television viewers that the veteran was in agony.

"I was going, 'My leg, my leg,'" Strug told reporters afterward. "Everyone was yelling, 'Come on, we need you.' But I was

telling them there was something wrong with me."

Experiencing great pain in her left ankle, Strug talked with Coach Bela Karolyi. Could she continue? Only she could answer this question.

"I felt like I had to do it," Strug said. "If I didn't, I didn't think we were going to win the gold. We were getting closer and closer to the Russians. I said to myself, 'The gold is slipping away. If I don't make this vault, everything we've all worked for falls apart.' So I said a little prayer. I said, 'I've done this vault a thousand times; let me do it one more time.' And I let the adrenaline take over."

Strug needed a score of at least 9.6 to insure gold for her team.

In the Olympic Stadium and millions of living rooms around the world, everyone watching cringed in dread. Since she could barely put any weight on her injured ankle, how could Strug possibly execute this

KAROLYI: THE MAN BEHIND THE CHAMPIONS

Kerri Strug's courage and gymnastic talents personified those of the gymnasts coached by one man, her coach, Bela Karolyi. Among his most accomplished gymnasts are Nadia Comaneci, Julianne McNamara, Phoebe Mills, Betty Okino, Dominique Moceanu, Mary Lou Retton, Kim Zmeskal, and Strug.

Karolyi first gained worldwide fame in 1976 as the coach of Comaneci, who scored the first perfect 10 in Olympic gymnastics, then repeated the feat six times. Karolyi and his wife defected to the United States in 1981 during an exhibition tour by the Romanian team he had coached with great success in the 1976 and 1980 Olympics. After working menial jobs to make a living, a group of Houston businessmen approached him about coaching at a private gym. Eventually Karolyi bought the gym and built it into an elite facility for the budding American gymnastics movement. He parlayed that success into the U.S. head coach position for Olympic and international competitions.

Training under Karolyi, Retton became the first American to win an all-around Olympic gold in 1984. Zmeskal became the first American to win the world championship, in 1991. And of the six national champions between 1987 and 1992, only one trained with someone other than Karolyi.

Talk about success. Karolyi's coaching efforts produced 28 Olympians, nine Olympic Champions, 15 World Champions, 12 European medalists, and six U.S. National Champions.

"My biggest contribution was giving the kids the faith that they can be the best among the best," Karolyi told the Associated Press. "I knew that if the Americans could understand they were not inferior...then they can be groomed like international, highly visible athletes."

---

vault well enough to secure the gold?

"I kept looking at the coaches," Strug said. "I couldn't walk or anything. They were saying, 'C'mon, you can do it, shake it off.' I'm like, 'You don't understand. There's really something wrong with me.'"

Strug took a deep breath and then began her sprint down the runway. She hit the springboard and was catapulted into her vault. She flew skyward, twisted, then turned with the precision of a Swiss clock and the grace of gazelle and landed on the mat—hard! On impact she heard a crunching sound from her same ankle. She raised her arms and intense pain shot through her ankle—a

(From left) Dominique Moceanu, Kerri Strug and Shannon Miller earned the right to hear the Star Spangled Banner as gold medalists in Atlanta.

pain even more excruciating than before when she had first injured it. As she raised her foot in pain, the crowd of 32,048 cheered their collective approval. The vault looked good enough to get the win for Team USA.

Then came the score: 9.712. The Americans had won the gold.

Approximately fifteen minutes afterward, Karolyi carried her to the awards stand to collect the gold medal. As X-rays later revealed, she had sustained a severe, third-degree lateral sprain that included two torn ligaments. Yet in defiance of all reason, she had tuned out the pain.

And for her courage, Team USA was dubbed "The Magnificent Seven," but no one on the squad was more magnificent than Kerri Strug the day she beat the pain...and the *former* world's best gymnastics team, the Russians.

Chapter Thirty-six

Jim Abbott:
On the One Hand…

New York Yankees vs. Cleveland Indians
Yankee Stadium, Bronx, New York, September 4, 1993

On a dreary Saturday in September 1993, Jim Abbott stood atop the hill at Yankee Stadium. Kenny Lofton of Cleveland, the first batter of the game, waited on the lefty's 3-1 pitch. Abbott wound, kicked, and fired…*ball four!* The collective sigh of almost 30,000 fans made their sentiment clear—this had the makings of another awful day.

In his first season working for George Steinbrenner, baseball's most unforgiving owner, Abbott couldn't find a consistent rhythm. Now, on this soggy, overcast afternoon on September 4—with the Yankees desperately chasing Toronto for the division lead—his record stood at 9-11. Moreover, Abbott had struggled in his previous start, "and 'struggled' is putting it nicely," he said. In fact, he had been pounded so badly, allowing seven runs at Cleveland, that he bolted out of Municipal Stadium and punished himself with a three-mile run.

For this game, bullpen coach Mark Connor urged Abbott to alter his approach against the hard-hitting Indians, who featured six regulars with batting averages of .298 or higher. "The real adjustment was mostly trusting my pitches a little more and getting ahead in the count," Abbott said. After the leadoff walk, the bold approach seemed to work. Abbott erased Lofton on a double-play ball and then allowed just a harmless walk in the second inning. In a groove, he pitched 1–2–3 frames in the third and fourth. His day was brightening with every pitch.

For most of his life, Jim Abbott had tried to live a routine existence but of course there was something different about him. His well-publicized handicap—he was born without a right hand—had only inspired him to work harder to achieve his dreams. As a child in Flint, Michigan, he scoffed at his parents' suggestion to play soccer and refused to wear a prosthesis. He wanted to play baseball and football, and he did so with astounding results.

As a senior at Flint Central High School, Abbott whiffed 148 batters and allowed just 16 hits in 73 innings. He also smashed .427 with seven home runs. On the gridiron, he threw four touchdown passes in the state semifinal game. "I was fortunate to be a very competitive person," Abbott said, "which wasn't always pleasant but served me well when things heated up."

Being born without a right hand did not prevent Abbott from attaining success—and a memorable milestone—in the majors.

HOW DID HE DO THAT?

A person needs only one hand to throw a baseball, but how does a physically challenged pitcher hold his glove? Or field a ball? Or even swing a bat? Mastering these skills is what made Abbott a truly extraordinary athlete.

As a Little Leaguer, Jim learned how to throw and catch with the same hand. While throwing, he balanced a right-handed glove on the end of his right arm—then slid his hand into the mitt after releasing the ball. As a pitcher, he had to make the switch quickly in case of a comeback grounder. After catching or fielding the ball, Jim squeezed the mitt between his right arm and chest and pulled the ball out with his hand.

Though this was a seemingly cumbersome process, Abbott was a terrific fielder who committed only nine errors in 10 major league seasons. As for handling bunts, Abbott grabbed them bare-handed—and cleanly. In one high school game, eight straight batters bunted on him. He gunned down the last seven.

At the plate, Abbott's efforts were also extraordinary. A .400 hitter in high school, he once blasted a game-winning, 330-foot homer to center field. He went two-for-three in his career at the University of Michigan and two-for-21 with three RBI in the majors. Abbott could smoke the fastball, but "if they threw a curveball," he admitted, "I couldn't touch it."

Abbott became a star left-hander at the University of Michigan, and then won the gold-medal game in the 1988 Olympics. On April 8, 1989, he made his major league debut with the California Angels, becoming one of the few players in modern baseball history to skip the minors entirely.

Two years later, in 1991, Abbott went 18-11 for the Angels, finishing third in American League Cy Young Award balloting. After that season, however, his run of luck seemed to dry up. He posted a 2.77 ERA in 1992 but received only 2.55 runs of support per game—the worst support of any American League starter since the designated hitter rule had gone into effect in 1973. He finished 7-15. In December 1992, Abbott was traded to the Yankees, who hoped he could pitch them to the postseason for the first time in 12 years.

Unfortunately, Abbott sputtered through the first five months of 1993, posting an uncharacteristically high 4.31 ERA. It got to the point where catcher Matt Nokes sat next to him between innings so they could analyze his pitching. Nokes continued to "babysit" Abbott on September 4. However, after the lefty allowed nothing but two walks over the fifth and sixth innings, Nokes stopped talking to his pitcher. In baseball, that's the tradition when someone's throwing a no-hitter.

With one out in the seventh, Yankees third sacker Wade Boggs preserved the no-no with a diving stop of an Albert Belle groundball. By the eighth inning, Yankees broadcaster Dewayne Staats had told viewers to call their friends and neighbors. Jim Abbott was only six outs away from immortality.

An increasingly raucous crowd of 27,225 rose to their feet in the top of the eighth, inspiring their new hero. "The fans were so into the game and the potential no-hitter, that it was impossible to ignore what was going on," Abbott recalled. "Again it came back to focusing on the mitt and trusting the pitch—staying entirely in the moment and the process. 'This pitch to that spot.' It felt like the calm in the middle of a storm."

Abbott opened the eighth by whiffing rookie Manny Ramirez and then offsetting a walk with two groundouts. As the Yankees took the field in the ninth, up 4–0, New York manager Buck Showalter called bullpen coach Mark Connor, telling him to send in closer Lee Smith. Connor practically went berserk until he realized that the skipper was just joking.

Abbott's teammates, meanwhile, were on high alert. Nervous shortstop Randy Velarde said he could barely move. First baseman Don Mattingly had "huge

Williams hauled it in on the warning track.

Now just an out away from adding his name to the voluminous pages of Yankees history, Abbott was calm as Cleveland second baseman Carlos Baerga settled into the batter's box. As the third hitter in the Indians' potent lineup, Baerga would finish the 1993 season with 21 home runs and 114 runs batted in. Additionally, with dangerous young slugger Albert Belle waiting on deck, Abbott knew he could not risk walking Baerga and giving Belle a chance to come to the plate.

The Yankee Stadium crowd, already on its feet and in full throat, dialed the decibel level up even further. Because of Baerga's propensity to make contact and Abbott's less-than-overpowering pitch assortment, it would likely be the Yankee fielding, which had been so solid all afternoon, that would put the finishing touch on one of the most remarkable pitching performances in baseball history. Shortstop Randy Velarde and second baseman Mike Gallego in particular knew to be prepared, as Abbott's breaking pitches and cut fastball had been producing groundouts all afternoon.

Now the big question of the day, of Abbott's career, of his life—would Baerga dash Abbott's dream, the same dream that everyone who ever pitched a baseball dreamt of, a no-hitter...and at Yankee Stadium! He wound up, hesitated—and probably beckoned God's favor too—and let go. The pitch was on the way now. Swinging in the hopes of breaking up the no-hitter and perhaps even starting a rally, the Indians' best hitter made contact. A ground ball bounded its way across the diamond, right into Velarde's glove. An easy throw to Mattingly from the sure-handed shortstop, followed by a deafening roar from the Bronx faithful, and Abbott's place in baseball history was a done deal. The eighth no-hitter in Yankee history had just been pitched—thrown by a man with only one hand.

goosebumps on my forearms, and the hair on the back of my neck was standing up." Kenny Lofton, leading off the top of the ninth, tried to bunt his way on, earning a cascade of boos. Instead, he grounded out to second. Felix Fermin followed with a 390-foot blast to left-center, but Gold Glove centerfielder Bernie

Chapter Thirty-seven

Althea Gibson: She Was Somebody

Wimbledon Women's Singles Final, London, England, July 6, 1957

It was a blisteringly hot day. The mercury inched toward 100 degrees as the sun beat down on Wimbledon's fabled grass tennis courts that July afternoon in 1957. English royalty and society figures fanned themselves in the stands, their strawberries and cream all but curdling in the heat. Two people, however, seemed unfazed by the precipitous rise in temperature. Queen Elizabeth II, elegantly turned out in gloves and one of her trademark frilly hats, calmly ate her lunch on the clubhouse porch, simply too regal to do something downright common like perspire. Then again, she didn't have anything to prove like African-American tennis player Althea Gibson, making her landmark Wimbledon finals debut in torpor-inducing weather. Yet like Her Majesty, Gibson radiated poise and confidence, as if this were just another friendly match on the Harlem tennis courts of her youth, rather than the most prestigious Grand Slam championship in tennis.

Six years after becoming the first African-American player invited to compete at Wimbledon, Gibson won the toss to serve first against Darlene Hard, a blond and bubbly Southern California native. Although Gibson already had one Grand Slam title to her credit—the

Althea Gibson was strong at the net in her milestone 6–3, 6–2 Wimbledon victory over Darlene Hard.

1956 French Open—a Wimbledon victory would place her in truly rarefied company, alongside such tennis luminaries as Helen Wills Moody, Maureen "Little Mo" Connolly, and Alice Marble. That Gibson had made it this far was due in part to Marble, who had pressured the famously elitist and lily-white United States Lawn Tennis Association to open its long-segregated doors to Gibson in 1950.

"If tennis is a game for ladies and gentlemen," Marble wrote in a scathing editorial on Gibson's behalf in the July 1950 issue of *American Lawn Tennis Magazine*, "it's time we acted a little more like gentle-people and less like sanctimonious hypocrites."

These so-called gentlepeople now watched as Gibson served, stretching her lanky, nearly six-foot frame to send the ball hurtling across the grass court to Hard. Her sweaty ponytail plastered against her neck, Hard seemed undone by the withering heat. She struggled to keep pace with the former Harlem street kid with the "knock 'em dead" serve, but Gibson easily took the first set, 6–3, in just twenty-five minutes.

Toweling off in the break between sets, Gibson scanned the crowded viewing stands for her old friends Katharine Landry and Dorothy Parks. The three of them had met while competing on the all-black American Tennis Association tournament circuit in the 1940s. Of all the spectators, only Landry and Parks knew what Gibson had endured to reach Wimbledon—

After Althea Gibson's back-to-back victories at Wimbledon in 1957 and 1958, 32 years would pass before another African-American woman tennis player reached the Wimbledon singles final. In 1990, Zina Garrison defeated both Monica Seles and Steffi Graf in the semifinals to face veteran Martina Navratilova in the championship match, which Garrison lost, 6–4, 6–1. Since 2000, the powerhouse Williams sisters have dominated Wimbledon, where in 2002 they became the first sisters to play each other for the title since 1884.

Here are the statistics for the African-American women tennis players in the Wimbledon singles finals to date.

YEAR	WINNER	RUNNER-UP	SCORES
1957	Althea Gibson	Darlene Hard	6–3, 6–2
1958	Althea Gibson	Angela Mortimer	8–6, 6–2
1990	Martina Navratilova	Zina Garrison	6–4, 6–1
2000	Venus Williams	Lindsay Davenport	6–3, 7–6, (7–3)*
2001	Venus Williams	Justine Henin	6–1, 3–6, 6–0
2002	Serena Williams	Venus Williams	7–6 (7–4)*, 6–3
2003	Serena Williams	Venus Williams	4–6, 6–4, 6–2

score on tie-breaker

and the intense pressure she felt to be a trailblazer for African-Americans in tennis. It was a role that Gibson had always resisted. "I have never regarded myself as a crusader," she later wrote in her autobiography, *I Always Wanted to Be Somebody*. Yet here she was, ten years after Jackie Robinson joined the Brooklyn Dodgers, an African-American woman from the slums of Harlem on the verge of making sports history before a royal audience.

Gibson took her place on the court for the second set. To look at this graceful and quietly self-assured young woman with impeccable manners, you'd never believe that she had once been a hellion. But if not for tennis, Gibson might have ended up another casualty of the ghetto. Hers had been a hardscrabble childhood, punctuated by frequent beatings from her father and run-ins with juvenile authorities for chronic truancy. The tennis court became a refuge for the wild and undisciplined little girl, whose athleticism and competitive zeal caught the eye of Harlem bandleader Buddy Walker. Through his financial and emotional support, Gibson began playing at the upscale Cosmopolitan Tennis Club, an enclave of Harlem's black bourgeoisie.

Although her coarse behavior and antics scandalized many of the well-heeled club members, Gibson silenced her critics by chalking up an impressive string of ATA victories. Etiquette lessons would come later, courtesy of Gibson's patrons—two wealthy African-American physicians/tennis aficionados—who saw in Gibson the makings of a world-class champion. That is, once she learned the proper fork to use with dinner, improved her grammar, and practiced her curtsey.

Fortunately, whatever anxiety or pressure Gibson may have felt to succeed certainly didn't manifest itself in her game. Rushing the net in the second set at Wimbledon, she invariably got the volley. When Hard tried the same strategy, Gibson sent the ball careening past her from the backcourt. The Pomona College freshman, then ranked one of the world's 10 best women players, simply collapsed in the face of Gibson's effortless domination of the court. As routs go, it was relatively quick—Gibson took the second set 6–2 in just 25 minutes—but painless? Not for Hard, according to a *New York Times* reporter: "The game grew faster as Miss Gibson's service jumped so alarmingly off the fast grass that Darlene nodded miserably as her errors

mounted." The sport of kings had a new queen.

Accepting a congratulatory kiss on the cheek from Hard—an image that undoubtedly sent blood pressures skyrocketing across the Jim Crow–era American South—Gibson beamed as Queen Elizabeth II strode across the red carpet to present her with the championship gold salver. The full import of her groundbreaking victory was not lost on Gibson, that most reluctant of role models. As she later wrote in her autobiography, "Shaking hands with the Queen of England was a long way from being forced to sit in the colored section of the bus going into downtown Wilmington, North Carolina." But for now, she simply exclaimed, "At last! At last!"

Gibson got a kiss from Hard, her finals opponent, after becoming the first black player to win Wimbledon's gold plate.

Chapter Thirty-eight

Bleeding Red, White and Blue

Summer Olympics, Baseball Final, United States vs. Cuba
Sydney, Australia, September 27, 2000

Team USA manager Tommy Lasorda had skippered the Los Angeles Dodgers to four World Series. But this, he said, "was bigger than Major League Baseball." While most Americans lay sleeping, the USA baseball team faced the Cuban national team in the gold medal game of the 2000 Olympics in Sydney, Australia.

Ever since President John F. Kennedy attempted to overthrow Fidel Castro's communist government in 1961, the Cuban dictator had prided himself on fielding a better national baseball team than the United States. Meanwhile, the patriotic Lasorda bled not just Dodger blue, as he used to say, but red and white too.

"I asked each and every player on that team before the tournament, why are you here?" said Lasorda. "And to a man, they said they were here to represent our country. And I tell you, I wanted to give every one of those boys a hug."

As the players lined up for pregame introductions—Cubans down one foul line, Americans on the other—personal as well as political tension filled Olympic Park's baseball stadium. Earlier in the Games, Cuba had pounded the U.S. 6–1 in a game that featured a bench-clearing skirmish. After Lasorda shook hands with Cuban manager Servio Borges at home plate, the battle for international baseball supremacy was set to begin.

Though each team entered the championship game with 7-1 Olympic records, the U.S. was an overwhelming underdog. Lasorda's club was an unusual mix of recent major league draft picks, including championship game starting pitcher Ben Sheets, and former big league players, including ex–Toronto Blue Jays catcher Pat Borders.

The Cuban team, meanwhile, was dubbed the "Big Red Machine," a takeoff on both its communist country and its resemblance to the great Cincinnati Reds powerhouses of the mid-1970s. In the two previous Olympics, Cuba had gone 18-0 en route to gold medals, outscoring opponents 213–75. Moreover, since 1951, Castro's pride and joy had won 16 consecutive World Cup tournaments. This year's squad featured slugger Omar Linares, who had blasted three home runs in the 1996 gold medal game, and fireballer Maels Rodríguez, who launched 100-mph strikes.

While the U.S. lacked Cuba's talent, it boasted a Hall of Fame manager in Lasorda, who had led the Dodgers to World Series titles in 1981 and '88. Still a rah-rah motivator at age 73, Lasorda skippered an

Ben Sheets was brilliant against Cuba, allowing just three broken-bat singles.

enthusiastic, cohesive team that consistently rose to the occasion. A year earlier, USA had qualified for the Olympics with a strong showing at the Pan American Games, where it finished second to Cuba.

Lasorda's troops opened the Sydney Games with a 3–2 nail-biting win over Japan, thanks to a 13th-inning

"Nothing in baseball has ever touched me like that," Team USA manager Tommy Lasorda said.

Sheets (28), Sean Burroughs (10) and Anthony Sanders did not hold back after stunning Cuba 4-0 to win Olympic gold.

homer by Mike Neill, who had mustered four hits in the majors. The U.S. followed with routs of South Africa (11–1) and the Netherlands (6–2) before a tight game with Korea, in which USA's Doug Mientkiewicz broke a tie with an eighth-inning, game-winning grand slam. After a 4–2 triumph over Italy (on Italian-

ᔐᔑ

At the medal ceremonies, Lasorda and his motley collection of ballplayers beamed with pride. "I've played on championship teams," said Lasorda. "I've managed championship teams. To see those guys jumping up and down with flags wrapped around them and gold medals being placed around their necks while the National Anthem played, I just cried."

ᔐᔑ

American Lasorda's birthday), USA lost to Cuba in a bitter battle marred by a spiking of Borders at home plate. The U.S. wrapped up the round-robin play with a 12–1 humiliation of host country Australia.

With a 6-1 record, the United States earned a spot in the semifinal contest against Korea—a game that hinted at USA's destiny. After eight innings and a two-hour rain delay, Mientkiewicz abused Korea again, belting a walk-off homer in the bottom of the ninth. America's new Olympic hero waved his arms in elation while his mates hugged each other Lasorda-style.

Ben Sheets, the Milwaukee Brewers' recent No. 1

pick, earned the start in the gold medal game against Cuba. Sheets, just 22, had nerves of steel. "He was the kind of guy we knew the Cubans could not intimidate," Lasorda said. "Because that's what they liked to do. They liked to try to intimidate you."

The Cubans, indeed, had little love for the Americans. Many were bitter that several of their stars had defected to the major leagues in recent years. The U.S. players showcased their pride by draping the American flag behind their bench. In the first inning, Neill broke the tension with a solo home run.

With a one-run lead, Sheets mowed through the Cuban lineup, one that entered the game with a .344 average in the tournament. With his cap tugged low, Sheets induced the Cubans to beat sod with his biting sinker. "He had great stuff that day," Lasorda recalled. "Unbelievable stuff."

In the fifth, Borders—the World Series MVP for Toronto in 1992—laced a run-scoring double to make it 2–0. Enter flamethrowing Rodríguez, who drew oohs from the Aussie crowd when his 100-mph fastball was recorded on the scoreboard. Nevertheless, Rodríguez loaded the bags for 31-year-old Ernie Young, a former Oakland A's outfielder. Young smoked a 98-mph pitch back through the box. Two runners crossed the plate, greeted by ecstatic mates who poured from the dugout.

Staked to a stunning 4–0 lead, Sheets continued to cruise. At one point, he retired 11 in a row. Through eight innings, with the score still 4–0, Sheets had allowed just three hits—all broken-bat singles. Only one Cuban had reached second base. In the ninth, Sheets struck out the first two batters, with Luis Ulacia throwing his helmet in frustration.

When Yasser Gomez flew out to left, with Neill making a stylish sliding catch, Sheets fell to his knees and raised his arms in triumph. For the first time ever, the United States had claimed Olympic gold in "America's game." The euphoric U.S. players huddled together, then took a victory lap around the field. Lasorda hugged his coaches with the American flag draped over his shoulder.

THE U.S. OLYMPIC BASEBALL TEAM ROSTER

PLAYER	POSITION	AGE	ORGANIZATION	LEVEL	OLYMPIC STATS
Position Players					**BA-HR-RBI**
Brent Abernathy	2B	22	TB	AAA	.385-0-4
Pat Borders	C	37	TB	AAA	.429-0-2
Sean Burroughs	3B	20	SD	AA	.375-0-1
John Cotton	IF	29	Col	AAA	.185-0-6
Travis Dawkins	SS/2B	21	Cin	AA	.000-0-0
Adam Everett	SS	23	Hou	AAA	.043-0-0
Marcus Jensen	C	27	Min	AAA	.167-1-5
Mike Kinkade	C	27	Bal	AAA	.207-0-3
Doug Mientkiewicz	1B	26	Min	AAA	.414-2-8
Mike Neill	OF	30	Sea	AAA	.219-3-5
Anthony Sanders	OF	26	Sea	AAA	.167-0-1
Brad Wilkerson	OF	23	Mon	AAA	.216-1-1
Ernie Young	OF	31	StL	AAA	.385-1-8
Pitchers					**W-L/ERA/IP**
Kurt Ainsworth	P	22	SF	AA	2-0/1.54/11.2
Ryan Franklin	P	27	Sea	AAA	3-0/0.00/8.1
Chris George	P	22	KC	AAA	0-0/0.00/3.2
Shane Heams	P	24	Det	AAA	0-0/7.71/2.1
Rick Krivda	P	30	Bal	AAA	0-1/18.00/2.0
Roy Oswalt	P	23	Hou	AA	0-0/1.38/13.0
Jon Rauch	P	21	CWS	AA	1-0/0.82/11.0
Bobby Seay	P	22	TB	AA	0-0/0.00/0.2
Ben Sheets	P	22	Mil	AAA	1-0/0.41/22.0
Todd Williams	P	29	Sea	AAA	1-0/0.00/5.0
Tim Young	P	26	Bos	AAA	0-0/0.00/0.1

At the medal ceremonies, Lasorda and his motley collection of ballplayers beamed with pride. "I've played on championship teams," said Lasorda. "I've managed championship teams. To see those guys jumping up and down with flags wrapped around them and gold medals being placed around their necks while the National Anthem played, I just cried. It just touched me. Nothing in baseball has ever touched me like that."

Chapter Thirty-nine

Proud Warriors

NBA Finals, Golden State Warriors vs. Washington Bullets
Oakland Coliseum, California, and Capital Center, Landover, Maryland, May 1975

You might say the 1975 Golden State Warriors were the Rodney Dangerfield of the NBA. Like the great comic, they just "didn't get no respect." And on the night of Game 4 of the Warriors–Washington Bullets playoff series, like Dangerfield's trademark line, the Warriors were looking at two major dissings. The first negative was the Ice Follies; the second, a karate tournament.

Because of the Follies and karate, the Warriors couldn't find a place to play one of their Finals home games. The Warriors possessed so little clout—and their appearance in the 1975 NBA Finals was so unexpected—that the executives of the Oakland Coliseum refused to host Game 4 of the Warriors–Bullets series because the Ice Follies already had been booked for that date. The alternative site, the Cow Palace, also was no-go; a karate tournament wasn't about to take a back seat to the NBA's Warriors.

As fate would have it, the NBA allowed the Washington Bullets to decide how to split the first four games. Washington chose to play Games 1 and 4 at home and 2 and 3 on the road. *Whatever,* sighed the Warriors. By this point in the season, they were used to second-class status.

Prior to the 1974–75 campaign, prognosticators

slotted Golden State for fourth place in the Pacific Division. Many felt the club wouldn't make the playoffs. After all, this was a team that couldn't even sign its No. 1 draft picks in each of the previous four seasons.

Head coach Al Attles, a player and coach for the Warriors since 1960, was used to making do with less. In 1974–75 he molded an eclectic mix of players into a hardworking, hustling unit that won 48 games—tops in the mediocre Western Conference. Attles emphasized a pressure defense that required a deep bench. Golden State was one of the few teams in NBA history to have 10 players averaging at least 10 minutes per game.

"Pro basketball had always been about eight people," Attles said. "You played your best guys. Our way was such a departure.... We played aggressive defense, so we needed a lot of people. A lot of guys got into the ballgame."

Ray, a 6'9" center, was among the Warriors' overachievers, battling for 10.6 rebounds per game. Jamaal Wilkes, a confident rookie out of UCLA, surprised fans with 14.2 points and 8.2 boards per outing. Guards Charlie Johnson and Butch Beard also averaged in double digits in scoring, while Beard shut down opposing point guards.

But among all the Warriors, only Rick Barry was a genuine star. An unparalleled shooter, Barry poured in 30.6 points per game in 1974–75. Many felt that an East Coast bias was the only thing that prevented him from winning the NBA MVP award that year.

Golden State won its first two playoff series in

George Johnson of the Warriors (right) *stole a rebound from Bullets All-Star Wes Unseld during Golden State's 92–91 win in Game 2.*

1975, but each was a war. The Warriors staved off the Seattle SuperSonics in six games. But at the end of the series, Golden State players had to battle an angry Seattle crowd in which two fans tried to start a fight with Barry and Beard.

In the Western Conference Finals, the Warriors outhustled a more talented Bulls team, but Chicago took a 16-point lead in the second quarter of Game 7. Golden State responded with a ferocious defensive effort,

holding the Bulls scoreless for the final seven minutes of the game. The Warriors roared back to win 83–79.

Nobody gave Golden State a chance in the NBA Finals, which some were calling the greatest mismatch in Finals history. The Washington Bullets had won 60 regular season games and most recently eliminated the mighty Boston Celtics for what some called the real NBA championship series. Pundits theorized that Washington's towers of power—future Hall of Famers

WHO WERE THESE GUYS?

An NBA axiom is that a team needs three superstars to win the championship. The Warriors, however, defied league logic, prevailing in 1975 with one star, Rick Barry, and a deep but largely unrecognizable supporting cast. Coach Al Attles employed not star power but depth and defense to wear down opponents. Here's a brief look at Golden State's top nine players in 1974–75:

Rick Barry, F, 30.6 PPG
A bull's-eye shooter who topped 30 PPG four times in his NBA/ABA career. Earned induction into the Basketball Hall of Fame.

Jamaal Wilkes, F, 14.2 PPG
A surprisingly productive rookie in 1974–75. Went on to become a 20-PPG scorer for the Lakers during their dynasty years in the 1980s.

Butch Beard, G, 12.8 PPG
Solid distributor and big-time defender. His career faded after his championship season with Golden State.

Charlie Johnson, G, 10.9 PPG
Topped 10 PPG in 1974–75 for the only time in his career. Ironically, helped Washington to

the NBA title in 1978.

Clifford Ray, C, 9.4 PPG
Small but tenacious in the paint. Achieved 10 RPG for the fourth straight (and last) season in 1974–75.

Jeff Mullins, G, 8.2 PPG
Topped 20 PPG four straight seasons for the Warriors beginning in 1968–69. Was a shadow of his former self by 1974–75.

Derrek Dickey, F, 7.7 PPG
Snatched 6.9 RPG for the championship-bound Warriors despite being listed at a mere 6'7", 218 pounds. The 1974–75 season was the best of his five-year NBA career.

Phil Smith, G, 7.7 PPG
Learned the ropes as a second-round rookie in 1974–75. Would blossom into a 20-PPG scorer a year later.

George Johnson, C, 4.4 PPG
A young, 6'11" center who skied for boards and blocks. Would mature into one of the top shot-swatters in the league in the late 1970s with New Jersey.

Wes Unseld and Elvin Hayes—would humiliate counterparts Ray and Wilkes. "A lot of people were predicting a sweep," Attles said.

The series unfolded as planned in Game 1, with the host Bullets leading by 14 at the half. But again, Golden State stormed back thanks to its fierce defense and deep bench. The once unwanted Charles Dudley, who had earned a tryout with Golden State only because GM Lou Mohs owed somebody a favor, played big minutes. Rookie Phil Smith, who was asked "Who *are* you?" by a reporter after the game, scored 20 points off the bench. The Warriors rallied to win 101–95.

Eerily, the pattern continued in Game 2. Down 13 points this time, Golden State rode Barry's 36 points to a 92–91 victory. Washington could have won it but missed two shots in the last six seconds.

"A lot of prognosticators couldn't believe it was happening," Attles said.

The Warriors made it happen by grabbing loose balls, getting back to prevent easy baskets, and swarming the boards. While Golden State lacked dominant rebounders like Unseld and Hayes, they had—as Attles put it—eight guys grabbing eight each.

Golden State didn't need another astonishing comeback to win Game 3. Thanks to Barry's hot hand (38 points) and yeoman work by reserve George Johnson (10 points, nine rebounds), the Warriors cruised 109–101. Through three games, Golden State's bench had outscored Washington's 115–53.

As the series switched to Washington for Game 4, the Warriors remained focused. "Not one word was uttered about winning the championship," Attles recalled. "And I told the team: 'Regardless of...what people think about you...no matter what anyone says about you or writes about you, you win one more game, and no one can ever take what you've done away from you. Never.'"

Unseld, who said Washington needed to win at least two games to avoid a summer of humiliation, wanted this game as badly as the Warriors did. The intensity reached full boil in the first quarter, when an ugly fight led to the ejection of Attles. Down 14, Golden State again came back, wearing down

Phil Smith (20) came off the bench in Game 1 to score 20 points for Golden State.

Washington with its pressure defense. Beard scored the last seven points of the game, including two free throws that clinched a 96–95 win.

The Warriors thus became just the third team ever to win the NBA Finals in four straight. As Attles said, a lot of people had predicted a sweep. "They just never dreamed," he added, "it would be the sweep it wound up being!"

Chapter Forty

Paul Lawrie: Close to Home...Where the Heart Is

British Open Golf, Carnoustie, Scotland, July 15–18, 1999

Pummeled by near gale-force winds and surrounded by dense, waist-high rough, Carnoustie Golf Links is not a hospitable place for a leisurely round of golf. The 7,361-yard course in Scotland inspires fear. There's not a pro alive who doesn't loathe the place, but they all respect it.

Legendary Walter Hagen may have called it the greatest golf course in Great Britain, but that's *his* opinion. Most golfers share the sentiments of Phil Mickelson, who didn't hold back in his withering assessment of Carnoustie: "I've never seen fairways as penalizing as that for a major championship. You might as well stick red hazard posts down the fairways."

No wonder they call it "Car-Nasty."

Playing the "killer links" at Carnoustie has been the undoing of many world-class golfers—and, sometimes, the making of a new champion. It was here, where his countrymen have played golf since the 1500s, that Scotsman Paul Lawrie forever left obscurity.

Having grown up virtually in the shadow of Carnoustie near Aberdeen, Lawrie had little interest in golf as a youth. His passions were soccer, snooker, and rugby. At 17 he dropped out of school to work at a nearby golf course. Soon Lawrie became an assistant under the late Doug Smart at Banchory, near Aberdeen, where the club has now named the 14th hole after him.

Since turning professional in 1986, Lawrie had played a

Scotland's Paul Lawrie overcame a 10-stroke deficit in the final round to conquer the 1999 British Open.

spectacularly erratic game of golf. However, there had been occasional flashes of brilliance, including finishing in a tie for sixth at the 1993 British Open at Royal St. George's. On his last shot of that tournament, he had holed a 3-iron for an eagle, which gave him a final-round score of 65. After that fine showing, however, Lawrie's game went into a steep decline. What had once inspired him now felt like a particularly onerous chore. A string of losses, coupled with performance issues, led him to consider quitting the play-for-pay circuit to become a club pro. At least then he'd be assured of a steady income to support his wife and children.

Lawrie prevailed in a three-way playoff to win his first major title.

Still, he wasn't quite ready to let go of his dream—not just yet. Rather than go the practical route, Lawrie decided to continue his playing career. His decision eventually paid off on the European Tour, where he won the 1996 Open Catalonia and the 1999 Qatar Masters. But since he had to go through a qualifying round just to get into the 1999 British Open, nobody gave him a chance to win the storied tournament, the British Open, coveted by the best golfers in the world.

At the time of the 1999 Open, Lawrie was ranked a humbling No. 159 in the world. During the tournament's first three days, Lawrie surprisingly held his own, posting scores of 73, 74, and 76; then again, he wasn't exactly dazzling either, trailing the leader, Frenchman Jean Van de Velde, by 10 shots heading into the final day of play. Even those close to Lawrie didn't put much stock in his chances. The only family member to show for Sunday's round was his brother. And what the rest of the family missed! That day, Lawrie put on a show for the ages.

Carding five birdies and just one bogey for the day, Lawrie posted a 67 to finish at six over, trailing Van de Velde by just three shots now.

After completing his round, Lawrie hung around the putting green, waiting for the possibility of someone choking and giving him a win, or perhaps a tie, requiring a playoff. Although he knew the chances were remote, he couldn't quite bring himself to leave. He continued to putt—and to dream.

Suddenly, Van de Velde's image on a big-screen TV near the putting green captured Lawrie's attention. The tournament leader had stepped to the 18th tee with a three-shot lead, minutes away from becoming the first Frenchman since Arnaud Massy in 1907 to win the British Open. At this pivotal moment, with victory all but assured, Van de Velde made a colossal blunder: he elected to hit with his driver off the tee.

The result was catastrophic. He pushed the ball right, near the 17th tee. Compounding the problem by not laying up, Van de Velde then grabbed a long iron and attempted to reach the green. Again the ball went right, ricocheting off the grandstand and into a thick rough. The tournament still was his if he chopped the

The famed Claret Jug was awarded at Carnoustie to a man who grew up just a stone's throw from the venue.

Paul Lawrie claimed the British Open title at Carnoustie Golf Links, which is one of the world's oldest sites for golf and easily one of the toughest.

Golf is recorded as being played on the land at Carnoustie as early as 1527 and many believe the sport was played there even before Columbus discovered America. The first club was formed at Carnoustie in 1839, where the original course had just 10 holes.

Carnoustie is like many links courses in that it is built upon useless wasteland. Carnoustie's Championship Links has meandering berms and pot bunkers, slippery slopes on fairways and greens, diabolical rough—and many days golfers must negotiate these dangers in the wind and rain, creating even more difficult obstacles to overcome. Another unique aspect of Carnoustie's random design is the fact that no two consecutive holes face the same direction, meaning wind, rain, and hill slope are different on every hole.

Despite all the trouble golfers face while playing holes No. 1 through No. 15, Carnoustie saves the most treacherous stretch for the end of the round. Holes No. 16 through No. 18 have earned a notorious reputation as the "toughest finish in golf," making no round—or lead—safe until one is sitting comfortably in the bar at the 19th hole.

Just ask Jean Van de Velde.

---

ball back to the fairway, but he elected to go for the green. This time the ball found water. After taking his penalty stroke, the seemingly cursed Van de Velde hit his fifth shot toward the green and the ball landed in the right greenside bunker. Miraculously, the Frenchman escaped the bunker and sank an eight-foot putt for a triple-bogey seven and a spot in a playoff with Lawrie and Justin Leonard.

As if Sir Isaac Newton had been counseling the golf gods about equal and opposite reactions, Lawrie found himself in a sweet spot. His game was getting better and better and Van de Velde's obviously was falling apart. But would the trends last into the playoff?

The playoff began at the 15th hole with a steady rain pouring down. All three players hit bad drives that turned into bogeys for Lawrie and Leonard and a double-bogey for Van de Velde. On 16 all three bogeyed before Van de Velde and Lawrie each sank birdie putts on the 17th giving Lawrie a one-shot lead with one hole remaining.

Unlike Van de Velde had done earlier in the day, Lawrie played 18 with aplomb, splitting the middle of the fairway with his drive before hitting his approach shot to within six feet of the pin. Seemingly cursed, Van de Velde played the hole poorly again, making double-bogey.

As the cheering from the rain-drenched gallery reached decibel levels unusual for even the British Open, Lawrie calmly watched as Leonard joined Van de Velde in bogeyland on the final hole.

It would have now taken a collapse as monumental as Van de Velde's to deny the Scotsman the win. But enough strange things had already happened on this day. Lawrie had to sink his birdie putt. Now there was a mere four feet between him and one of the greatest upsets in modern golf. Unshaken, Lawrie addressed the ball, got the line, and with a plunk it hit the bottom of the cup. He had done it! The British Open was Paul Lawrie's. The Scotsman won on his own turf, so close to home he could almost throw the ball there.

Not since the 1956 Masters, when Jackie Burke Jr. came from eight strokes behind to defeat Ken Venturi, had a golfer made such an astonishing comeback in a major tournament.

Chapter Forty-one

Dikembe Mutombo: Eight Plus One Equals a Ten

NBA Western Conference Playoffs, Seattle SuperSonics vs. Denver Nuggets

Seattle and Denver, April–May 1994

Zaire, the former Belgian Congo, now the Democratic Republic of the Congo, is a hot, fly-infested place. Until 1974 it was famous—shall we say infamous—for little more than civil wars and genocide. But it was "the Rumble in the Jungle" that put it, and fight promoter Don King, on the map, and George Foreman on the canvas. After that famous Ali fight, though, there wasn't much to celebrate.

Dikembe Mutombo changed that. From this West African nation famous for its pygmy warriors, the 7'2" giant, who speaks English, French, Spanish, Portuguese, and five African dialects, would put the Third World nation on center stage in the world of sports.

Now, as center for the Denver Nuggets, the West African and his teammates knew they were out of their league and that Seattle would make easy work of them. All the fledgling Nuggets ever expected from the playoff was a little experience.

But Seattle never thought the Nuggets would be

Dikembe Mutombo's eighth block of the game, against Detlef Schrempf in the closing minutes, helped the Nuggets to a 98–94 win and the biggest upset in NBA playoff history.

particularly easy, though the SuperSonics finished the 1993–94 season with a franchise-record 63 victories. And the Nuggets, their first-round playoff opponent, was the *eighth*-seeded and had sneaked in with a barely respectable 42-40 record. But for Seattle, Game 1 vs. Denver was like a gentle sailboat ride on Puget Sound. Behind explosive superstars Shawn Kemp and Gary Payton, the Sonics breezed to a 62–37 halftime lead and a 106–82 blowout victory.

Denver's front line of Mutombo, LaPhonso Ellis, and Brian Williams combined for just 14 rebounds. "I'm going to put some cayenne peppers in Dikembe's and LaPhonso's pregame meals," said Williams afterward. "I'm going to get them mad and hot."

Seemingly, a jug of Tabasco sauce would not have given the Nuggets the oomph they needed to compete with the super Sonics. Seattle, the No. 1 seed in the Western Conference, had led the league in victories. Coach George Karl boasted All-NBA players in Kemp (18.1 points and 10.8 rebounds per game) and Payton (16.5 points and 6.0 assists per contest). Moreover, guard Nate McMillan led the NBA in steals while Detlef Schrempf, Ricky Pierce, and Kendall Gill each averaged more than 14 points a game.

If the Sonics lineup wasn't already enough to make any opponent run and hide, three of the five first-round games would be played at the Seattle Center Coliseum, where the Sonics had gone 37-4 on the season. And there was other history too: no No. 8 seed had ever defeated a No. 1 seed since the playoffs were expanded to 16 teams in 1984.

Though the Nuggets had improved since their 24-58 season in 1991–92, they sorely lacked experience in pressure situations. In fact, they were the youngest team in the entire NBA. Denver head coach Dan Issel, a former Nuggets scoring legend, had to rely on a stable of young pups to compete with Seattle's pedigreed show dogs.

Of Denver's eight top players, four had been selected in the last three drafts: Mutombo, Ellis, guard Bryant Stith, and forward Rodney Rogers. The 7'2" Mount Mutombo was the best of this quartet, leading the NBA in shot-blocking in 1993–94—although critics panned his offensive game.

Denver's other four regulars had all overcome obstacles. Guard Mahmoud Abdul-Rauf, their leading scorer (18.0 points per game), battled Tourette's syndrome. Forward Brian Williams, suffering from clinical depression, had admitted to attempting suicide before finding help. Reggie Williams had signed with the Nuggets after being released by San Antonio. And Robert Pack, a

dynamic backup point guard, had never even been drafted.

It was no surprise, then, that Seattle cruised to easy victories in the first two games. The Sonics, who loved to turn rebounds and turnovers into fast-break buckets, romped to a 13-point halftime lead in Game 2. The Nuggets traded baskets in the second half and lost by 10, 97–87. Seattle needed just one more win in the best-of-five series to move on.

As the series shifted to Denver, Issel told his players that they had nothing to lose. "To be honest," he admitted to the press, "we just wanted to get some playoff experience this year." For Game 3, however, the momentum clearly shifted.

The young Nuggets were absolutely energized by the McNichols Sports Arena crowd, which hadn't hosted a playoff game in four years. They played spirited, pressure-free basketball. The Sonics, meanwhile, came out flat, allowing Denver to roar ahead 41–26. On the strength of Reggie Williams's

Mutombo pulled down the final rebound and took the game ball with him after a defensive performance for the ages.

Denver's upset of Seattle in the 1994 playoffs did not surprise a particular contingent—those who intimately know Dikembe Mutombo. The man known as Mount Mutombo because of his mammoth frame can also, it seems, move mountains. Following are some his most remarkable accomplishments.

- In his NBA career, Dikembe has led not just Denver to the later rounds of the playoffs but the Atlanta Hawks, Philadelphia 76ers, and New Jersey Nets as well.
- In his first 11 NBA seasons, he averaged in double digits in scoring and rebounding every year.
- He became the first man ever to win four NBA Defensive Player of the Year awards.
- His off-the-court contributions have been even more gigantic. A native of the Congo, Mutombo exceeded his dream of being a doctor: He donated and raised millions of dollars to build a new hospital in his hometown of Kinshasa, the nation's first new, fully equipped medical facility in 30 years.
- Dikembe, who speaks nine languages, also has served as an international ambassador for UNICEF. Mutombo has supported many charities, including the Global Polio Eradication Initiative.
- At a fund-raiser for his hospital, Mutombo said, "When you take the elevator up to reach the top, please don't forget to send the elevator back down, so that someone else can take it to the top. This is my way of sending the elevator down."

31 points, the Nuggets won 110–93.

In Game 4, Denver slowed the pace, frustrating the energized Sonics. Down by four late in the game, the Nuggets rallied to force overtime, then overwhelmed Seattle in the extra session to win 94–85.

Seattle was now 39-4 at home, but that statistic seemed irrelevant for the series finale in Game 5. The Nuggets now felt like world-beaters, while the favorite Sonics faced elimination and humiliation. "I can't deny the butterflies felt like rocks," said Sonics coach George Karl.

For much of Game 5, the Nuggets dictated the tempo. Offensively, they slowed the pace while setting up high-percentage shots for their big guys— Mutombo, Ellis, and Brian Williams. Seattle tried to disrupt Denver with a full-court press, but the Nuggets maintained their cool, committing just 11 turnovers.

On the other end, Mutombo and Brian Williams sealed off the post area, holding powerful forward Shawn Kemp to just six second-half points. Mutombo made a defensive statement with eight blocked shots, while Williams grabbed a stunning 19 rebounds—five more than Denver's whole line had managed in Game 1.

Robert Pack took advantage of an ailing Payton, scoring 23 points, including 10 in the fourth quarter.

The Sonics, desperate to avoid the "chokers" label, nearly lost in regulation, saved only by a last-second layup by guard Kendall Gill.

In overtime, Seattle moved ahead 94–93 on a bucket by Kemp with 2:29 to play. However, thanks largely to two in-your-face rejections by Mutombo, the Sonics didn't score again. The Nuggets got all the offense they would need from a slashing Ellis, who scored on a layup while being fouled by Payton. Ellis canned the free throw to give the Nuggets a 96–94 lead. Mutombo swatted away a layup attempt by Schrempf, and then, after a 24-second violation on Denver, also rejected the high-flying Kemp's attempted five-footer. It was Mutombo's eighth block of the game.

While two free throws by Robert Pack provided the final score of 98–94, it was the defense of the man who had averaged 4.1 blocks per game in the regular season that made the difference in the end. When the final buzzer sounded, it was, fittingly, Mutombo who ended up with the final rebound.

The 7'2" center from the Congo, the ball still in his hands, lay with his back on the floor—his eyes closed and a euphoric smile upon his face. He knew that the Nuggets had just pulled off the greatest first-round upset in NBA history.

Chapter Forty-two

The Neutral-Zone Trap and the Devils

Stanley Cup Finals, New Jersey Devils vs. Detroit Red Wings
New Jersey and Detroit, June 17–24, 1995

Detroit is an urban landscape pockmarked with potholes. They form as melted ice that seeps deep into the pavement as the harsh winter of the Great Lakes takes its toll on the city's infrastructure. Yet with all the melted snow that drains southward from nearby Canada each spring, there had been a 40-year drought in the Motor City. It was that long since the Wings had won the Stanley Cup.

Down 2–1 in Game 1 of the 1995 Stanley Cup Finals, the Detroit Red Wings couldn't get the puck out of their own end against the New Jersey Devils. With less than seven minutes remaining, Detroit's Slava Fetisov passed the puck to Ray Sheppard, who—with no other options—dished it back to Fetisov. The Red Wings were stuck in their own end, victims of New Jersey's dreaded neutral-zone trap.

"It's like walking around a mousetrap," Red Wings forward Shawn Burr said in the *Sporting News*. "You almost feel like a mouse and have to try to stick your finger into the trap to try to get the cheese."

In the Finals, the Devils utilized their infamous defensive scheme to clamp down on the mighty Wings. In Game 1, New Jersey limited the Western Conference's highest-scoring team to just 17 shots, Detroit's lowest output of the season, in a 2–1 triumph. The Devils followed with 4–2 and 5–2 victories, then got the brooms and champagne ready for Game 4.

This series wasn't supposed to go this way. The Red Wings were the NHL's new glamour team, with Detroit earning the coveted nickname

Goalie Martin Brodeur showed his hang time after New Jersey completed its surprising four-game sweep of Detroit.

"Hockeytown." In 1994–95, a season shortened by the owners' lockout, the Wings sported the best record in the NHL at 33-11-4—compared to 22-18-8 for New Jersey.

Scotty Bowman, the winningest coach in NHL history and hoister of six Stanley Cups at the time, manned Detroit's bench. On the ice, his stars shone like diamonds on championship rings. Captain Steve Yzerman was en route to 700 career goals. Paul Coffey reigned as the highest-scoring defenseman ever. And center Sergei Fedorov had been named league MVP a year earlier.

Moreover, Detroit boasted the league's largest crowds and best tradition, as fans flung octopuses onto the ice after playoff victories. Meanwhile, the respect-starved Devils had spent their 13-year existence in hockey purgatory. In the New York area, they always had been third banana behind the New York Islanders and New York Rangers. In 1983 Wayne Gretzky had even called the Devils a Mickey Mouse organization, prompting derisive laughter (and opposing fans with Mickey Mouse ears) around the league.

Yet Devils coach Jacques Lemaire liked the low profile. The man who had won eight Stanley Cups with Montreal as a defensive-minded center—winning five Cups, ironically, under Coach Bowman—took over the reins of the Devils in 1993. In spring '94, he led New Jersey to Game 7 of the Eastern Conference Finals, where they lost in double-overtime to the Rangers. The agony of that defeat inspired his troops to practice even harder. Lemaire, working with committed, team-oriented players, perfected the neutral-zone trap, which was all puck fans were talking about in spring 1995.

Here's how the trap worked: An opposing puck-carrier, after corraling the rubber in his own end, would be forced to the boards by a New Jersey forward, usually the center. There he would be harassed by a Devils winger, while New Jersey's weak-side winger and two defensemen would clog the neutral zones. The puck-carrier was now trapped. If he tried to pass the puck sideways through the sea of red, a Devils forward easily could intercept it, triggering a breakaway.

Contrary to public perception, the Devils were much more than a team with a gimmick. Defenseman and captain Scott Stevens was a perennial All-Star, Martin Brodeur was impenetrable in goal, and Neal Broten and Stephane Richer averaged a point per game. Meanwhile, Claude Lemieux was becoming one of the NHL's greatest money players. In the 1995 playoffs, he lit the lamp 13 times in just 20 games.

New Jersey "trapped" the ultimate prize, Lord Stanley's Cup.

As a team, New Jersey was exceptionally fast, big, and aggressive.

The Devils' combination of talent, tenacity, and teamwork—and the trap—helped them overwhelm their first three playoff opponents in 1995. They began with a five-game rout of Boston, shutting out the Bruins three times. After losing their next game to Pittsburgh, they put the clamps on Mario Lemieux's high-scoring outfit, winning four straight while yielding just five goals.

❧❧

The Devils were so focused that they went 8-1 on the road over the three series.

❧❧

Even the rugged Philadelphia Flyers couldn't break the trap, falling in six games. The Devils were so focused that they went 8-1 on the road over the three series.

As a result of the shortened season, Western Conference teams hadn't played Eastern teams during the 1994–95 campaign. Thus, the Red Wings were facing the Devils for the first time all season, and they weren't prepared for what they saw.

In Detroit in Game 1, fans greeted the Devils during introductions with cries of "Who cares?" Yet all game long, the Wings mucked through the neutral zone as if they were marching across New Jersey swampland. Not only did the Wings lose 2–1, but they could muster only one shot in the last nine minutes.

Prior to Game 2, Yzerman promised that the Wings would not be held to 17 shots again. He was right. They managed 18, and they lost 4–2. Disappointed Wings fans packed up their octopuses and went home. The series moved to New Jersey.

The Red Wings tried to speed up play in Game 3, hoping to buzz-saw their way through the trap. But the Devils could play at a breakneck pace as well. They pushed ahead of Detroit 5–0 and won 5–2. "There wasn't much neutral-zone trapping going on there, was there?" Stevens told the *Sporting News.* "I guess we even played exciting hockey."

The Red Wings were a proud group of veterans, and they played for a franchise that was as hungry for a championship as any in the league. But they faced a hole from which only two teams had ever clambered— a three-games-to-none deficit in a best-of-seven playoff series.

Despite this, Detroit was determined to make a statement against the New Jersey defense that had trapped their way to the brink of winning the Stanley Cup. Lemaire's defensive brainchild had worked in the first two games of the series, and in the third the Devils had simply outgunned their increasingly disheartened foes. But now, with their backs against the wall, the Red Wings would summon every ounce of speed left in their skates and finesse left in their sticks.

In the first eight minutes, the Wings staged an all-out assault on Brodeur. The Devils struck first on a goal by Broten, but Detroit was quick to respond. Only 55 seconds later, Federov pushed his own rebound past Brodeur to tie the game. Shortly thereafter, Detroit's Paul Coffey made it 2–1 Red Wings with a shorthanded goal—exactly the type of play that Lemaire's defense was designed to prevent. The coach would not let his players be disheartened, however, and Shawn Chambers came back with just over two minutes left to play in the period to tie the game at two apiece.

With the score still knotted at two at the beginning of the second period, Detroit's high-powered squad turned up the intensity to previously unseen levels. Given a man advantage after a penalty on Ken Daneyko, the Red Wings seemed to momentarily overwhelm the well-trained New Jersey penalty-killing machine. In the span of four minutes, five Detroit shots made it to the front of Brodeur's crease. And each time, the Devils' All-Star goalkeeper rose to the occasion. With each

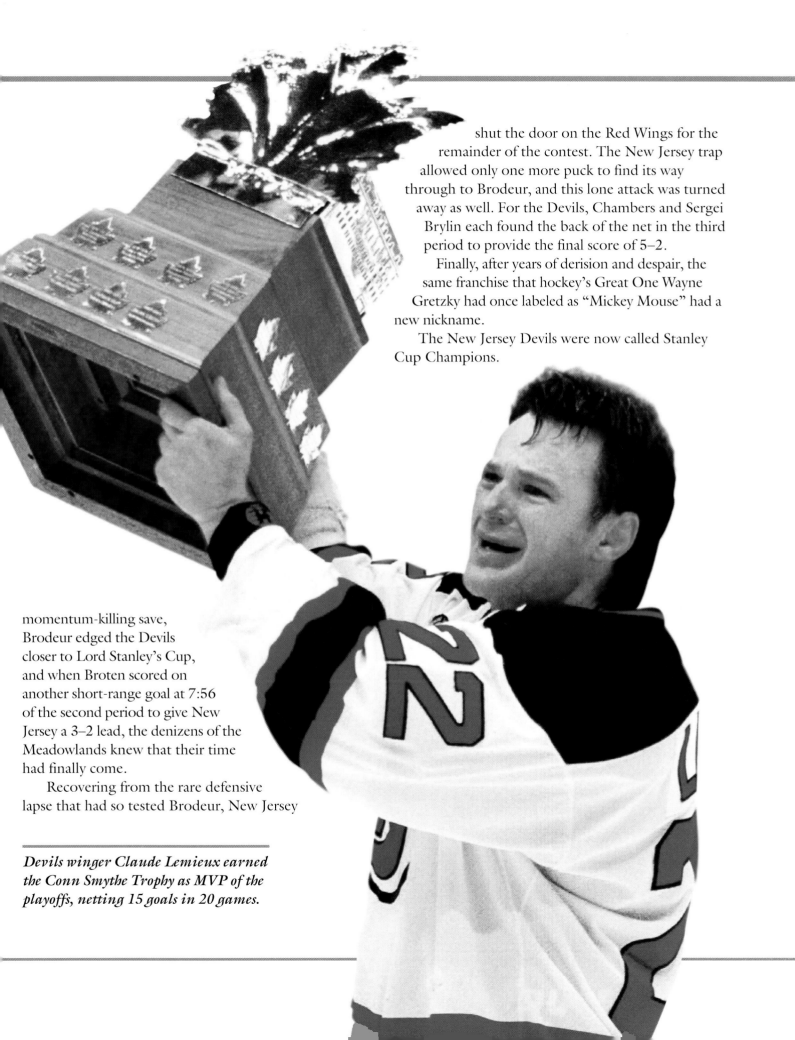

shut the door on the Red Wings for the remainder of the contest. The New Jersey trap allowed only one more puck to find its way through to Brodeur, and this lone attack was turned away as well. For the Devils, Chambers and Sergei Brylin each found the back of the net in the third period to provide the final score of 5–2.

Finally, after years of derision and despair, the same franchise that hockey's Great One Wayne Gretzky had once labeled as "Mickey Mouse" had a new nickname.

The New Jersey Devils were now called Stanley Cup Champions.

momentum-killing save, Brodeur edged the Devils closer to Lord Stanley's Cup, and when Broten scored on another short-range goal at 7:56 of the second period to give New Jersey a 3–2 lead, the denizens of the Meadowlands knew that their time had finally come.

Recovering from the rare defensive lapse that had so tested Brodeur, New Jersey

Devils winger Claude Lemieux earned the Conn Smythe Trophy as MVP of the playoffs, netting 15 goals in 20 games.

Chapter Forty-three

Lasse Viren:
The Finns Are Flying Again

Summer Olympics, 10,000 Meters Final, Munich, Germany, September 3, 1972

I t is cold in Finland. So cold, even the Finns—a breed accustomed to the Arctic winters—can't stay warm, at least not when it comes to track and field. In short, most track fans assumed that the Finns' glory days were long over.

In April of 1966 Arthur Lydiard arrived there to access the situation. The New Zealand distance coach, reputed to be the best in the world, arrived in Karhula on a cool spring day, cool that is for early spring in northern Scandinavia—15 degrees below zero.

The visiting coach led 28 promising Finnish track athletes on a 25-kilometer run. As he glanced over his shoulder, his eyes beheld a revolting sight—only *two* runners had stayed with him. The other 26 were back at the clubhouse drinking coffee and warming themselves in the sauna.

A Finnish coach told Lydiard, "Well, you've seen it for yourself."

Lydiard's assessment was quick and succinct—the Finns had become soft; they had no *sizu* as they say in Finland, or "guts," the nearest English translation.

It wasn't surprising that as they entered the 1972 Munich Summer Games, Finland had not captured a single gold medal in distance running since the 1936 Games. Nineteen thirty-six culminated the glory days of the 1920s when Paavo Nurmi conquered any opponent who dared walk onto the same track. Finland craved the arrival of another such legend, someone who could hoist the hopes and dreams of the nation renowned for their distance running.

It wasn't long after the Kurhula incident that the coach met Finnish distance runner Lasse Viren, then on the A-grade team (for competitors under age eighteen). Like others of his ilk, Viren had a dream, a dual dream: becoming a national hero—and, closely related to it, to be awarded stipends so he could leave the brutal Finnish winters and train in warm weather. Viren didn't want to be like the typical aspiring Finnish runner, who simply ceased training in the cold months.

It was Lydiard who changed Viren's dream, at least the second part of it. The coach told everyone, including the press, "These young men were not hard like their forefathers and that if they wanted to

Dick Quax and Klaus-Peter Hildenbrand failed to catch Lasse Viren in the 10,000 meters four years later in Montreal, where the fleet Finn won two more distance goals.

be good runners, they would have to get out and train in the winter." The press gave his advice abundant coverage.

Lydiard adopted the Finns' outer track uniform to keep out the cold air, running with a cushion of warm air between the suit and the body. The zipper was used as a makeshift thermostat.

Some of the more accomplished Finnish runners didn't go for the program: Jouko Kuha, for one, whose habit was training in the winter in exotic climes—Majorca, the Canary Islands, and Brazil among them. But his career only got so far, having set a world record, but never having won an Olympic or European medal. Though Kuha was quick to reject Lydiard's advice, at least one young runner took the coach to heart, Viren.

Viren opted to train in winter in his frozen homeland, sometimes finding reindeer trails to run on. On some days, he'd run completely out of Finland, crossing over into the bordering Soviet Union. His workouts were relentless, and the cold winters merely meant more clothing, never less training.

By age 23 he would resurrect the phrase "Flying Finns" as Finnish distance men were known during their heyday from 1912 to 1936, a period in which the Finns took 24 Olympic championships and dominated the world. Finland's fall from grace coincided with Russia's 1939 invasion and the war that followed. During its aftermath Finland had not been able to recover.

Viren would have three chances to prove his worthiness for comparisons to the mystical Nurmi and distance runners past. He was entered in the 5,000 and 10,000 meters and the marathon. Just one race into the sequence, Viren's legacy would be established forever.

The 10,000 meters is a grueling test of endurance and speed. The contestants race around a track for close to 30 minutes and often sprint to the finish. The Munich Games brought forth an esteemed field for the 10,000 meters final after 18 runners had bested Billy Mills's Olympic record of 28:24.4 (set in 1964 Tokyo Games) in the qualifying heats.

Viren brought an unknown commodity to the international field. He'd finished 17th in the previous year's 10,000 meters final during the European Championships held in Helsinki. Several weeks prior to the Olympics he'd improved his 10,000 time to 27:52.4—a Finnish national

Even after following his 10,000-meter victory with another gold medal in the 5,000, Finland's Lasse Viren found the strength to raise his arms in triumph.

record—and he'd set a world record in the obscure two-mile run with a time of 8:14. The hopes of Finland were fueled, but nobody considered Viren the favorite, not in a field with American distance icon Frank Shorter and Miruts Yifter of Ethiopia. Viren just plain lacked experience.

Based on the preliminary 10,000 meter races, all expected a blistering final. And from the outset, the forecast appeared to be an accurate one. Briton Dave Bedford led the first lap, posting a time of 59.9. Despite Bedford's rabbit start—which saw the first mile run in 4:15—he couldn't shake his competitors, which included Yifter, Emiel Puttemans of Belgium, Mariano Haro of Spain, Shorter, and Viren. The leading pack passed the two-mile mark in 8:44, an early, though unreliable, indication that a world record might be in the cards.

In an instant the entire complexion of the race changed. Just prior to reaching the halfway point, Viren realized he was too close to Puttemans and raised an arm for balance. The maneuver slowed Viren, making him a hazard for Shorter.

"When Viren lost his balance, I was positioned behind and outside of him," Shorter told *Runners World* magazine. "As he backed toward me, I instinctively extended my left hand, to keep him from hitting me. I knew he was going down. I wanted to be able to block him so our legs wouldn't tangle. But we never actually touched."

Shorter managed to avoid a collision, but others were not so fortunate.

Suddenly Viren tripped. As he went down, his unstable legs crossed paths with Tunisia's Mohamed Gammoudi, the bronze medalist in the 10,000 at the 1968 Mexico Games. The two went reeling into the infield. Despite the accident, the leading pack didn't break stride. Viren and Gammoudi remained dazed...and *down*.

Viren got to his feet first; Gammoudi followed. Both were seemingly out of the race, yet amazingly they gave chase to catch the pack. Miraculously, in less than half a lap, Viren caught the leaders. Young and inexperienced, the Finn just didn't know he was supposed to be finished, nor did he know that the extra energy he exerted making up for his fall would ultimately cause his leg muscles to fail. The 44-year-old Gammoudi understood the reality. He dropped out.

But young Viren had the audacity to believe he was back in contention.

"When I'd seen him before the race, Viren had the attitude of a man who would win," Shorter said. "Once he fell, I think he realized immediately that it did not cost him that much."

By the 6,000 meters mark, Viren bounded to the front of the pack, but the race was hardly over. The lead seesawed between Viren and Yifter. Bedford dropped way behind the leading pack by 8,000 meters, while Shorter, Haro, Puttemans, and Viren remained grouped together, cautiously awaiting any kind of move.

Undaunted, Haro surged to the lead with two laps remaining, but Viren was staying right with him. In a gutsy move, Viren went for the lead early and with 600 meters remaining he got there. When the bell sounded for the final lap, front-runner Viren had a three-meter lead over Puttemans and Yifter trailed by 10. Approaching the final turn, Viren kicked into overdrive with Puttmans on his shoulder. But Viren refused to lose, running the final lap in 56.4 seconds en route to winning the gold medal with a time of 27:38.4, good enough to break Ron Clarke's world record. He had done it, the gold was his, and the Finns were once again flying.

When Viren took his victory lap he was joined by an ecstatic group of his countrymen waving Finland's flag. Before the '72 Games were complete, Viren would add a gold medal in the 5,000 meters, completing the rare "5 and 10 double."

There's more, if you can believe it. The day after his victory in the 5,000, Viren, on a whim, decided to try his hand at the Marathon, a race he'd never competed in. The judges allowed him to enter the competition and, incredibly, the Finn placed fifth, two spots behind the bronze medalist.

Chapter Forty-four

Goran Ivanisevic: The Crazy Croat

Wimbledon Men's Singles Final, London, England, July 4, 2001

Looking more like Dracula than an athlete, Goran Ivanisevic sports some high-profile tattoos. There is a rose on his left shoulder; the right one bears a shark, representing the wild man's self-proclaimed split personality. Which side will come out at the Wimbledon finals no one knows for sure. Ivanisevic only assured everyone, "It's under control."

Uncertainty and unpredictability are the Croatian's hallmarks, but a more dependable measure of what's to come seemed to be already written. Before today, the train carrying the "Crazy Croat's" tennis career seemed to have pulled into the station for the final time.

Ivanisevic, a 125-to-1 shot at this year's Wimbledon, had accomplished a lot in his career. Twenty-one titles for starters, and reaching the finals at Wimbledon three previous times, having lost once to Andre Agassi in 1992 and twice to Pete Sampras, in 1994 and 1998. Though for seven years he held the rank of No. 2 player in the world, he'd fallen to the rank of 125th and didn't appear capable of getting his game back together. The previous November, Ivanisevic had to withdraw from a tournament after demolishing all of his rackets in a raging outburst. Three weeks before, the madman of the Balkans hit bottom when he lost to little known Italian veteran Cristiano Caratti.

But how much history would factor into the final

no one knew. If the specters of his convoluted past reincarnated, his dreams would be blown away like autumn leaves in a gust of wind.

A few days earlier, most tennis fans regarded the veteran from Croatia as not even being fit to play at the 2001 Wimbledon. He'd lucked out just getting in—the All England Club extended him a wildcard invitation for past excellence at Wimbledon.

To get to the final he had to nurse a sore shoulder, despite which, the Croat had made quick work of his first three opponents. Sweden's Fredrik Jonsson lost to him 6–4, 6–4, 6–4 in the first round; Spain's Carlos Moya lost 6–7, 6–3, 6–4, 6–4, which earned Goran a spot against up-and-coming Andy Roddick of the United States, a match heralded in England as "All-American Boy Faces Crazy Croat."

Goran's booming serve dismantled Roddick with 41 aces—five short of his Wimbledon record and eight shy of Richard Krajicek's world record. Most likely both records would have been shattered had Ivanisevic not kept his victory to four sets, winning 7–6, 7–5, 3–6, 6–3 to send the young American packing.

Ivanisevic sank to the ground in jubilation after defeating Patrick Rafter, but fatigue could easily have had a similar effect after a marathon fifth set that wound up 9–7.

He continued to march through the field. Britain's Greg Rusedski was finished off in three sets; Russia's Marat Safin required four. But Britain's Tim Henman, who many said would end the Croat's fairy tale when they met in the semifinals, was no wham-bam-send-on-the-next-guy cinch. Their match was, by all accounts, one of the most bizarre semifinals in all of tennis.

It started off normal enough. Ivanisevic took the first set from Henman 7–5, and then the Brit won a second set tiebreaker 8–6 to even the match. Henman went up 2–1 with a 6–0 win in the third set. By now, many were sure that Wimbledon was the Croat's curse, as sure as the Bambino was the Boston Red Sox's.

Then the gods cast their benevolent eyes on Ivanisevic. Seemingly ready to fall again, Ivanisevic got a little help from up above...and it came in biblical proportions. The heavens literally opened up, in the form of a match-delaying rainstorm, which eventually extended the match to three days (that's no typographical error, *three days!*). Upon returning to the dampened grass of Centre Court, Ivanisevic beat Henman in the fourth-set tiebreaker 7–5 and took the fifth set 6–3.

Goran Ivanisevic had reached the final for the *fourth time* in his career.

Australia's Patrick Rafter would be his opponent, an adversary with some

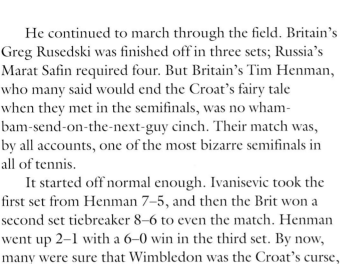

Goran Ivanisevic secured a Wimbledon trophy after three previous unsuccessful trips to the final.

powerful baggage—the Aussie had lost in the final the previous year and he was back to right the wrong. Adding to the Croat's challenge, Rafter had been looking formidable as he earned this year's reprieve. Some of his fans who came from Australia even slept on the lawn, maintaining a vigil.

Ivanisevic wasn't exactly in dreamland either. "Maybe two hours I slept," Ivanisevic said. "I woke up 1:30 in the morning. I thought, 'It's 9 o'clock.' I see 1:30. Okay, let's go back to sleep…I was so nervous."

Centre Court had become a cauldron of support for the sentimental favorite from Croatia, but the Australian fans enthusiastically waved their country's flag in support of Rafter. Each cheering section shouted the other down with every close call.

Adding drama to the event was Ken Rosewall's record of failed Wimbledon attempts. If Ivanisevic lost, he would tie Rosewall for the most losses in a Wimbledon final. "I just heard that ten minutes before I went on the court," Ivanisevic said.

Determined not to set such a dubious record, Ivanisevic took two of the first three sets before having to face a final hurdle after Rafter throttled him 6–2 in the fourth set. Ivanisevic began to talk to himself.

"I said, 'This is your last chance, you're going to win it, you just have to keep cool, you can't afford to be crazy in a Wimbledon final,'" he said.

The self-proclaimed crazy became cool as a cucumber. He sat two points from defeat serving at 6–7, love–30 in the fifth set. Managing to recover from the deficit, he broke Rafter in the next game with a forehand service-return winner. The fifth set went six more games, making it the longest fifth set in the tournament's history.

In the final game, Ivanisevic blew three match points—two through double-faults.

The air was thick with suspense now. Either one of the biggest upsets in tennis history would happen within seconds, or one of the biggest disappointments.

Unbeknown to Ivanisevic, there was trauma in the stands, a calamity rivaling the dash of a lifetime dream come true. At that very moment, Ivanisevic's 58-year-old father, Srdjan, a university lecturer, was suffering

In pain and fearful for his life, his father watched his son lob the ball in the air and mightily swing his racquet.

chest pains. Having just had a heart bypass and told by his doctor to avoid stress, the elder Ivanisevic was convinced he was going to die now, right there in the crowd of anxious fans whose every eye was fixed on his son attempting to make sports history.

As Rafter awaited Ivanisevic's serve for the match point and the championship, the elder Ivanisevic prayed, not for his life, but for a little time, even seconds would be enough. At all costs, he had to keep from passing out or keeling over, knowing full well there would be bedlam in the stands, breaking his son's concentration and dashing his dream of being the first wildcard to win Wimbledon.

"I knew it was OK to die *after* the match but not during it," he told himself.

In pain and fearful for his life, his father watched his son lob the ball in the air and mightily swing his racquet.

In a fraction of a second that must have seemed like a lifetime to the Ivanisevics, the ball made contact with his strings. Two lives now hung in the balance as the ball sailed over the net. Rafter lurched forward to return the serve.

With a mighty forehand the Australian smashed the return…*into the net!*

The Crazy Croat had won Wimbledon.

The new champion leaped into the stands and clambered through rows of seats to throw his arms around his father. Minutes later, pressing the Wimbledon trophy to his lips, he gazed back into the stands at his father, whose eyes were swelling with tears. Through his pain, Srdjan's smile said it all: His son had just become the first Croatian to win Wimbledon.

Chapter Forty-five

Tenley Albright:
America's First Ice Princess

Winter Olympics, Women's Figure Skating Final
Cortina, Italy, February 3, 1956

Like a surgeon's scalpel, the blade of Tenley Albright's left skate sliced through the three layers of her right boot, ripping open a vein and scraping the bone at her ankle joint. A deep, searing pain seized the pretty, 21-year-old figure skater as she lay on the ice at Cortina's outdoor rink, the fabled Dolomites of northern Italy looming behind her. You couldn't ask for a more picturesque setting for the 1956 Winter Olympics figure skating competition, but at the moment, Cortina's beauty was understandably lost on Albright. Two weeks before the Olympics, America's best hope for its first gold medal in women's figure skating was being helped off the ice. Given the debilitating severity of her injuries, it seemed highly doubtful that she would be able to skate, let alone be well enough to win the event.

A doctor's daughter on leave from premed studies at Radcliffe College, Albright harbored no illusions about the extent of her injuries. Although it cheered Albright to know that her father was en route from Massachusetts, she was pragmatic about her chances for a full recovery before the competition began. With its daring flourishes and acrobatic leaps choreographed to

Offenbach's *Tales of Hoffman*, Albright's free skate program was immensely challenging, both physically and artistically. The judges would be none too impressed if she favored her right ankle or grimaced in pain throughout the three-minute program.

Albright knew that her injuries would eventually heal and that she'd skate again. There had been no such certainty ten years earlier, however, when she had been stricken with polio. At eleven, the vivacious and athletic little girl had been confined to her bed, like the thousands of other childhood victims of the polio epidemic. In 1946, the Salk Vaccine was still eight years away, so doctors had relied on the "Sister Kenny treatment" to soothe Albright's pain and relax her constricted muscles. Soft wool cloths were soaked in hot water, wrung dry of excess water and tightly wrapped around her legs. The low-tech brainchild of an Australian bush nurse, the Sister Kenny treatment had certainly alleviated Albright's suffering, but it had only been the first step in a long, arduous recuperation. What had once been effortless now required intense concentration and physical stamina that would tax someone twice her age.

Slowly, with uncommon patience and a high toler-

Albright gained fame with her gold medal skate in one of the most inspiring settings anywhere,
an outdoor ice sheet in Cortina, Italy, in the shadow of the Dolomites.

ance for pain, Albright had regained the full use of her legs and resumed skating. Four months later, she won the Eastern Junior United States Ladies Figure Skating

competition. By 1956, she had won six consecutive United States women's singles titles, the world championship, *and* a silver medal at the 1952 Winter Olympics

THE LONG TRADITION OF AMERICAN GOLD

Prior to Tenley Albright's gold medal win at the 1956 Winter Olympics, American women figure skaters had been the proverbial bridesmaids in this event. European skaters, most notably Sonja Henie of Norway (and later Hollywood), dominated the competition until Albright and Carol Heiss took the gold and silver, respectively, at Cortina D'Ampezzo, Italy. While Albright retired shortly after her Olympic win to resume her premed studies at Radcliffe, Heiss would subsequently win the gold medal at 1960's Winter Games in Squaw Valley, California.

In an event that probably generated more buzz than any other in Olympic competition, the 1994 "Tonya & Nancy" showdown at Lillehammer stands as the most notorious scandal in recent Olympic history. Despite being knee-capped by a metal-baton wielding associate of Tonya Harding's husband, Nancy Kerrigan recovered to skate her way to a silver medal. The disgraced Harding finished 10th.

Since 1956, fourteen Americans have won medals in women's figure skating. Here are the medalists, in chronological order.

YEAR	SKATER	SITE	MEDAL
1956	Tenley Albright	Cortina D'Ampezzo, Italy	Gold
1956	Carol Heiss	Cortina D'Ampezzo, Italy	Silver
1960	Carol Heiss	Squaw Valley, California	Gold
1960	Barbara Roles	Squaw Valley, California	Bronze
1968	Peggy Fleming	Grenoble, France	Gold
1972	Janet Lynn	Sapporo, Japan	Bronze
1976	Dorothy Hamill	Innsbruck, Austria	Gold
1980	Linda Fratianne	Lake Placid, New York	Silver
1984	Rosalyn Summers	Sarajevo, Yugoslavia	Silver
1988	Debi Thomas	Calgary, Alberta, Canada	Bronze
1992	Kristi Yamaguchi	Albertville, France	Gold
1992	Nancy Kerrigan	Albertville, France	Bronze
1994	Nancy Kerrigan	Lillehammer, Norway	Silver
1998	Tara Lipinski	Nagano, Japan	Gold
1998	Michelle Kwan	Nagano, Japan	Silver
2002	Sarah Hughes	Salt Lake City, Utah	Gold
2002	Michelle Kwan	Salt Lake City, Utah	Bronze

Albright (left) *settled for second in the 1956 World Championships in Garmisch, Germany. She congratulated winner Carol Heiss* (center) *and bronze medalist Ingrid Wendl.*

fellow American Carol Heiss and Austrian Ingrid Wendl, then Dr. Albright was going to make sure that she had the best medical care available.

As expected, the surgery went smoothly. When the competition began days later, Albright was back on the ice, performing with a grace belying the fact that she was still in a considerable amount of pain. At times, the stress on her right ankle must have been unbearable, yet Albright bore it stoically through the compulsories and short programs. The true test would come in the free skate program.

Spectators circled Cortina's outdoor rink to watch Albright perform. As the first few bars of Offenbach's operatic score poured from the speakers, Albright gave herself over to the lushly romantic and dramatic music. There was no sign of pain or anxiety in the opening moments of her boldly skated program—just breath-taking assurance and athleticism. Yet for the spectators familiar with the 1951 film version of *Tales of Hoffman*, the injured skater's choice of music had acquired an eerie relevance. For in this full-length cinematic ballet inspired by Offenbach's opera, the hero falls in love with a mechanical ballerina named, oddly enough, Olympia. The exquisite creation of a magician, Olympia bewitches the hero with her sylphlike grace, only to spin faster and faster out of control before collapsing. Realists in the stands would have scoffed at drawing any parallel between Albright and this fictional character, but even they watched the plucky American skater nervously, tens-ing every time she landed her full weight on her right ankle. Would Albright's injured right ankle suddenly give way, shattering her confidence and ruining her gold medal chances, in a sad case of life imitating art?

Perhaps to assuage their own nerves, the spectators began humming along to the music halfway through Albright's program. It was an extraordinary display of support for Albright, who finished the program to thun-derous applause and 10 first-place scores from the 11 judges. Through an unforgettable combination of talent, artistry, and grit, Albright had dispelled any fears that she would suffer a collapse like that of her ballet counterpart. She was no Olympia—just an Olympic champion.

in Oslo. Watching her execute dazzlingly intricate jumps on the ice, you'd never believe that just ten years prior, Albright could not walk three steps unassisted.

Two days after Albright's fall in Cortina, her father arrived in the gorgeous mountain resort town to perform emergency surgery on his daughter's ankle. Normally, Dr. Hollis Albright would have refrained from treating a member of his own family, but that unwritten rule of medical ethics didn't apply here. There was simply too much at stake for him to entrust his daughter's care to an unknown doctor, far from home.

She had devoted the last ten years of her life to figure skating in tireless preparation for this opportu-nity. If she were to compete against her archrivals,

Chapter Forty-six

Laura Wilkinson: What's a Broken Foot Compared to a Broken Heart?

Summer Olympics, Women's Platform Diving
Sydney, Australia, September 24, 2000

aura Wilkinson stood on the 10-meter platform, waiting to be announced to the crowd. In a few seconds, the willowy Texan would make her next-to-last dive. It was one of those proverbial "stop and smell the roses" moments for the 23-year-old. From atop the board, she surveyed the spectators below until she located all that mattered in the world to her, perhaps as much as the gold medal itself— her family, her coach, and finally her teammates. With their faces imprinted on her mind's eye, she could now make what would be the most important dive of her life

This one would be no lead-pipe cinch—an inward 2 from the pike position—and if it wasn't just right, she would lose her tenuous hold on first place. No American woman had taken the gold medal in the 10-meter platform diving since 1964. Yet despite the tremendous pressure to end the 36-year drought in

Opposite: *The pressure of diving in the Olympics was nothing for Wilkinson, a former gymnast who had broken three bones in her right foot just months before the Sydney Games.*

Laura Wilkinson and her coach, Ken Armstrong, celebrated the first U.S. gold in 10-meter platform diving since 1964.

the event, Wilkinson appeared almost uncannily calm.

She knew what to do: "stay in the moment," breathe evenly, focus on positive imagery, and clear her mind. But how could she do that with a broken foot? Pain was the only thing she could think about.

Months earlier, Wilkinson had broken three bones in her right foot while executing somersaults on a mat during warmup activity. Since the U.S. Olympic Trials were then only two months away, she had elected to postpone surgery and deal with the pain. Under the watchful eye of coach Ken Armstrong, she had continued to train upward of six hours daily, wearing an ensemble of casts before finally having all of them removed just 10 weeks after her injury. Even though she had been freed of the cast, the pain in her foot remained constant. Simple things, like climbing the ladder to reach the platform, proved excruciating. The first time she had tried to climb the ladder following her injury, it had taken almost 10 minutes to reach the top. Doctors had fitted her with a protective shoe—actually a kayaker's boot—to cushion her injury, so she could climb the ladder free of pain. Upon reaching the top of the platform she would cast her shoe aside.

Armstrong believed the injury actually fueled Wilkinson with a sense of urgency. After she won the Olympic Trials in June, it was full speed ahead for the Olympics—even if she continued to labor with a broken foot.

Heady stuff for a former gymnast wearing a Speedo.

Until she was 15, Wilkinson had assumed that her future lay in gymnastics. But around that time, she came to the conclusion that she'd taken the sport as far as she could. A jock at heart, she had then tried every sport imaginable before falling in love with diving. Nothing compared to the sheer exhilaration of launching herself off the diving board into the water below, her lithe body slicing through the air like a missile toward its target.

Although most serious divers start training at a younger age, the teenager found that many of the muscles and skills she'd developed in gymnastics translated well to diving.

Wilkinson drew strength from her religious faith, which soothed her mental outlook and helped her deal with stress. Many times before a dive, she would recite her favorite biblical passage, Philippians 4:23: "The grace of the Lord Jesus Christ be with your spirit." She believed with all her heart that God was looking after her pursuit. Frankly, she'd need all the heavenly assistance *He* could spare to prevail against the top-flight competitors.

The biggest threat came from China. Indeed, the landscape of women's platform diving had changed drastically since the Chinese began pursuing the sport with an intensified diligence. From 1924 to 1956, U.S. women platform divers had claimed 17 of 21 available medals. Prior to the Sydney games, Chinese women divers had taken the gold medal in three of the last four Summer Olympics.

After the preliminaries of the Olympic platform diving, Wilkinson trailed by 40 points. Prior to her third dive of the competition, she stood in fifth place behind the insurmountable challenge brought forth by the Chinese divers. Specifically, the Houston native found herself trying to catch Sang Xue and Li Na, the latest Chinese divers to dominate the sport. Still, Wilkinson carried a sense of confidence.

"I had my best, toughest list of dives ever," Wilkinson said. "I thought it was possible, if I didn't miss a dive."

Wilkinson executed a solid reverse 2 tuck on her third dive, which brought four 9.5 scores and a very respectable total of 75.33. She then caught a break. Sang and Li tanked their dives, scoring 47.04 and 53.10 respectively. Suddenly, the American diver found herself in first place. Now all she had to do was keep from getting rattled, no easy prospect considering the dive required her to perform a maneuver similar to the one in which she broke her foot. During the preliminaries, she had botched the dive not once, but twice. Now, this very dive would determine whether she would win the gold medal.

Anticipating her takeoff, Wilkinson was replaying what Coach Armstrong had whispered to her moments earlier: "Do it for Hilary."

Hilary Grivich, a former national team gymnast,

Wilkinson flashed the smile of a gold medal winner who had beaten the odds.

had followed Wilkinson's same path by moving from the pommel horse to a diving board. Best friends, the pair had grown up together, attending the same high school and the same college. Then, three years before the 2000 Summer Olympics, Grivich had been killed in a car accident.

Never before had Armstrong mentioned her lost friend, but the effect on Wilkinson was profound, providing clarity and perspective. She smiled. Philippians 4:23 had been announced, and Hilary remained in her heart. The time had come to put aside all the pain and fear. She went for it.

It was perfect!

One dive remained, but the degree of difficulty paled in comparison to the dives she'd used to take and maintain the lead. Once again, she performed flawlessly and entered the water with barely a ripple, even though the pain in her broken foot was excruciating.

With her three straight nearly flawless dives, Wilkinson had left no room for a comeback from the dynamic Chinese duo. The injured Texan leapfrogged four of the world's finest divers to claim the gold medal.

Despite the pain, she never considered quitting. Succumbing to the agony would have dealt her a devastating blow and she knew it from the very outset of the pain. Simply put, after all her years of preparation, what's a broken foot compared to a broken heart?

Chapter Forty-seven

Dan Jansen: The Heartbreak Kid

Winter Olympics, 1,000 Meters Speed Skating Final
Lillehammer, Norway, February 18, 1994

The Hamar ice rink in Lillehammer, Norway, was a huge shell that looked remarkably like the upturned hull of an ancient Viking ship. Perhaps its architecture was no coincidence. Perhaps the ghost of a genuine Viking mariner of old was sending a message, and if he was, it surely would be directed at speed skater Dan Jansen, an experienced navigator in a storm. The young American would soon be navigating to save his very life. An athlete has to do that sometimes. With so many failed attempts to win Olympic gold, it was now coming down to one last chance—one final race.

Jansen's talent was never in question. In fact, these 1994 Olympic games in Lillehammer were the fourth of his career. Unfortunately, success eluded him at every turn and he became known as the "heartbreak kid" of the Winter Olympics.

The youngest of nine children, Jansen practically grew up on the ice. His family home was a block away from the outdoor speed skating rink in West Allis, Wisconsin, where he donned his first pair of skates at four. He was winning regional meets by age eight and national meets at 12. In 1984 he made the Olympic speed skating team headed for Sarajevo, Yugoslavia.

Jansen placed fourth in the 500-meter race at those Winter Games, missing the bronze medal by just sixteen hundredths of a second. While friends and fans mourned his near-miss of a medal, Jansen took pride in his accomplishment, savoring his standing as fourth best in the world. Little did he know, it was to be his best Olympic showing for the next decade.

Jansen quickly made his mark in the speed skating world, winning the 500- and 1,000-meter races at the 1986 World Cup Championships and taking top honors at the World Sprint Championships in 1988.

The Winter Olympics were held in Calgary that same year and expectations were high for Jansen to medal. But while Jansen was at the top of his form physically, he was near rock bottom emotionally. Who could blame him? He received word the morning of his first race that his sister Jane had just died of leukemia.

Knowing that she would want him to skate, Jansen took his place for the 500-meter race—and jumped to a false start. His second attempt began with a slow start and quickly deteriorated from there. Since speed skaters move at high speeds, slipping goes with the territory and most skaters catch themselves and go on. But a complete fall spells disaster. For Jansen, one of the worst days of his life suddenly got worse. Ten seconds into the race, his left foot went out from under him. He was unable to right himself and went careening across the ice, into another skater and hitting the pads surrounding the rink.

Still hurting four days later, Jansen lined up for the

1,000-meter race, dedicating it to his sister Jane. He started well, making it through 800 meters before the unthinkable happened. He caught an outer edge and went down. Jansen's second Olympics was over—and he never even crossed the finish line.

The 26-year-old Jansen trained harder than ever and went on to win first place at the 1992 World Cup leading up to the 1992 Olympics in Albertville, France. Almost as if he were

Jansen's skate in the 1,000 was virtually flawless—a stark change from his 500-meter performance days earlier.

After a 1,000-meter race he dedicated to his late sister, Jane, Jansen reacted to a world record time of 1 minute, 12.43 seconds.

jinxed, Jansen lost his balance in a turn. He narrowly missed a bronze medal in the 500 and finished a disappointing 26th in the 1,000.

With the 1994 Olympics just two years away Jansen sought advice from sports psychologist Jim Loehr, whose clientele included many other ill-fated athletes. Recognizing that Jansen was pinning his hopes on the 500-meter race, Loehr convinced him to appreciate the longer sprint and to approach it with a new strategy— and a new attitude.

As the Lillehammer Games approached, Jansen was once again in top form. *Time* magazine dubbed him "the greatest sprinter on long blades in the last decade."

Heavily favored to win the 500, Jansen started fast, going strong into the backstretch. Then on the final turn, he lost control of his left skate, touching his hand to the ice to steady himself. On a longer race, the misstep might not have mattered, but in such a short race, it made a world of difference. Jansen came in a disappointing eighth.

So here it was. His career came down to one final sprint. Never his best event, the 1,000-meter race was Jansen's last hope for gold.

During warmups, Jansen skated around that giant hull of an arena, feeling much like the ancient mariner with one squall left to conquer. Trying to shake a feeling that something was not quite right, Jansen decided he needed to feel more fatigued. He hit the stationary bike for 15 minutes and followed up with a short jog.

Commentator Eric Heiden, a former gold medalist himself, noted that as many as 10 skaters had a chance to win this race. Jansen's top competition was Igor Zhelezovsky of Belarus and Sergei Klevchenya of Russia. Both skated in the first pair, posting medal-worthy times of 1:12.72 and 1:12.85.

Going in the fourth pair, Jansen felt a sudden jolt of energy right before the gun signified the start of the

His first Olympic gold medal and thoughts of his sister made Jansen's trip to the stand more emotional than most.

୨ରେ

During warmups, Jansen skated around that giant hull of an arena, feeling much like the ancient mariner with one squall left to conquer.

୨ରେ

race. "I knew I was ready," he later said in his auto-biography. And he was. Jansen was paired with Junichi Inoue of Japan and both skaters came out fast. Jansen reached the 200-meter mark with a competitive time of 16.71. When the skaters changed lanes at the 400-meter point, he crossed over and got a brief boost by riding Inoue's slipstream going into the turn.

Jansen was skating smoothly, maintaining an even rhythm as he went into his second-to-last turn, only 300 meters from the finish, where Klevchenya almost went down earlier. Hugging the inner lane, the turns are tighter and the force seems greater—both of which increase the risk of falling. And Jansen did slip—but briefly. The crowd gasped as his hand grazed the ice. He lost two or three hundredths of a second, but he stayed calm. When his coach held up a card that read 26.5—his time for the first 400 meters—Jansen knew he was on pace for a medal, and after the final turn, he let loose on the last 50 meters. As he crossed the finish line, the noise in the arena was deafening. The crowd saw the time before he did...1:12.43—good enough for a gold medal *and* a new world record.

Jansen skated a much photographed victory lap with his seven-month-old daughter in front of an emotional crowd. A lot of hard work and a few highly publicized failures were now behind him. He had finally conquered his demons, and had tasted success. It was time to come home.

Chapter Forty-eight

Sarah Hughes: The Fend-for-Herself Ice Princess

Winter Olympics, Women's Figure Skating Final
Salt Lake City, Utah, February 19, 2002

ℒℴℂ

The night before her final program, Sarah Hughes donned her good luck charm, an old T-shirt given to her by Peggy Fleming, the gold medalist from the '68 Olympics.
Superstitious, yes, but on the eve of an event for which you've been preparing for a lifetime, you just can't take any foolish chances. This was as important as lacing up your skates "just so."

Sarah Hughes had been lacing up her skates since age three. It was requisite to race her brothers on the backyard rink built by her father at their home in Great Neck, New York. The future Olympian also had to make her own arrangements to get to practice, a consequence of her mother, Amy's, long battle with cancer beginning when Sarah was 12.

By then, the fend-for-herself ice princess won the U.S. junior figure skating championships and had subsequently evolved into an independent sort, not the usual thing for the daughter of an Ivy League–educated attorney with six children.

"I started skating because I love to skate—and I love to compete," Hughes will tell you. It probably didn't hurt that her father was a skater too. John

A teenager from Great Neck, Hughes wore a gold medal around her own neck after her first Olympics.

Hughes played hockey at Cornell University and had even tried out for the Toronto Maple Leafs.

Even as a young child Sarah had a wish that she

With the bulk of the pressure on the likes of Michelle Kwan and Irina Slutskaya, American Sarah Hughes came through with the performance of her life.

A DAY IN THE LIFE OF SARAH

What does it take to be a champion? In Sarah Hughes's case, becoming a champion figure skater required a lot of work. For two and a half years leading up to her winning the gold medal at the 2002 Winter Olympics in Salt Lake City, Hughes's five-day-a-week training regimen was very rigorous.

The day began by piling into the car with her mother, Amy, who drove Sarah to the skating rink.

Once on the ice, Sarah went about her paces from 10:45 to 11:45 before taking a light lunch.

After the half-hour break, she returned to the ice to skate from 12:15 to 1:45. (Saturdays she limited herself to a 90-minute workout.)

Following her set daily regimen Sarah engaged in regular weight and conditioning drills with a private trainer.

Sarah also took a Pilates class, a low-impact stretching and strengthening system.

Of course, Sarah went to school every day too, often getting special attention to fit with her training, which obviously interfered with regular classes.

Evenings were for homework. She did enough of it to maintain an A average, and is currently a student at prestigious Yale.

ice, a joy that seemed to translate into consistency that could be plotted like a graph showing the steady progress toward achieving a goal.

At age 13 she finished fourth in the nationals; at age 14, she finished third; at age 15, she finished second. When she made the U.S. Olympic team at age 16 she had never won a U.S. or world senior championship. In fact, even qualifying for Team USA was precarious. At the trials, at which she finished third, she failed to complete a scheduled triple Salchow–triple loop combination, which kept her

expressed more than once: "My dream is to be in the Olympics and get a gold medal. I can't wait for that to happen." With that goal at an early age, she plotted a course few children dare to make the blueprint of their youth.

Throughout the process Hughes had continued to display a rarely seen joy going about her paces on the

from finishing ahead of Michelle Kwan and Sasha Cohen. But it earned her a spot on the 2002 Winter Olympic team where she'd compete with the world's best in Salt Lake City.

Satisfaction from making the team never translated to complacency. Hughes turned to her coach, Robin Wagner, to help concoct a plan to win the Olympic gold.

The plan involved the recognition that she already had the basic ingredients of an Olympic-caliber figure skater—elegance coupled with athleticism. But that wasn't enough even though she had remarkable ability to execute exceptionally clean jumps without landing on her backside…and she made few mistakes overall. *But there was nothing eye-catching about her performance*. She simply lacked glitz. All of which was about to change when she met Alex Goldstein.

Goldstein, a recognized expert in editing music for figure skaters, would tweak the soundtrack for Hughes's long program that Coach Wagner had helped her select. Originally the music made a smart transition from Ravel's *Daphnis and Chloe* to Rachmaninoff's Piano Concerto No. 2 for the final 90 seconds of the four-minute program. After a little snip or two here and a little cut there, Rachmaninoff got his walking papers and they decided to let Ravel continue to play, a progression moving from flutes and violins to attention-grabbing cymbal crashes near the end. *That's glitz!*

Accompanying the change in music was a speed injection into the choreography of Hughes's program, a new, shorter hairdo, and several options for the dress she would wear; all trimmings to highlight her skating ability. Straight ahead, the short program waited.

Fighting off a case of backstage jitters, Hughes finished the short program in fourth place. Most of her problems stemmed from technical flaws in her jumping. When executing a triple Lutz, she took off from the wrong edge of her skate, which led to the judges teeing off on her when calculating her technical marks.

Hughes pulled off seven triple jumps in her winning skate.

She would be the second of the final six skaters to take the ice at the Salt Lake Ice Center. She had not given up on the idea of winning a gold medal, but the chances looked remote for leapfrogging pre-Olympic favorites Michelle Kwan of the United States and Irina Slutskaya of Russia, in addition to teammate Sasha Cohen, who had finished in front of Hughes at the nationals. Perhaps this sense of not being able to better her plight helped soothe her nerves. What did she have to lose, save the butterflies in her stomach?

Her brilliance on the ice was magnificently amplified by the riveting, Goldstein-inspired music that dazzled the crowd as she passionately danced to each frolicsome passage. In the process she perfectly executed seven triple jumps, five in combination. So fine were her triple-triples that Hughes let out a giddy shriek when she finished the last one of two in her program.

Hughes's program, though spectacular, had merely signaled the beginning of a night of figure skating. Much suspense remained for the outcome of the competition.

When Cohen flopped, Hughes knew she had at least a bronze. Kwan then faltered with two major errors in a lackluster program. Finally, Slutskaya did nothing to curry the favor of the judges.

"Sarah was able, with a good free-skate, to put a little pressure on the girls coming after her," Wagner said. "We were really just thinking about getting the bronze. I know Irina and Michelle are both strong competitors, very strong-willed, and I think we both felt they'd put out fairly good performances."

The sum total was that the competitors, who followed Sarah, just couldn't one-up her performance and Sarah's score subsequently shot from fourth to first place. She was now the gold medalist. The young woman from Great Neck had nailed the biggest performance of her life and the crowd adorned her with flowers and cheers. Wagner met Hughes when she stepped off the ice and turned her around to face the crowd so she could bask in the magnificent canvas she had painted on the ice.

Who knows? Perhaps that T-shirt from Peggy Fleming really did have magical powers.

Chapter Forty-nine

Jim Morris:
The Middle-Aged Rookie

Texas Rangers vs. Tampa Bay Devil Rays
The Ballpark, Arlington, Texas, September 18, 1999

Texas can be hot in summer. Hotter than a two-dollar pistol. And today was one of those days, a sweltering June afternoon, right around 100 degrees.

But it was the moment of truth for the soon-to-be old man of baseball rookies, 35-year-old Jimmy Morris. Because his wife was at work that day, Morris arrived at a Tampa Bay Devil Rays tryout in Brownwood, Texas, with three kids and a stroller. Crusty scout Doug Gassaway, who had just watched 70 so-called ballplayers while away his time in the agonizing heat, had little patience with Morris, an aspiring pitcher, who was showing his age now in the Texas heat.

"I looked at him and said, 'C'mon, Jimmy, I'm hot and I'm tired,'" Gassaway told the *Tampa Tribune.* "Let's get this over with so I can go home."

Morris, his hair thinning and sporting a middle-aged

Opposite: *His second major-league pitch gave Morris an 0-2 edge in the count against the Rangers' Royce Clayton. His next delivery was strike three.*

Morris became baseball's oldest rookie since 1970, earning his way to the big leagues as a 35-year-old former high school coach and teacher.

paunch, unleashed his first pitch…at 94 mph. Gassaway couldn't believe it. He asked the guy next to him if the radar gun was broken. Morris then upped the next pitch to 96 mph. Then 95. Then 12 straight at 98. Said Morris: "A scout came up after I was finished and said, 'Do you know you were throwing 98?' I was shocked."

Gassaway had never seen anything like it. By the time Morris lugged his kids back home, messages lit up his answering machine: The Devil Rays wanted to see him pitch again in two days. Morris had suddenly become a blue-chip baseball prospect—again.

For Morris, the son of a Navy officer who moved his family from base to base, life often had been a struggle. He found solace on the ballfields, where he could boom punts 50 yards and fire whistling fastballs. While pitching in junior college in 1983, he was drafted by the Milwaukee Brewers in the first round. His big-league dream, however, eroded with each passing season. Meager wages, endless bus rides, major elbow surgery, and a blown shoulder caused him to hang 'em up in 1987.

After baseball, Morris and his wife, Lorri, settled in San Angelo, Texas. While Lorri worked in the admissions office at Angelo State University, Jim took college classes and worked for the Texas Youth Commission, transporting juvenile offenders around the state. He also regained his arm strength by throwing batting practice to the Howard Payne University baseball team.

Morris was so impressive that the Chicago White Sox gave him another shot, assigning him to Class A for 1989. Jimmy was elated to be back in uniform, but his 90-mph fastball wasn't good enough. His pitches came in fat, and the young sluggers teed off. Morris retired, again, after the season.

With baseball seemingly out of his system, Morris donned football pads for Angelo State, for whom he led the NCAA Division II in punting. Over time, Lorri gave birth to three children while Jimmy got a job teaching science at Reagan County High School in Big Lake, Texas.

In 1999 Morris took over the Reagan County High School baseball team, and often inspired his players with talks about chasing their dreams. Morris's players, impressed by his still smokin' fastball, told their coach that he should pursue his dream too. They made him a deal: If they won their district championship, he would try out for a major league team. He agreed, and they won the title, so on June 19, 1999, Morris trudged with his three children to the tryout at Howard Payne University.

Gassaway signed the 35-year-old "prospect" to a professional contract. First, Morris went to a rehab camp "to work off all the Famous Amos cookies," he said. He then was off to Double-A Orlando, while Lorri—still working full-time—stayed with the kids. Recalled Morris: "There were times when I said, 'What are you doing? You have a wife and kids at home—you must have a screw loose.'"

However, after just three games and a 1.80 ERA for Orlando, Morris was promoted to Triple-A Durham to play out the season. He pitched 18 games with mixed results, and after the last game he packed his truck to go back to Texas…until Durham manager Bill Evers called him into his office. The Devil Rays had phoned, he told Morris. He was going to The Show, with his first game against the Texas Rangers on September 18.

Lorri and the kids drove for four hours to The Ballpark in Arlington, Texas. "I already got my tears out when I saw him in the bullpen," Lorri told the *Tampa Tribune*. "He looked so happy in his uniform and on the field, that smile on his face."

With the Rangers leading by a big margin and the Devil Rays light-years out of the pennant race, manager Larry Rothschild called Morris's number with two outs in the eighth inning. "Larry and [catcher] John Flaherty were talking to me on the mound," Morris said, "and I had no idea what they were saying to me, because I'm fulfilling my dream in front of 45,000 people."

Morris faced only one batter, All-Star Royce Clayton. Throwing nothing but smoke, he got ahead 0-2. Morris recalled: "I remember thinking, 'He's late.' I can do this. Next pitch, chest-high fastball—they ring him up. Strike three!"

That night, back in his hotel room, Jim ordered pizza for everyone. Still riding a high, two nights later, he outgunned the Anaheim Angels, setting down sluggers Jim Edmonds, Mo Vaughn, and Tim Salmon in succession. In five games in 1999, Morris

After Jim Morris's major league debut in 1999, representatives from numerous motion picture studios contacted the Devil Rays about movie rights. The Walt Disney Company won out, and by spring training 2002 *The Rookie* was in theaters nationwide.

The film is, more or less, an accurate portrayal of Morris's rise to glory. Even the most amazing occurrences—such as the scout checking the radar gun for damage after Jim recorded 98-mph readings—really happened. Still, some of the events, for dramatic or practical reasons, were fudged.

First of all, the role of Morris was played not by a fuzzy-faced 35-year-old (like Jim) but by a clean-shaven 47-year-old Dennis Quaid. The actor looked good in blue jeans during the tryout scene, but in truth Morris wore softball pants that day. Director John Lee Hancock abandoned reality completely when he had Quaid throw a fastball past a roadside speed-display board. Not only did Morris never do this, but such a contraption cannot detect and record the speed of a thrown ball.

In his major league debut, Quaid strikes out Royce Clayton on three pitches. Morris needed four, which included a foul ball—deemed too hard to shoot by Hancock.

Despite the discrepancies, Morris loved the film. So too did fans and critics. *The Rookie* grossed more than $75 million before Labor Day, and it won an ESPY as the best sports movie of 2002.

Dennis Quaid protrayed Jim Morris in the 2002 Walt Disney movie, **The Rookie.**

retired 15 of the 21 batters he faced.

In 2000 the Devil Rays used Morris as a situational lefty, and he posted a respectable 4.35 ERA in 16 games. After the season, a sore elbow forced him into his third retirement. This time, however, Morris did not retreat into obscurity. On March 26, 2002, Walt Disney Pictures premiered *The Rookie*, the fairytale story of a pitcher whose dream came true.

"Absolutely living a dream," he said of his very first major league pitch in 1999. And what the sports writers reported was pretty dreamy too—his fastball that evening was estimated at 95 miles an hour.

Chapter Fifty

There Must Be a Lackey Among the Angels in Baseball Heaven

World Series, Anaheim Angels vs. San Francisco Giants
Anaheim Stadium, Anaheim, California, and PacBell Park, San Francisco, California
October 19–27, 2002

G ame 7 of the World Series is a no-man's-land where you could die or be miraculously resurrected from the dead. Let's face it, no ball team wants to be here, not if you ask them when they clinch the pennant.

The most remarkable thing about Game 7 is that it belongs to no one, no ballclub that is. It is a gift from the baseball gods, their gift to fans, not to mention a bonus to the television networks that can sell commercials for three-times retail.

But with this Game 7, one of the ball teams actually did get a present, a serendipitous gift only the Angels appreciated fully, or at least one of them, hitting coach Mickey Hatcher. "I *wanted* San Francisco to score first," he said. "That's a good sign." And that's what happened. In the second inning the visiting Giants jumped ahead 1–0.

Hatch knew what was happening well—that falling behind frequently sparked the Angels into comeback mode. The Angels' Rally Monkey, now a national phenomenon, had a ritual when they erased a deficit. The little simian creature would dance on the video scoreboard, while Edison Field would buzz with human energy.

And the Angels had a ritual too—they pumped adrenaline in a comeback, like a basement sump pump working double-time in a flood. They had been near enough to the basement enough times before this Series, they practically had an elevator on order from Otis.

In this, the highest-scoring World Series in history, a single run was almost irrelevant. Sure enough, for the seventh time in the 2002 postseason, the Angels caught up with the team they trailed in the next half inning, as catcher Benji Molina doubled in a run. Then, with the bases loaded in the third, Garret Anderson rifled a shot into the right-field corner. David Eckstein scored, Darin Erstad scored, and they waved in Tim Salmon too. Anderson's bases-clearing double made it 4–1, as 44,000 championship-starved Angels fans whacked their thunder sticks and frantically shook their lucky stuffed monkeys.

It was amazing how confident these Angels had become, especially within the context of their woeful history. A 1961 expansion team, the Angels made the playoffs only three times over their first 41 seasons—

and never reached the World Series. Anaheim finished 41 games out of first place in 2001 and returned in '02 with basically the same cast of characters. If that wasn't enough, rumors persisted that the Walt Disney Company was about to sell the club. "This team's been through so much," Erstad told ESPN.com, "we just said, 'Enough's enough!'"

In 2002 Angels players came together for the common cause. Under the guidance of manager Mike Scioscia, the no-name pitching staff posted the most saves

Mighty-mite second baseman David Eckstein was a hard-charging personi-fication of the Angels' spirit.

and the fewest runs allowed in the American League. Though lacking home run blasters, the Halos manufactured runs with line drives, steals, and well-placed bunts. No team fanned less often. Defensively, the Angels ranked second in the league in fielding average. This winning combination helped Anaheim amass a franchise-record 99 wins and clinch a playoff wildcard berth.

Several players captured the spirit of this destined team. Pint-sized second baseman David Eckstein, 5'6", scored 107 runs while leading the AL in sacrifice hits (14) and hit-by-pitches (27). The unassuming Anderson, quietly productive since the mid-1990s, blasted .306 with 56 doubles and 123 RBI. And Erstad, a self-punishing, diving-all-over-the-place center-fielder, scored 99 runs before erupting for huge numbers in the postseason.

In the AL Division Series, Anaheim pulled a shocker. On the strength of comebacks in Games 2 and 3, the Angels ousted the New York Yankees three games to one, ending New York's string of four straight World Series appearances. The Angels lost Game 1 of the AL Championship Series to Minnesota, but then reeled off four straight victories. A 10-run rally in the seventh inning of Game 5 shot the Halos to the World Series.

Incredibly, not one player on the Angels had ever been to the Fall Classic. In fact, two of Anaheim's post-season stars, reliever Francisco Rodriguez and starting pitcher John Lackey, had opened the season in the minor leagues. With an explosive fastball, Rodriguez fanned 15 batters in 10 innings in the ALDS and ALCS while going 4-0 in relief (thanks, of course, to Anaheim rallies). Lackey, a 6'6" Texan, tossed 10 shutout innings in the first two postseason series.

Still, neither pitcher had ever seen the likes of slugger Barry Bonds of the San Francisco Giants, Anaheim's nemesis in the World Series. A year earlier, Bonds had smashed a major league–record 73 home runs, and in 2002 he copped the NL batting title (.370) while conking 46 homers. With pitchers afraid to pitch to him, he accumulated a MLB-record 198 walks.

Perhaps due to jitters, the Rally Monkey failed to work his magic in Game 1 of the Fall Classic, as the Giants hung on for a 4–3 win at Anaheim. In true form, the Angels bounced back with triumphs in Game 2 (11–10, thanks to Tim Salmon's two home runs) and Game 3 (10–4). San Francisco also proved resilient, winning Game 4, 4–3 and Game 5 in a rout, 16–4.

When the Giants went up 5–0 in the seventh inning of Game 6, thanks in part to a homer by Bonds—who batted .471 with four longballs in the series—the Angels seemed doomed. After all, no team had ever overcome a five-run deficit in an elimination game to win the World Series. Yet, with the Rally Monkey going ape on the scoreboard, the Angels pulled off the mother of all comebacks. A three-run homer by Scott Spiezio and a two-run double by Troy Glaus led to a jaw-dropping 6–5 victory.

Lackey started the Series finale, trying to become the first rookie starter since Pittsburgh's Babe Adams in 1909 to win a Game 7. Poised and throwing strikes, Lackey yielded just one run in five innings. With the fairytale script going as planned, the Angels entered the ninth up 4–1, but trouble loomed. Closer Troy Percival allowed two runners to reach base with one out.

There was nothing the Rally Monkey could do. Salmon said he prayed to God, hoping he'd side with Angels. Jackie Autry, widow of the original owner, could barely watch. Percival responded by striking out Tsuyoshi Shinjo, but one batter remained. On the first pitch, Kenny Lofton belted a flyball high into the night sky—and deep. Erstad drifted back, within 10 feet of the warning track.

"I remember saying to myself, 'This is the hardest catch I've ever made,'" Erstad said afterward. "I said, 'Just use two hands like your dad taught you.'"

When the ball descended into Erstad's glove, the Angels became the first team ever to go from 41 games out one year to World Series champions the next—marking the greatest *season* comeback ever.

While the Rally Monkey became a national phenomenon in fall 2002, the Angels' lucky charm had made her world premiere on June 6, 2000. With Anaheim trailing (of all teams) San Francisco that day, the Angels' video crew debuted something new on the JumboTron: a clip of a hyper-monkey from the film *Ace Ventura: Pet Detective*. The Angels came back to win the game, scoring twice in the last inning.

Not long after, the Angels hired their own monkey, Katie, the capuchin featured on the TV show *Friends*. They taped her jumping around and then displayed it on the JumboTron to spark rallys in the late innings.

According to RallyMonkey.com, the furry primate was responsible for seven successful comeback victories in 2000. (For the monkey to get credited with a victory, the Angels had to win at home after being tied or trailing in the seventh inning or later.) The monkey earned 16 victories in 2001, but in 2002 she really went bananas. She sparked Anaheim to 27 late-inning comeback triumphs, including six in the postseason!

By October of that year, the Rally Monkey had joined Benji, Flipper, Curious George, and Seabiscuit among America's most beloved animals. At ballgames and online, vendors hawked stuffed Rally Monkeys as well as T-shirts, caps, beach balls, and seat cushions featuring the little primate's image. When the Angels came back from a 5–0 late-inning deficit to win Game 6 of the World Series, the Rally Monkey forever secured her place in baseball lore.

The Rally Monkey was everywhere in October 2002 as Anaheim fans went bananas over their team.

Photo Credits